e-Government

THE USE OF INFORMATION AND COMMUNICATION TECHNOLOGIES IN ADMINISTRATION

Eric E. Otenyo and Nancy S. Lind

YOUNGSTOWN, NEW YORK

Printed in the United States of America

ISBN: 978-1-934844-17-5

Library of Congress Control Number: 2011944924

Requests for permission should be directed to:
permissions@teneopress.com, or mailed to:
Teneo Press
PO Box 349
Youngstown, New York 14174

e-Government

Table of Contents

List of Boxes

List of Figure and Tables

Acknowledgments

First, we owe many thanks to the numerous scholars and practitioners whose ideas contributed to our understanding of this emerging field of study. We are grateful also to the individuals and organizations who allowed us to use their materials.

Eric Otenyo is grateful for the encouragement of Fred Solop and Michael Stevenson of Northern Arizona University. Many thanks to Todd Johnson, Debbie Jo Maust and Corrina Ikakoula for sharing stories on the use of ICTs in the workplace. Finally, Otenyo owes much gratitude to his extended family, especially Margaret O. Matanda, Pamela E. Otenyo, and Nancy N. Siage. He dedicates this work to them.

Nancy Lind is grateful to all of the friends and family who have believed in her over many years, including former dean Gary Olson, who provided considerable encouragement in a time of need. Lind owes much gratitude to her family, especially Robert and Camille Lind, Thomas Lind and her little Shadow and Ebony. She dedicates this work to them.

Both authors extend their sincere thanks to all who reviewed this book and worked diligently to see it through the production process. Special thanks are owed to Robert Maranto, Pam LaFeber, and Edward J. Miller, who provided detailed reviews of earlier drafts.

e-Government

Chapter 1

Understanding e-Government

Defining e-Government

Establishing the definitions of e-government is our first task. Similar to public administration, it is difficult to arrive at a precise and widely accepted definition of e-government. In January 2009, a Google search for the terms "e-government definition" generated an astounding 136,000,000 results! Fortunately, from the hundreds of definitions and extrapolations available, we can delineate the emerging field and practice from other fields. For starters, consider the following examples:

- E-government refers to one aspect of digital government: the provision of governmental services by electronic means, usually over the Internet. E-governance, in contrast refers to a vision of changing the nature of the state. (Garson, 2006, pp. 18–19)
- Electronic government, or e-government, is the use of information technology, in particular the Internet, to deliver public services in

a much more convenient, customer-oriented, cost-effective, and altogether different and better way. (Holmes, 2001, p. 2)

- In its broadest sense, electronic government, more popularly referred to as e-government, is the use of information and communications technologies by governments to operate more effectively and transparently; to provide more and better information and services to the public; and to facilitate the participation of individuals, businesses and groups throughout society in their own governance. Another more succinct way of putting this may be that e-government is the use of electronic technology to facilitate better and more open government and governance. (Curtin, 2007, p. 2)
- E-government is the use of information and communication technologies (ICTs) to improve the activities of public sector organizations. Some definitions restrict e-government to Internet-enabled applications only, or only to interactions between government and outside groups. Here, we do not—all digital ICTs are included; all public sector activities are included. (Heeks, 2004)
- E-government refers to the use by government agencies of information technologies (such as Wide Area Networks, the Internet, and mobile computing) that have the ability to transform relations with citizens, businesses, and other arms of government. (World Bank, 2009)
- E-government (from electronic government, also known as e-gov, digital government, online government or in a certain context transformational government) refers to government's use of information technology to exchange information and services with citizens, businesses, and other arms of government. The legislature, judiciary or administration to improve internal efficiency, the delivery of public services, or processes of democratic governance may apply e-government. The primary delivery models are Government-to-Citizen or Government-to-Customer (G2C), Government-to-Business (G2B) and Government-to-Government (G2G) and Government-to-Employees (G2E). The most important

anticipated benefits of e-government include improved efficiency, convenience, and better accessibility of public services. (Wikipedia, E-government, 2009)

- Electronic government is a generic term for Web-based services from agencies of local, state and federal governments. Such websites provide a wide variety of services to the public and have been extremely helpful in reducing internal paperwork. For example, the myriad of forms that government agencies require can typically be downloaded from a website. When information on the site is clearly indexed and explained, the number of support calls is dramatically reduced compared to the days before the Web. (Free Dictionary, 2009)
- E-government is a generic term that refers to any government functions or processes that are carried out in digital form over the Internet. Local, state and federal governments essentially set up central websites from which the public (both private citizens and businesses) can find public information, download government forms and contact government representatives. For example, there are many states within the United States that offer online filing of state income taxes every year, which reduces the amount of paperwork, streamlines the process and speeds the amount of time that taxes are filed. E-government also refers to the standard processes that different government agencies use in order to communicate with each other and streamline processes. (Webopedia, E-government, 2008)
- By definition, e-government is simply the use of information and communications technology, such as the Internet, to improve the processes of government. Thus, e-government is in principle nothing new. Governments were among the first users of computers. But the global proliferation of the Internet, which effectively integrates information and communications technology on the basis of open standards, combined with the movement to reform public administration known as New Public Management, has for good reason generated a new wave of interest in the topic.

E-government promises to make government more efficient, responsive, transparent and legitimate and is also creating a rapidly growing market of goods and services, with a variety of new business opportunities. (Gordon, 2008)

- The term "e-government" focuses on the use of new ICTs by governments as applied to the full range of government functions. In particular, the networking potential offered by the Internet and related technologies have the potential to transform the structures and operation of government. (OECD, 2005)

E-government has transformed the meaning of bureaucracy as street-level bureaucrats employing a wide variety of technologies are transformed into screen-level bureaucrats (Bovens & Zouridis, 2002). Conditioned by the revolution in information and communication technologies, e-government and e-commerce encompass new ways of human behavior at the level of acquiring and providing services from government agencies or buying and selling things in the commercial sector. The use of information and communication technologies (ICTs) has transformed the way government does its business; it is nothing short of a revolution.

These broad efforts at defining e-government identify it with the use of ICTs in the provision of public services. While this assumption reflects the central mission of e-government, it limits the entire spectrum of possibilities and visions for e-government. Numerous indirect governmental activities and services are captured by this expanded vision. New formats of interactive, computer-mediated technologies (non–Internet-based services) add to the complexities of the role that ICTs play in the functioning of government.

From the perspective of public administration, e-government goes beyond the simple association with online and web services. Internationally, governments have invested millions of dollars in technologies beyond e-mail and the Internet. E-government is about changes in how public services are delivered, and can be differentiated from e-commerce, the electronic exchange of money for the purchase of private goods and services. E-commerce is often associated with e-business plans and is thought of as a strategy for delivering "faster, better, and cheaper" services to members of the public (Holmes, 2001).

The story of e-government, however, is incomplete without an understanding of e-democracy, which is subsumed under the larger concept of governance. Because public administration in Western countries exists within the framework of democracy, the unlimited possibilities of electronic communication for political recruitment, interest articulation, aggregation, mobilization, and public decision making support the cause of administration in numerous ways. Foremost is the role of e-democracy in the election of political leaders who form and shape the public policies that administrators are mandated to implement. In tandem with general administration is e-management—the use of ICTs to improve critical operating tasks and processes such as maintaining staff records, budgeting, and managing information for executive decision making. In addition, e-democracy enables the public to participate in its government in many direct and indirect ways.

The Internet

The Internet is the most visible venue of e-government. The Internet is a global information system of unique address defined and linked together by Internet Protocol (IP). The Internet is supported by Transmission Control Protocols (TCP) and is accessible either publicly or privately. Most people, including the Supreme Court in *Reno v. ACLU* (1997) conceive of the Internet as a system of computers networking with each other. Of course these computers are programmed or operated by people. The Internet is also identified as a network of networks, all freely exchanging information. The most widely recognized aspects of the Internet are electronic mail (e-mail) and the World Wide Web, but it includes other services such as Gopher and UseNet (Stone, 1997). While e-mail refers to the techniques for transmitting electronic messages over a computer system, the web is simply the "universe of documents and files written in hypertext that are accessible from servers connected to the Internet" (Klotz, 2004, p. 2).

Dr. Vannevar Bush did much of the work that led to the establishment of the Internet. Bush had been the director of the Office of Scientific Research and Development during Franklin D. Roosevelt's presidency. Bush designed some analog precursors to modern computers and wrote an article speculating that a machine for retrieval of data similar to the modern-day computer was feasible. While he was at MIT, his research developed the differential Analyzer, a device capable of solving differential equations, an idea that led to the development of digital circuits. He also led the organization that oversaw scientific research for military purposes. The Internet has origins in the late 1960s, when the United States Department of Defense (DoD) developed a digital project to connect computers located in various regions of the country. The Internet, as a communication device, supported the country's aspirations as a global power. Eventually, the project expanded to nonmilitary organizations.

Unlike previous communications technologies such as the telephone, telegram, and radio, digital computing was integral to military applications from its infancy. The original computers, the British Colossus machines, were designed during World War II to help the Royal British Army read encrypted German messages. Computing history attributes the creation of these devices to the leadership of several engineers and mathematicians, including Tommy Flowers, Harry Fensom, Bill Chandler, Sid Broadhurst, and Max Newman. The prototype, Colossus Mark 1, worked for a limited time in 1943 but was quickly replaced in 1944 by a vastly improved Colossus Mark 2.

The question of who invented the computer is not one with a simple answer. During the 1960s, conventional wisdom attributed the invention of the computer as we know it today to the pioneering work of Dr. John Mauchly and Dr. J. Presper Eckert on the Electronic Numerical Integrator and Computer (ENIAC) at the University of Pennsylvania. However, following a lengthy trial which granted ENIAC's patent rights to Mauchly and Eckert, the courts named Dr. John Atanasoff of Iowa State University inventor of the digital electronic computer. There is much credibility to Atanasoff's claim to have been responsible for the idea of the interaction of logic circuits in the computing elements (Smiley, 2010).

Smiley, Atanasoff's biographer, showed that Mauchly had visited Ames, Iowa, in 1941 and "spent considerable time with the machine, he understood it fully, and in substantially every detail" (2010, p. 177). Smiley pointed out that Atanasoff worked closely with Clifford Berry, a like-minded engineer who at age 11 had already built a ham radio (Smiley, 2010). Ultimately, the contacts between all these mathematicians and engineers can be said to have contributed to the creation of the first computer devices to resemble those we know today. These formed the basis of the Atanasoff-Berry Computer (ABC), which was a forerunner of, and huge influence on, the subsequent devices built at University of Pennsylvania (Burks and Burks, 1988; Mollenhoff, 1988). The real answer to the question of who invented the computer is that many inventors contributed to its evolution. It is best to see the computer as a complex piece of machinery made up of many parts, each of which can be considered a separate invention.

By 1952, Drs. Mauchly and Eckert, working at the University of Pennsylvania, received a patent for their work on ENIAC. Its purpose was to compute World War II ballistic firing tables (ACSA, 2004). This statement accompanied the patent of ENIAC:

> With the advent of everyday use of elaborate calculations, speed has become paramount to such a high degree that there is no machine on the market today capable of satisfying the full demand of modern computational methods. The most advanced machines have greatly reduced the time required for arriving at solutions to problems which might have required months or days by older procedures. This advance, however, is not adequate for many problems encountered in modern scientific work and the present invention is intended to reduce to seconds such lengthy computations. (Weik, 1961)

Clearly, the invention was about speed and efficiency—core values that administrators continue to embrace.

According to Gates (1995), ENIAC was more like an "electronic calculator than a computer, but instead of representing a binary number with on and off settings on wheels the way a mechanical calculator did, it used vacuum tube "switches" (p. 26). He added that although "ENIAC weighed 30 tons and filled a large room" and "stored only the equivalent of about 80 characters of information," it was an ancestor of today's computers (p. 27).

Another powerful computer, the Universal Automatic Computer (UNIVAC), was commissioned by the U.S. Census Bureau to support census activities. It was also designed and developed at the University of Pennsylvania by the creators of EINAC, Drs. Mauchly and Eckert. UNIVAC became the first commercially available computer after the Eckert-Mauchly Computer Company, which was later purchased by Sperry Rand Corporation, produced one for Prudential Insurance. In 1986, Sperry Rand and the Burroughs Corporation merged to form Unisys Corporation. Unisys continues to contract with the federal government, including the DoD, for various computer-related services. For example, it supplied the Army's RFID In-Transit Visibility system, which provides instant access to information about equipment and supplies, enhancing readiness and safety (Unisys, 2009).

Although Unisys has continued its partnership with DoD, the mainframe UNIVAC computers were discontinued in the mid-1950s. The International Business Machines Corporation (IBM) developed a newer generation computers that were widely tied to the defense industry, and became a key supplier of mainframe computers during the Korean War. Continuing its partnership with the federal government and DoD, IBM became the leading producer of mainframe computers in the 1970s.

In 1973, IBM successfully moved computing into the hands of single users through the SCAMP project. The company's General Systems Division created a prototype device dubbed "Special Computer, APL Machine Portable" (APL stands for "A Programming Language") which many industry analysts consider the first personal computer (International, 2009). This device, which users could program or use to run various "canned" applications, became the prototype of the IBM 5100 portable computer. IBM continued to supply other market-leading products such as the 1403 printer, a breakthrough product in the 1960s. From 1968 through the 1970s, IBM held more 65 percent of the world's computer mainframe market (Stone, 1997, p.163). IBM played an important role in the development of computing and e-governance in general.

American Telephone and Telegraph (AT&T) was another important company in early computing. Though associated with telephones, AT&T increasingly integrated computer software for internal use. It competed with IBM in the general area of communication and developed instruments with interconnecting capabilities. Most telecommunications companies at that time had worked on applications to improve the capacity to connect telephones to computers. By 1969, AT&T had developed a sophisticated operating system, UNIX, one of the first operating systems to be written in programming language, which greatly improved its capacity to integrate these services. AT&T continued to be a leader in the development and design of sophisticated systems to transmit and receive data over the telephone. Later, AT&T and other innovators improved on computing and data transmission capabilities and changed the way telecommunications operated.

In the meantime, the advent of Intel's microprocessor in 1971 ushered in a new era of discovery in microelectronics. The microprocessor facilitated the development of the modern computer and subsequently the Internet. Stone (1997) argued that it was one of the most important inventions of the twentieth century. The use of dedicated microprocessors for calculations allowed other microchips to solely store data, greatly increasing the efficiency of computer systems. In brief, the telecommunications-computer interface, more than any other invention, laid the groundwork of the modern Internet. Intel and other microprocessor manufacturers provided the vision for numerous other applications, including the invention of handheld devices, modems, and peripheral devices for transmission of a vast amount of computer-generated information (p. 182).

Defense matters remained at the core of the search for better computing devices and expansion of the early computer networks which would become the Internet. The Soviet Union's launch of Sputnik-1, the world's first orbital spacecraft, in 1957 spurred the U.S. federal government to expand research in technology and communications. The federal government feared that the telecommunications network could be vulnerable to disabling attack by an enemy. As a result, it established the Advanced Research Projects Agency (ARPA) under the purview of the DoD. Because the tradition of contracting out was established early at ARPA, further developments in telecommunications can be traced to the inventive collaborators already described.

ARPA established that an alternative telecommunications system was necessary to forestall any possibility of destruction of the nation's command and control network. As in the administrative concept of redundancy, multiple nodes would safeguard the command systems when a single node was attacked. The Rand Corporation provided the idea of packet switching, that is, breaking digital analog messages into multiple, smaller packets. By 1969, these ideas culminated into the ARPANET system, which linked university departments engaged in defense research to each other and to the DoD e-mail.

E-mail as we know it emerged in late 1972 from similar collaboration between the DoD and private contractors. Historians report that computer engineer Ray Tomlinson, then working for DoD-contracted Bolt, Beranek and Newman, is credited with inventing Internet-based e-mail. Starting in 1968, he had been experimenting with a program called SNDMSG that the "ARPANET programmers and researchers were using on the network computers (Digital PDP-10s) to leave messages for each other" (Bellis, 2011). The early version of SNDMSG was a local program with limited outreach capabilities. It could only be used to leave messages on the computer that one was working with. At this time, computing was accessible through mainframe terminals. There were no modern personal computers. Tomlinson developed a file transfer protocol, which he called CYPNET, that enabled SNDMSG to transfer electronic messages to any computer on the ARPANET network (Bellis, 2011).

By 1972, ARPA contractors successfully developed programs and protocols that would run e-mails on the ARPA network. In 1982, the network conversion to TCP and IP permitted distributing large amounts of information and postings via e-mail. The Internet had become a reality, and it began to spread like wildfire. However, usage of networked computing was limited until the end of the Cold War in 1991, when the

World Wide Web emerged as a powerful information and communication system, easily accessible to the general public.

Although government Internet sites are often considered elements of the e-government universe, not all government websites are part of this phenomenon. Various technologies are applied in this emerging system. There is a distinction between application of non-Internet and Internet-based technologies, as shown in box 1.1.

Box 1.1. *Non-Internet and Internet Technologies Related to e-Government.*

Non-Internet technologies	Internet technologies
Telephone and other interactive devices that enable services such as interviews to be conducted	MyGov information (E-Service) centers notifying customers when driver's licenses will expire
The provision of government services by telephone (such as by call centers) to check status of applications, touch-tone applications	E-mail and mass Listserves (computer-mediated communication); Electronic Data Interchange Systems (EDI)
Fax machines	**Internet tax software packages**
The use of mobile phone (and PDA) communication technology (such as text messaging [SMS] and MMS, as well as 3G, WiMAX, GPRS, and Bluetooth)	Customer data information packages; law enforcement data banks for criminal elements including sex offenders; public records including marriage and death certificates
Surveillance systems, tracking systems, RFID, CCTV, biometric identification, road traffic management, and regulatory enforcement systems including radar devices	Weather reporting systems, citizen survey systems, council minutes, tender documents, welfare assistance program case updates, AMBER Alert systems
Smart cards, identity cards, and other near field communication applications	Cyberspace meetings (virtual meetings), discussion bulletins, chat rooms, professional networking sites
Polling station technology (where non-online e-voting exists)	Polling station technology (where online e-voting exists)
Television and radio-based delivery of government services (this often has an interface with the Internet), Digital Audio Broadcasting, digital TV, and high-definition TV	Satellite TV and radio broadcast–based delivery of government services, often transmitted through Internet cables or wireless technologies

In sum, many advances in computing continue to take place. The modern Internet emerged after much investment from DoD and the work of a number of universities in enhancing applications to include civilian uses. Meanwhile, the web has become the most visible face of the Internet. By 1994, the leading company in popularizing the web was Netscape Communications, which developed popular web browsers. Later, Microsoft successfully developed other easy-to-use and inexpensive browsers, thereby becoming the largest player in the business.

There are several frameworks that illuminate our understanding of e-government: the ecology of public administration, the state transformational context, the organizational culture perspective, the communication context, and the technical design perspective. These frameworks are drawn from various literatures and have different conceptions of the role of e-government in contemporary public administration.

ECOLOGY OF e-GOVERNMENT

One of the most significant variables conditioning e-government practices is its ecology—the mutual relationships between objects and their environment. Gaus (1947) and Riggs (1961) gave meaning to the concept of ecology for public administration. Their assumption was that the principles and practices of an administration were shaped by its environment. Gaus (1947) discovered the importance of the ecology of public administration after raising concerns about societal change and the interactions between society and public administration. Riggs (1961) elaborated that changes in administrative behavior were often related to corresponding economic, social, and political processes. The emergence of e-government can be partially understood in the context of its ecology. This perspective has significant theoretical import. E-government is itself an independent variable affecting the larger social environment.

The starting point for analyzing the significance of environmental factors in public administration is to explore organizational theory parameters and contextualize the roots of the ecology of public administration in its traditional and broader meaning. In terms of contemporary organization theory, the environment plays a crucial part in structuring the behavior of public officials. The study of organizational environments focuses on how external forces can impact the operations of an organization. Pfeffer (1998) argued that though the environment impacts organizations, not every organization is impacted by every event, not even technological changes. Further, each organization is influenced by the constraints of its environment. Thus technological advances bring both positive and negative changes to public agencies.

Scott (2003) believed that an organization's environment evolves over time, and that the organization adapts to this change to survive. Adaptation perspectives have observed that organizations scan the prevailing environment for opportunities or threats and formulate appropriate strategic responses. Individual countries adapt at different rates to shifts in technology. Adaptation rates vary according to each country's social, technical, political, and economic situation. As organization theorists have noted, the ability to adapt is constrained by "structural inertia" (Hannan & Freeman, 1977). Different public agencies opt to arrive at equilibrium by employing varied sets of strategies. Governments of poor countries, worried about control of the Internet, have sought to create international organizations to moderate domain names and regulate access to suit the needs of their own regimes.

Countries such as China have expressed their disappointment with the proliferation of blogs and Internet discussion boards that support prodemocracy dissident activities. Not surprisingly, an advanced democracy like the United States is remarkably uncomfortable with increased use of the Internet by terrorist groups plotting to disrupt economic life. Efforts at controlling challenges posed by environmental forces are well explained by organizational theorists. As Pfeffer and Salancik (2005) noted, managers must understand the context of the behavior of an organization to facilitate managing and controlling it. They must recognize that organizations are dependent on environmental forces and will use these forces to their advantage in natural and rational attempts at self-preservation. What is important to recognize is that "organizations create and appropriate knowledge, know-how, and meaning from their environments" (Scott, 2003, p. 101). Public security agencies in various countries react differently to these environmental variables. Similarly, Downs (1967) recognized this dynamic by asserting that technology influences both external and internal aspects of the bureau.

Public administrators have tended to delineate the environment in terms of its societal specifics, political order, economics, and technological factors. Contemporary scholarship can add globalization to these environmental factors as an aspect of the economic mosaic in which administration occurs. As for the political environment, the domination of conservative governments, as well as the high priority accorded to public security, especially the terror alert system, no doubt are factors administrators contend with today. Let us briefly examine some of these factors.

Social Changes

Social changes influence public administration immensely. We will first discuss social conditions involving the consumption of ICTs. In *The Third Wave*, Toffler (1981) made the case that human civilization had reached an irreversible epoch in which information was more abundant than ever. New information technologies were restructuring education, scientific research, and government affairs. He correctly noted that the new civilization was based on a mass media with immense interactive capabilities. Toffler stated that

> Humanity faces a quantum leap forward. It faces the deepest social upheaval and creative restructuring of all time. Without clearly recognizing it, we are engaged in building a remarkable new civilization from the ground up…What is now is nothing less than a global revolution, a quantum jump in history. (pp. 10–12)

Toffler (1981) popularized the idea of the "electronic cottage," which underscores the general idea that though the Industrial Revolution had taken people out of their homes, the information technologies revolution allowed them to return. Clearly, those who telecommute find much meaning in Toffler's ideas. Some lifestyles have been transformed by the opportunities afforded by IT. In education, literally hundreds of education programs are now online, and open universities and online colleges offer various degree programs that are changing the way we learn.

Castells (1997) reiterated that from paleontologists' viewpoint, the history of human society and life in general is stable but punctuated at rare intervals by major events. The advent of IT is one such event. According to Castells (1997), a new paradigm of social organization exists in which our material culture is organized around these new information technologies. With the emergent Information Age, human agents have developed numerous social networks and communities, of which the more familiar include Myspace, Facebook, and Twitter. Because these are communities in a literal sense, they must be regulated and hence have attracted the interest of public administrators. For instance, it is no secret that human resource managers often visit the Myspace and Facebook networks to understand the "fit" of a potential recruit.

Likewise, for security reasons, Internet police follow activities of suspicious individuals who frequent these social forums. Cybercops are employed to patrol the electronic beat (Clark, 1994). Hackers are known to attack social sites and penetrate important government sites, including the DoD (Tang, 1997). In addition, Lyon (1997) found that these cyberspace communities are beyond the scope of our understanding of the self and society. Because of that realization, the challenge for administrators, especially those with expertise in e-government, cannot be underestimated.

From a managerial standpoint, additional changes in society are worth mentioning. Hines (1994) recognized that ICTs have influenced workers in at least two fundamental ways. First, the technologies enable most workers to efficiently manage their records and other work-related information. For example, farmers can use smart technologies to compute the degree of ripeness and yield of their crops, as well as to locate their livestock. Second, workplace design has changed to accommodate the new technologies. For example, police officers use a wide range of computer-mediated technologies, including GPS systems, to manage traffic problems. In addition, automated traffic management systems have made it easier to monitor speeding vehicles. Police officers are able to use handheld or wrist-based computer devices to summon nearby patrol cars for assistance in the pursuit of criminals. In all workplaces, automation is the norm rather than the exception. The danger of this is the technophobia experienced by those who are not ready to embrace new technologies and perhaps the more serious problem of administrators leaning too heavily on technological determinism. The latter is an assumption that all human problems can be neatly analyzed and solved through computer-mediated devices.

Leading scholars introduced the concept of the "global village" in the 1960s in response to the replacement of older technologies by electronic media. This replacement reinforced the theory of technological determinism (McLuhan, 1962). McLuhan argued that the masses were too passive and unlikely to prevent the richer members of society from manipulating behavior driven or afforded by the emergent electronic media. By contrast, Hiltz and Turoff (1993) saw the unfolding world with a less frictional evaluation of human agency and predicted more cooperative work between the elite and the common man.

Scholars recognize that communication within the Internet creates both opportunities and challenges. Public administrators, particularly regulators, must be concerned about the ensuing challenges. Some of the more obvious ones, which demand policy intervention, are issues of child molestation, pornography, and all manner of fraudulent activities. These social dimensions of ICTs impact how institutions function (Street, 1992). Sociological studies recognize that rapid changes in ICT production outstrip the human ability to adapt. This leads to questions such as whether or not the Internet changes the way we socialize and do business.

Forester (1992) and other observers of the social scene contend that information technologies have not necessarily increased leisure time. Instead, the vast majority of workers appear to be working harder and for longer hours than ever before. While opportunities for leisure within the context of the Internet have been expanded, the average worker puts in more hours now than at any other time in history, thanks to the universal presence of computers.

From a sociological perspective, ICTs have implications for human relationships. In some cases, "people skills" are being lost, because almost all transactions take place within virtual media. There are also numerous psychological problems associated with computer-mediated communication devices. Psychologists believe that some managers suffer from a "communicaholic" disorder in which they persistently are in touch with their subordinates through handheld computer devices such as the Blackberry and iPhone.

Another set of problems has much to do with the fact that the computer has made it possible for the public to have access to millions of resources that provide information on all human conditions, activities, and problems almost instantaneously. The information revolution has led to a phenomenon known as "infoglut" or information overload. At the beginning of this chapter, the point was made that searching Google for the terms "e-government definition" returns more than a million links; this is one example of the scope of the infoglut. From a government and public administration perspective, infoglut negatively affects decision making. With over 21.4 million websites added in 2010 alone, the volume of information available to users can be overwhelming to public administrators (Royal Pingdom, 2011).

The next set of issues is associated with the influence of the Internet on social processes, especially in terms of its impact on moral values. Hundreds of websites carry messages that promote one cause or another. Recent pressures affect how we define marriage and workplace sexual harassment. Already there has been frustration that TurboTax packages designed to help clients file taxes electronically did not use inclusive language. This omission resulted from the software creators' assumption that partners filing jointly are marriages of one man and one woman, as understood by the dominant culture, unfortunately leaving out those whose partners are of the same sex.

Additionally, public bureaus have to contend with an increasing segment of the population whose first language is not English and who come from diverse backgrounds. Diversity is a broad concept that includes those who believe or do not believe in intelligent design, school prayer, abortion, and the right to choose. It is not just about race or ethnicity. Most societies have significant immigrant populations, and administrators are tasked with creating unbiased administrative systems responsive to the needs of all—a growing challenge to e-governance. E-government practices must therefore be understood in terms of this dynamic.

Political Changes

E-government has to contend with legal issues such as personal privacy but also issues of control of and access to ICTs. The prevailing explanation from critical theorists is that ICTs favor those with power and reinforce existing power structures, and only those with the capabilities and resources to enjoy technological advances can enjoy the full benefits of e-government and other ICT applications.

It is necessary for public administration to understand all elements of e-government as a part of this complexity. Take, for example, the authentication systems that permit e-governance. While these are administrative devices for control, the use of digital signatures presents significant policy and administrative procedure concerns.

It has been argued that Public Key Infrastructures (PKI) at the core of ICTs invariably shift accountability to private software developers. PKI enables users of unsecure networks to exchange data through a secured trusted authority. The PKI provides a digital certificate that authenticates messages. When the key is discovered or intercepted by unauthorized persons, messages are decrypted and compromised. This aspect of the bureaucratic control model is often at odds with the notion of representativeness in government and challenges its core assumptions. This is not surprising because from the outset cyberspace has been a contested domain (Loader, 1997). Government attempts at controlling online activities are often perceived as an affront to individual liberties.

Political issues are a source of concern to the extent that there are both domestic and international debates over the domination of U.S. academics and engineers in the control of Internet delivery systems. At the domestic level, for example, the control of Internet providers and the near monopoly of a few corporations in the hardware and software industries raise political questions of governance, especially as the Internet becomes embedded in our lifestyles. Among the largest of these companies, all of which have faced endless litigation, are giant corporations such as Microsoft, EarthLink, Yahoo, and AOL (formerly a division of Time Warner Inc.).

Major telecommunications giants, including Verizon, wield a combination of political and market influences that shape domestic policies. For instance, Verizon effectively campaigned to prevent independent municipal networks in Pennsylvania when several city authorities wanted to set up low-cost local broadband services. The corporation claimed that the government has an unfair advantage over corporations and other commercial service providers. Several special interest lobbyists backed Verizon and persuaded city authorities to sign legal agreements granting the incumbent telecom company automatic priority as a citywide service provider (Chen, 2004). Several other states passed laws that limit the ability of local governments to participate in building telecommunication networks in their jurisdictions. While there has always been concern over the amount of power and influence that these companies have in social and economic systems, public pessimism about their profit motive has become increasingly significant (Laudon, 1977).

Internationally, there are significant concerns over the domination of domains and the entire Internet system by the United States. The Internet is not controlled by a centralized international body but is basically managed by an American private-sector nonprofit organization called the Internet Corporation for Assigned Names and Numbers (ICANN) established in 1998 (Cukier, 2005). Most Third World countries view this as an aspect of U.S. hegemonic control over the world's communication systems. Following intense debates, United Nations Secretary General Kofi Annan ruled that the United Nations would not take control of domain name management, despite rumors that it would do so. Instead, ICANN would remain in charge of technical management of the Internet, and individual countries would own their code domains. The United Nations established an Internet Secretariat in Geneva to serve as a coordinating body for Internet governance issues.

If ICTs are a part of how governments provide services, then citizens are entitled to representation in e-government rule-making processes and the implementation of supporting policies. When representativeness is missing, the question becomes whether e-government undermines the social contract between the public and administrative service providers. This is by itself a huge problem for democratic governance. Likewise, the use of e-government as the main avenue for political recruitment and selection poses significant problems for the underclass, such as in several countries that have implemented Internet voting.

Nonetheless, the place of e-democracy is now enshrined in the popular conception of how government works and is an integral part of the e-government movement. Volumes of literature speak to the issue of increased contact between representatives and their constituents through e-mail services (Davis, 1999; Goldschmidt, 2001). The Internet has also provided opportunities for direct political action through protest and mobilization (Grossman, 1995; Morris, 2000; Norris, 2001). Electronic media have changed the way rulemaking is done, especially by enhancing public feedback processes (Shulman, 2005; Schlosberg & Dryzek, 2002).

Economic Changes

Contemporary economic factors that impact e-governments include the growing federal budget deficit, competition from China in the manufacturing sector, and rapid globalization. The budget issue is reinforced by the common persistence of cutback management practices. As Levine (1978) illustrated, public organizations live in environments where they must "tighten their belts." They must strive to widen their revenue bases and develop incentives to prevent disinvestment.

A similar argument is expressed by Caiden's (1981) thesis that budgeting occurs amidst uncertainty and instability. She asserted that budgeting faces challenges of instability arising from uncertainty in three areas: continued quests for budget reform, problems in forecasting, and the erosion of accountability. The latter has continued to be a major problem in recent years, as the U.S. Government Accountability Office (GAO) has continued to report cases of misuse of public funds through unwise expenditures. High installation costs, budgeting uncertainty, and cutback management all affect procurement and servicing of ICTs.

Globalization is an aspect of the internationalization of trade and finance and the transfer of technology from one region to another. It is not uncommon for policy makers and administrators to speak of a global economy. Globalization also includes the proliferation of a global "info-structure" which has expanded due to advances in satellite and communication systems. The relationship between ICTs and globalization is well documented (Castells, 2000; Ohmae, 1995). Globalization as an aspect of the environment in which public administration occurs presents special challenges. First, component manufacturing for computers and other ICTs is often dispersed globally, with several software and hardware companies are located in India and East Asia. The sheer volume of interconnectedness and interdependence of public officials globally is equally significant (Luke & Caiden, 1999).

Globalization has both national and local impacts. Public administrators are forced to contend with both the intended and unintended consequences of these changes. For example, the issue of cyberthieves forces local, state, and federal law enforcement officials to use resources to ensure cybersecurity. The bureaucracy must be adequately prepared to manage public resources within an economy that has a global frame of reference.

Comparative studies have indicated that e-government is an important component of the management of trade patterns and activities. Most government trade ministries use data available on the Internet for this purpose. The Internet continues to be a source of general information about potential products from countries wishing to engage in global markets. Information available on the Internet includes product availability, investment risks, business climates, foreign exchange rates, and shipping directories. The Internet has addressed the problems of dispatch and delay that previously worked against trading partners and is an inexpensive means of receiving important up-to-date information and documentation.

A shift away from statism and the reification of private providers of services previously associated with the state apparatus is occurring in tandem with the change in economic imperatives. State transformation literatures are enormously important in assessing the full impact of e-government and e-services. State transformation has been largely occasioned by changes in ICTs. The state has changed in its mandate and outreach due to globalization. To some extent, state power has declined, because it has had to share influence with non-state actors such as transnational corporations and nongovernmental organizations NGOs, both of which have an enormous presence on the Internet.

Besides diminished influence, state transformation has shown other dynamics. Through ICTs, citizens have access to multiple political centers to which they can hold allegiance. Global citizens can network through ICTs with more ease than ever before possible. The very fact that, for example, Europeans have shifted their identities from local to state to union membership itself signifies a diminished sense of statehood.

State transformation is most apparent in changes in its ability to perform certain functions. In the new economic thinking, how regulation is conducted has changed. As has been shown in the United States, e-rulemaking can produce overwhelming public participation that is mostly attributed to the existence of new technologies. State transformation occasioned by the forces of globalization has led to fragmented levels of decision making. Even in poor countries, cybercafés make it relatively easy for members of the public to voice their opinions against oppressive regimes and seek support globally. Ironically, terrorist groups fighting for all manner of causes have found these same technologies advantageous for raising funds and conducting outreach programs outside the state purview.

It can be said that ICTs are actively driving the evolution of the state by forcing it to accept and coexist with more non-state actors (Boyer, 1990; Kamarck, 2004). Yet the state has only begun to adapt by transforming itself, often painfully. A significant aspect of the broad idea of state transformation is the change in the state's economic mandate. The economic environment affects how public services are delivered and provided. It is instructive to note that e-governments are flourishing at a time when the ideologically touted idea of big government is under scrutiny.

Significantly, public trust in government declined while privatization and partnerships between NGOs and private- and public-sector entities became more prominent in providing services. Economic policy reflected these important changes, and all of these changes were aided by the increased accessibility of ICTs.

Technological Changes

In their account of the role of technology in the growth of the administrative state and public bureaucracy, Milakovich and Gordon (2004) underscored the salience of new information technologies. They contended that during the 1990s, the field of public administration and management witnessed significant growth in the use of technology, thereby affecting budgetary outlays. Significant amounts of time were allocated to training programs to enable administrators to use these new technologies. The growth in these technologies clearly outpaced employee skills. The most vivid developments were in the area of IT. Milakovich and Gordon (2004) argued that IT led to the emergence of e-government, which "takes the IT concept further by integrating disparate information sources into a one-stop web 'portal' for improving access to information about government; for example, www.Firstgov.gov" (p. 11).

The technological environment through which e-government functions is an indirect product of a cultural bias which places Western society at the core of the Industrial Revolution. The West developed a blind faith in technology and its resultant innovations. Values that hindered absorption of new technology were quickly discarded. Among the most visible features of the technological orientation of the culture is the continued promotion of consumerism. Evidence shows that consumption of Internet-based products is increasing. E-government is an aspect of this tradition. The range of available products and their usage is growing exponentially. The most obvious growth in the industrial world is that of computer-based information technologies.

The communication landscape has been complicated by the coexistence of the traditional broadcasting and telecommunications industries. Convergence of these industries in areas such as Internet telephony complicates the social context of these technologies. These technologies offer different services but have far-reaching consequences for administrators wishing to create order through regulatory measures. One might contend that there is merit in creating a forum for industry-level convergence on issues of service quality. The literature recognizes that infrastructure management requires administrative oversight (Mansell & Silverstone, 1996; Winseck, 1998).

Challenges to quality service provision include the risk of creating uneven access for members of the public and the reliability of information carried by growing outlets. Frequent concern has been expressed for providing access to the greatest majority of the public. Therefore, public resources continue to be used to address these issues through nontraditional service delivery approaches such as cross-subsidizing efforts. In radio broadcasting, public radio directly appeals to the public for contributions to fund programs. Eventually, the crossbreeds between broadcasting and Internet media will move in this direction. A regulatory framework will continue to evolve through the leadership of the Federal Communications Commission (FCC) and to a small extent the Federal Trade Commission (FTC).

ORGANIZATIONAL CULTURE

O'Leary (2006) pointed out that the concept of organizational culture is as significant as the concept of organizational environment. Organizational culture refers to many variables including observed behaviors, group norms, shared meanings, values, and physical arrangements in organizations. The reform ethos, which seeks to enhance organizational performance, is part of the culture of public organizations. To a considerable degree, organizational culture, once established, must be sustained, at least for a while. Khademian (2002) stated, "to sustain a culture requires an understanding of the commitments driving change" (p. 133).

The National Partnership for Reinventing Government (NPRG) under the Clinton administration was certainly about changing the culture of public organizations. The administration made full use of contemporary ICTs by providing well-developed reinvention websites. For example, the reinvention site had more than 3,000 reinvention documents including older, historical documents as well as new ones added every week. The site's search engine provided unlimited links to reinvention documents and websites across the federal government. The National Performance Review's website also provided features such as a reinvention toolbox, a reinvention calendar, and a lab database. It also archived the President's executive orders and memoranda on reinvention, the Government Performance and Results Act, and the status of all National Performance Review recommendations. Reinvention meant changing the fundamental transformation of public systems and organizations to create greater efficiency and effectiveness in service delivery. It was about replacing bureaucratic systems with entrepreneurial systems.

One goal of the program was to reinforce American national pride through the slogan "America@Its Best," which "read like an e-mail address to emphasize the commitment to greater public access through the expanded use of information technology and the Internet" (Milakovich & Gordon, 2004, p. 40). Increased application of ICTs was an important part of the reinventing movement, which itself was aimed at changing organizational culture in public agencies (Shafritz, Ott, & Jang, 2005). Thus, to understand e-government, one must conceptualize the emergence of ICTs as an aspect of movements to reform the organizational culture of federal government agencies.

As Shafritz and Russell (2003) observed, the culture that exists in organizations is but a smaller version of a societal culture. Organizational culture is a construct that helps predict behavior in organizations.

Studies of intergenerational issues speak of the Generation Xers and the large impact that technology has had on their lifestyles. They are a population cohort that is computer savvy and has little to no recollection of life without computers. Such is the extent to which ICTs have permeated our worldviews and civilization. Issues of the use of technology are transmitted by default to new generations through powerful marketing strategies coordinated by corporations. We cannot understand the logic of these technologies and their role in e-government outside of its organizational culture context for at least three reasons.

First, powerful organizations, often with interlocking directorates, shape and form our consumption patterns (Bagdikian, 1997). They advertise and sell electronic gizmos including advanced ICTs. Government agencies as well as private sector interests become instant consumers of these symbols of modernity and civilization. Desires are increasingly manipulated through powerful conveyors of information—television and other electronic and print media. Soon we find that we cannot function without updating our computer software. The more we rely on information technologies, the more manufacturers wish to offer increasingly sophisticated innovations. Of course, to perpetuate dependency on these instruments of control, powerful advertising by the corporations fills a great part of what we consume as news. The net result is that we are socialized to consume products shown on the Internet and in other technological communication outlets.

Second, successive governments, including the administrations of Bill Clinton, George W. Bush, and Barack Obama, have continued to prioritize the development of technologies for managing government data banks more efficiently. By default, all reforms that improve efficiency in government promote a culture based on ICTs. Information and communication technologies are in large measure considered an essential feature of modern government. Governments, although conservative and rule bound by nature, do not necessarily wish to be left behind in the use of technologies that permeate the entire social fabric. Thus, also wishing to take part in the utilization of ICTs as symbols of modernity, as well as advance more practical ends, many government agencies established websites in the 1990s, cementing the place of ICTs and e-government in the contemporary social mosaic.

Third, e-government by itself is the avenue through which a great deal of professional socialization takes place. Without doubt, the extensive use of Listserves and e-mails increases the visibility of e-government practices. Professional associations increasingly post interactive training activities that in turn reinforce the use of ICTs. Public administrators are socialized to be members of virtual and cybercommunities that are both formal and informal. Cultural symbols of bureaucratic organization include a host of technological devices such as teleconferencing equipment, fax machines, touch-tone telephone–based communication systems, agency-based Listserves, and other electronic gadgets considered essential to the functioning of modern organizations.

The very existence of ICTs has provided public administration with a wide array of its technical vocabulary. Starting from the word e-government, a host of key phrases that inform contemporary speech are attributed to the new environment. Just for example, some of the everyday words associated with e-government and ICTs include e-mail address, electronic file, portal, Listserve, Netiquette, password, cyberspace, cyberlanguage, telecities, network, technopolis, and so forth. A huge shift in our language base has occurred, with e-government becoming a primary conveyor of an emerging lexicon. The images of public organization now include these e-government artifacts.

Communication in the Context of Public Administration

Our conceptual understanding of the importance of e-government's links within public administration begins with an overview of the role played by technological innovations in ensuring that information flows from administrators to the public as well as in the reverse direction. Information typically refers to data that are meaningful for decision making. The type of data of interest to administrators is useful for understanding provision and acquisition of public services. Communication must occur before information becomes useful for the policy maker, implementer, and consumer of public policies. Policy goals are clarified through communication systems. Communication is the interactive process through which information and meaning are exchanged between sources and receivers. It is absolutely essential in all organizational settings. Most experts on organizations assert that effective communication is the foundation for effectiveness in any type of organization.

Communication plays a crucial role in the manner in which organizations are structured and function, and public administrators know that policy implementation cannot be successful without good communication skills. Since Barnard (1938) wrote the classic *Functions of the Executives* we have known that successful public management is dependent upon good communication. Today no public administrator ignores how he or she communicates with both internal and external parties who interact with the organization she or he leads. Public organizational leaders know that both data and information are available, that data are raw information that must be internalized, reorganized into information, and transmitted throughout the organization.

To a large extent, e-government is about the use of the vast technological resources including telephone conferencing, mobile phones, e-mails, BlackBerry hand units, data storage and retrieval equipment, and a host of other recent innovations. For example, agencies use Internet technology to automate internal processes on "intranets" and give employees an opportunity to be connected by e-mail to friends and family all over the world. The advantages and disadvantages of these inventions are discussed in various administrative forums and need not repeat here.

E-mail is the most visible and widely used form of computer-mediated communication (CMC) (Huang, 2002). In government as in the business sector, it is used for a host of communication activities including "marketing, intelligence gathering, negotiating, relationship building, and payment processing" (Huang, 2002, p. 193). One of the major strengths of this approach is its ability to provide immediate feedback in a multidirectional format. However, in terms of information richness theory, e-mail lacks the attributes that make face-to-face conversation useful in the provision of street-level services.

TELECOMMUTING AND TELECONFERENCING

Another of the plethora of opportunities afforded by computer-mediated devices is the proliferation of telecommuting and teleconferencing. Numerous applications that fall under this class of technologies. The common characteristic is that most telecommuting and teleconferencing approaches are considered effective administrative means of saving energy and attendant commuting costs. Persons who commute to work incur thousands of dollars in travel-related expenses—vehicle maintenance, wear and tear on roads and bridges, and even activities such as parking lot snow removal, for example. Studies show that further costs are saved when agencies utilize video conferencing and interactive web-based seminars, known as webinars, rather than scheduling physical meetings. A webinar can take the form of a variety of interactions that include lectures, workshops, and presentations transmitted over the web. Although some interaction is possible through webcast platforms, most are typically one-way communications from a speaker to an online audience. Of course, interaction and question and answer sessions can be facilitated through handheld mobile devices and speakerphones. Voice over Internet Protocol (VoIP) has further added quality to the repertoire of communications devices. Web-based communication platforms include programs such Skype, Gizmo, and Vonage.

These devices are cheaper to operate than previously dominant platforms for long-distance voice communication such as the public switched telephone network. VoIP is quite versatile because it uses a variation of standard TCP/IP protocols to send data over the Internet. It has numerous advantages over older electronic meeting system (EMS) platforms. For example, VoIP can carry images, live videos, texts and has screen-sharing capabilities. However, one limitation of VoIP systems is that they require high-speed broadband connections to work best. A second weakness is in the design of the devices. Since VoIP uses SIP, a variation of the standard TCP/IP protocols, it was never engineered to support long live conversations, and is frequently susceptible to stutter and latency (Neagu, 2009). Without disregarding these limitations, the use of VoIP communication devices does not necessarily reduce the quality of deliberations conducted in virtual conferencing. Video conferencing provides opportunities for more participants in these synchronous meetings.

Numerous examples can be provided to illustrate the advantages of video conferencing. In the well-documented case of Nebraska's Division of Communications of the Department of Administrative Services, an estimated travel cost of $287,664 was saved by the state's "video conferencing network for a twelve-month period from October 1991 through September 1992" (Nebraska, 1994). Computations show that savings were accrued in staff time, mileage calculated from gasoline costs, and in some cases meals and lodging.

Savings accrued through teleconferencing are only an economic aspect of increasing use of web-based communication. These technologies also offer improved security over their predecessors. For example, in a case from Allegheny County, Maryland, teleconferencing was a logical step toward enhancing public safety. A report noted that:

> The bad economy and fears of terrorism led both companies and employees to want to spend less time traveling. Along the way, improvements in technology made folks realize that a well-done teleconference can be just about as good as an in-person meeting… A good example of the use of teleconferencing as a normal—not exotic—tool comes from the government. Late last month, the General Services Administration (GSA) said that it will open teleconferencing centers in 14 of its offices during the first two months of next year. The news isn't surprising in the context of the government's long-time commitment to telecommuting. Progress can be measured in many ways, and a pretty good one is how effectively criminals are being kept off the streets. If that is an accepted metric, teleconferencing indeed is doing well: The Maryland Department of Public Safety and Correctional Services aims to use teleconferencing to enable inmates to appear in court and participate in doctors' visits via teleconferencing. The system recently was unveiled in Allegheny County, Maryland. (Weinschenk, 2010)

Before moving on to applying a theoretical lens, we should add one more example of teleconferencing in a legal context. Previously, there was no law governing teleconferencing and the use of computer-mediated devices for holding meetings between participants located in different communities. Several jurisdictions now give decisions arrived at in teleconferencing environments as much weight as those made in face-to-face situations. The state of Tennessee exemplifies this emerging trend, because county commissioners, city councilmen and school board members across the state are able to confer with one another without violating the state's Open Meetings Act (Humphrey, 2009). Under the technological sunshine law (the Open Meetings Act), local elected bodies have the option of setting up a chat room on a government website. Officials can exchange messages and discuss pending issues without contravening regulations of government communication and transparency. Chat room meetings are becoming common even among college recruiters and will only grow in importance as premium high-speed connectivity proliferates. The Open Meetings Act included a provision to increase public access to chat room meetings through computers freely available in the public library systems.

The field of communications may provide the clearest lens for viewing e-government issues. Several authors discuss the context of e-government in terms of the role technology plays in achieving effective communication between service providers and consumers. The general aim of e-government initiatives is to make governments work better and more efficiently through reducing the size of the paper trail. This was a big part of the reinvention doctrine posited in the NPRG initiatives during the Clinton administration. Witness these passages from leading public administration textbooks:

- Communication technology greatly affects the flow and efficiency of communication in all directions. The Internet in particular has been an enormously important communication technology development that promotes horizontal and crisscrossing information flows. (LeMay, 2006, p. 293)
- Technology impacts modes of communication, formal and informal. In an era of faxes, computers, and Photostat machines, communication challenges will emerge that are even more complex, demanding, and technical. Cell phones, e-mail, and telephone answering machines contribute to the narrowing of the gulf between formal and informal communication distinctions. ...Despite the

downside of the information highway, Internet access has made communication between local government and citizens much easier nationwide. Public records access, personnel postings, permit applications, and legislative updates are available online in dozens of cities and counties... Advances in the use of information technology (IT) and the Internet continue to change the way that federal agencies communicate, use, and disseminate information, deliver services, and do business. Electronic government (e-government) refers to the use of technology, particularly web-based Internet applications. (Berkley and Rouse, 2004, pp. 240–241)

- Public administrators continue to expend much of their time and effort on those communicative tasks and on the growing number and diversity of communication, including e-mail messages, contracts, service agreements, satisfaction surveys, and other forms. The pervasiveness of communication extends beyond the managerial workday. (Stillman, 2005, p. 258)
- E-government holds great potential for facilitating the public's interaction with public administration. Agencies can use the Internet to disseminate reports, studies, rules, and information about their operations, procedures, and eligibility requirements for benefits. They can create electronic reading rooms to reduce the number of freedom of information requests they receive and process. E-gov initiatives can increase public participation in agency rulemaking and other decision making. E-gov can enable individuals to pay taxes and fees as well as apply for benefits and licenses electronically. In some cases, adjudication—especially appeals—can also be handled electronically. Because e-gov ordinarily reduces agency expenses, its use is limited primarily by imagination and technology. (Rosenbloom & Kravchuk, 2005, p. 472)
- Greater communication with public officials and administrators is possible through electronic mail, faxing, and audio-video conferencing... Although they vary in quality and ease of use, at present virtually all federal agencies and states and most local governments have established websites for access to service and

information. The White House launched First Gov in 2000, a website that currently provides a portal for citizens, business and organizations and federal employees to access a wide variety of information and governmental services ranging from apply for a passport or a student loan, obtain information on government contracts and rules, and access information and directories for federal agencies. (Denhardt & Denhardt, 2006, p. 412)

- The rise of desktop computers and the Internet in the 1990s led to a radically new approach to some of government's problems. Government officials began recognizing that citizens did not necessarily need to come to government to transact public business. The spread of always-on electronic connections made it possible to build systems to allow citizens to file their taxes, renew their motor vehicle registrations, check on traffic congestion, obtain a police report, pay a traffic ticket, or apply for a job... the government can enhance the ability of citizens to connect more easily with government. (Kettl & Fesler, 2005, pp. 132–133)
- There are two faces of e-government: internal and external. The internal face denotes the operations of government itself; for example using the Web for electronic procurement, electronic forms, and Web based management information systems. The external face refers to the online services offered to citizens and businesses, for example, community calendars, bill payment portals, and application forms for employment. While there are two distinct faces to e-government, they seldom represent independent initiatives. E-government then is in essence the overarching term for all efforts to use the Internet to simplify governmental activities for both the public and the public's employees. (Shafritz & Russell, 2003, p. 284)

Technical Design Changes

One of the central issues of design in information technology concerns evidence that most pubic organizations are not generating optimal value from their massive investments in IT (Starling, 2005). Failure is attributed to variables such as lack of leadership and poor design. The design of technology standards and operations management is crucial to ensuring the successful implementation of IT programs in the public sector. Information management must be considered in understanding the functioning of e-government designs. Increasingly, public administration experts point to the management implications of the designs of information and communication technologies as necessary ingredients for a successful e-government.

Another important and often ignored dimension of evolving technology is the cost of ITs to the organization. Costs are either direct, defined as budget outlays associated with acquisition of information and communication technologies, or indirect. Indirect costs described by Starling (2005) are as follows:

> Some costs are hidden. All the excitement about the benefits of computerization should not blind an administrator to the indirect costs associated with personal computers (PCs). Managers are now only beginning to quantify some of the unproductive behavior—call it "fiddling"—associated with the use of PCs. Some fiddling may eventually make a person more productive, such as learning to use a new program or reconstructing a file that was accidentally erased. But most of it is straight procrastination—the equivalent of sharpening pencils. And it costs organizations in time and salaries. (p. 568)

Design issues must also grapple with IT capabilities and whether technology within organizational structures should be centralized or decentralized. Administrators must avoid redundancy and maximize benefits while minimizing costs. Often technical support can serve several units or divisions of an agency. In some jurisdictions management of sensitive data requires the centralization of operations. The most recent responses to security concerns in the United States have forced greater interagency information sharing, in most cases, using centralized databases, or at least some degree of sharing between key consumers of security information including the Central Intelligence Agency (CIA), Federal Bureau of Investigations (FBI), local law enforcement officials, and the Attorney General.

In addition, issues of privacy and security are increasingly important. There is an ongoing national conversation in the United States about the trade-offs between individual liberties and governmental concerns for security.

Other related concerns include authentication and authorization issues. *The New York Times* recently reported growing concern with the issue of identity theft occurring over the Internet. The *Times* reported that cybercriminals had perfected electronic cons by developing malicious programs to infect computers and access vital information by logging keystrokes. The fraudsters "monitor Web access of online banking customers and start recording information only when the user enters the sites of interest to them" (Zeller, 2006). The programs transmit user names and passwords to gangs that steal millions of funds. Cybercriminals affect computers as much as virus writers do. E-government is not immune to these concerns.

The proliferation of firewall and Internet security technologies has not necessarily tamed the growth of Internet criminals. Design issues also require upfront investment in wireless security technologies and public education. Without proactive interventions, the promise of e-government can be costly.

Finally, another challenge of e-government is to design websites that conform to federal and state laws. Public agencies providing services through the Internet must deal with the issue of language barriers. Events such as Hurricanes Katrina and Rita, which devastated vast areas of Louisiana and Mississippi in 2005, required that the Federal Emergency Management Agency (FEMA) and other disaster management efforts describe available services in both English and Spanish. Though this has been done, design of Internet services in all aspects of government must continuously be sensitive to language and cultural representation. Adherence to simple rules of web design including simplicity, clarity, and sensitivity to digital access issues is a must, especially for regions such as those with Native American reservations where access can be problematic even in public libraries where connection speeds are slow.

KEY CONCEPTS

Communication
Computer-Mediated Communication (CMC)
Cutback Management
Democratic Governance
Design
Ecology
E-government
E-mail
Federal Communications Commission (FCC)
Federal Trade Commission (FTC)
Globalization
Information Technologies (ITs)
Internet
Internet Governance
Internet Telephony
Intranets
National Partnership for Reinventing Government (NPRG)
National Performance Review (NPR)
Organizational Culture
Organizational Environment
Privacy
Public Key Infrastructure
Regulatory Framework
Security
State Transformation
Technical Environment
Teleconferencing
Webinar

DISCUSSION QUESTIONS

1. What is e-government, and how important is it in the delivery of public services in your city or local government?
2. List the types of ICTs that are featured most prominently in government offices that you visit frequently. Why do you think these are the most frequent types used?
3. Discuss the merits of studying e-government within an organizational culture framework.

4. How important is the concept of environment or ecology of administration to our understanding of e-government?
5. To what extent is Internet technology disruptive? What are some of the opportunities and threats associated with the Internet? How have security and safety concerns affected how we understand the nature and scope of e-governments?

Internet Activity

Several names of authors in the emerging e-government field are mentioned in this book's first chapter. Using all the search engines available, locate some of the papers and reports they have published that are available online. Cut and paste their definitions of e-government in a word file and post your finding to other members of the learning community. You need to find at least three individuals.

CHAPTER 2

THE STUDY OF e-GOVERNMENT

In the past, organizations regarded technological changes as both opportunities and challenges. The most recent wave of technological change is in the area of information and communications. Similar to the past, governments have embraced the accelerating pace of development in ICTs. With these new technologies, there is a growing need in both academia and practitioner fields for students of public administration to understand this new, enhanced role for technology. It is, after all, ICTs that form the basis for e-government.

E-government plays an important role in the provision of public services and participation in governance. It remains a core element in administrative reform, which itself merits focused study. However, the degree to which reforms are fundamental or go far enough in changing the core essence of government is very much a subject of academic dispute. Kraemer and King (2006) examined the theoretical ideal of ICTs as an instrument of administrative reform and found that the adoption of newer ICTs reinforced existing administrative and political arrangements. What we can say is that e-government essentially structures the form of public service delivery to accommodate the new virtual spaces brought about by ICTs. Much like budgeting and human resource management, e-government is a tool of public administration. The quest for efficiency and effectiveness is the modus operandi of public administration reform, and the continuous improvement of available ICTs is perceived as the epitome of these values.

Still, e-government is a value choice that goes beyond efficiency and effectiveness and embraces other values such as transparency and representativeness in managing the work of government. Fountain (2001) observed that information technology, along with changes in organizational design, reduces the amount of red tape and accelerates the delivery of services for some members of the public.

In terms of a broad vision, e-government focuses on at least five broad goals aimed at improving the management of public service delivery. These goals are:

i. Knowledge management, especially improvements in storage and dissemination of information for better decision making
ii. Empowerment of citizens and delegation of decision-making authority to other organizational levels
iii. Enhanced economies of scale, especially in the area of planning and implementation of government programs (e-government initiatives save tremendous amounts of time and lower financial costs to the public.)
iv. Performance monitoring
v. Enhanced data sharing among numerous government agencies (Sharing data enhances quality coordination and improves strategic planning as well.)

E-government employs aspects of transparency and openness in government and is an aspect of the "good government" movement. Henry (2006) described good government as an old idea whose remnants continue to have a global appeal. Among the key values of good government are the desires for competency, democracy, and honesty. To the extent that e-government promotes responsiveness and efficiency, it is in line with the ideals of progress in modern government. Studies that explore efforts by public institutions to promote effectiveness and efficiency are therefore an important aspect of good governance. Research has shown that e-government has a positive effect on citizen confidence in government (West, 2004). Furthermore, though e-government may not necessarily increase citizen confidence in government, it does reinforce the public perception that governments promote efficiency. This is consistent with the argument that new technologies raise citizen expectations about government performance. A number of scholars, including Norris (2001), regard information technology as the most important component for increasing citizen participation and confidence in government institutions. Studying e-government, therefore, is an important part of understanding issues of civic engagement and democratic governance.

The study of e-government is still in its infancy. Information and communication technologies provide new opportunities for growth in the emerging field. At least three distinct phases of the development of this subfield of public administration can be identified.

The stages are not unusual in any field's evolution. The first phase was the formative stage and was concerned with boundary formation, discovery, and self-definition. The second stage involved boundary scanning and interconnectedness with other social sciences. At this stage, the field's evolution was informed by the successful launching of e-commerce. Arguably, e-commerce provided proponents of the government's reinvention movement with a template from which to expand initiatives to empower the customer or citizen clients. The third stage was organized around empirical data derived from practical applications of e-government. Much has been learned from "best practices" developed from the application of ICTs in different public sector settings. Let us consider the stages in some detail.

First, scholars grappled with definitional and theoretical issues including the subfield's boundaries. Researchers in the burgeoning subfield of e-government apply a variety of established theoretical lenses to study complex phenomena. Among the most popular overarching approaches are those derived from Weber's theory of bureaucracy. Bureaucratic approaches state that e-government is a manifestation of the reform ethos in public administration. Viewed from this perspective, successful implementation of e-government connotes innovation in public administration.

Other interesting theoretical lenses are network theories. In political science, network theories describe domestic policies and international relations from the point of view of interacting agencies (Kettl, 1993; Milward & Provan, 1998; O'Toole, 1997; Scharpf, 1993). Network theories in public administration explain interjurisdictional cooperation in both geographic and organizational space. In many of these formulations, organizations are self-correcting entities working in subsystems to optimize the achievement of different goals and missions. Frederickson's (1999) work on administrative conjunction argues that functional professionals carry out conjunction activities through loosely linked and coupled networks.

Essentially, functional professionals do not require hierarchical command or market pressure to conduct their business. Network relations arise because public organizations are interdependent and feed off each another, because they depend on exchange of resources and have integrated workflow processes. Decision-making mechanisms, even if decentralized, accept loose coupling and weak ties to conform to general ruling party policy platforms. From this perspective, one-stop portals and other applications of ICTs in e-government are studied as aspects of collaboration within and between government agencies and departments. Two other popular broad lenses in the study of e-government are stakeholder-based perspectives and diffusion of technology theories (Khosrow-Pour, 2008b; Lazer, 2002).

In the case of stakeholder theoretical frameworks, scholars examine aspects of e-government by studying the roles of various actors in the complex matrix of service delivery (Scholl, 2001). Stakeholder theories are associated with interest group theories in political science and apply a wide variety of perspectives to help us understand policy formulation and implementation. In the case of diffusion theories, scholarship examines the impact of computerization and informatics on the delivery of public services in online environments. Such studies are in turn based on a wide variety of sociological perspectives.

Seminal e-government scholarship from the second phase of this field's development is concerned with the derivation of e-government from precedents in e-commerce. E-commerce has distinguished itself as a set of mechanisms for buying and selling services and merchandise through electronic means. It also involves a wide range of marketing and end-to-end transactions between suppliers and consumers in a variety of technologies such as EDI, mail, and funds transfer. It involves specific types of transactions such as customer-to-customer (C2C), business-to-business (B2B) and business-to-customer (B2C) (Laudon & Laudon, 2003). These communication categories are mirrored in the e-government literature as government-to-government (G2G), government-to-citizen (G2C), government-to-employee (G2E), and government-to-business (G2B) formulations. Carter and Belanger (2004, pp. 11–12) observed, "both e-Commerce and e-Government systems support the electronic mediation of transactions over potentially great distances." Discussion of similarities or differences between e-government and e-commerce does not ignore the fundamental differences between public and private enterprise. Efforts within a section of the scholarly community aim to change government, but their efforts fail to change the fundamental nature of the work of government, especially its role in the core area of protecting the public interest, such as in regulation, security, and public safety. The drive for e-government is probably understood best in the context of the underlying goals and motives of ruling elites and society at large. Both stakeholder and technology diffusion perspectives support efforts to study emerging trends in how government works in an environment saturated with ICTs. Scholars often do not leave behind their values, and some clearly maintain an activist posture in their writing.

Much of the work carried out in this genre is associated with the drive to make the public sector function more like the private sector and increase efficiency in service delivery. Public opinion in America overwhelmingly supports the idea of government embracing electronic technologies in providing services in a similar manner to the private sector. The appeal is based on several factors including infrastructural savings and improved transaction costs. The reinvention movement in public service sees this model as applicable to ICT investments in government and seeks to apply some of its techniques and principles to measuring public organizations.

Third and most recently, e-government scholarship broadly addresses application strategies as well as growing ethical concerns including the digital divide, privacy, and security. These are central themes captured in hundreds of syllabi for courses in e-government. The focus on information technology security and accountability practices has increased because without data integrity, e-government would be unacceptable in a democratic setting. The widely held view is that e-government can only improves trust in government only if and when security and system integrity are ensured. A vast literature has mushroomed examining the context of trust and confidence in government.

PUBLIC ADMINISTRATION AND THE REFOUNDING ERA

Scholarship in the most prominent journals of public administration explores the close link between e-government and the evolution of public administration. E-government is perhaps the latest addition to the multidisciplinary family of public administration studies. E-government belongs to the refounding period of the larger discipline in the 1980s–1990s. The re-founding period of the broader field includes the much touted "reinvention of government" ideology. The reinvention movement, attributed mostly to Osborne and Gaebler (1992), seeks to make government work more efficiently. As Osborne and Plastrik (1998) explained, it is not synonymous with privatization. It is about transforming public agencies through changing their culture and power structures.

The Clinton administration actualized Osborne and Gaebler's (1992) ideas by encouraging debureaucratization and making government more customer-friendly. ICTs are considered a tool for reforming public bureaucracy, especially those geared toward deconstructing horizontal differentiation within government agencies and departments. In an executive order issued in 1999, President Clinton instructed agencies to design e-government systems that minimized institutional hierarchies and encouraged information sharing among federal agencies. The executive order was followed by the administration's implementation of Al Gore's National Performance Review's recommendation to make full use of computer systems to revolutionize the way public services are delivered. Support for reinvention of government through e-government innovation is also expressed in the assertion that information and communication technologies challenge past norms and capabilities of traditional bureaucracy (Bellamy & Taylor, 1998).

As we mentioned in Chapter 1, the increased use of computers and other information technologies is one of the fundamental characteristics of society today. The self-renewing nature of technology is a cornerstone of the reinvention movement. It represents a change from the resistance to change associated with bureaucratic practices by Burns and Stalker (1961) and other leading organization theorists.

Applications within the New Public Management Approaches

The refounding movement in American public administration occurred at the same time as the reinvention movement (NPM) in the 1990s. The movement was anti-statist. One of the goals of NPM is the pursuit of technological means for performing government work (Rosenbloom & Kravchuk, 2005). Information technologies feature most prominently in this emerging field. Savas (2005) noted that many processes and procedures in government are beginning to take advantage of the e-government technologies now abundantly available throughout the United States and other advanced countries. In the United States, citizens can now engage public service providers through the proliferation of information kiosks located in strategic places in urban settings. Public libraries have also become major points of access to e-government services. In some areas, public libraries are the de facto e-government access points, providing vital information on issues such as Medicare drug plans, welfare benefits, assistance programs for children, disaster relief, and even information on public housing. For example, the Florida Department of Children and Families requires needy members of the public to complete benefits applications through online outlets accessible in public libraries. Part of the reason for reaching out to needy families through public library access is the concern for continuous access to the Internet and other elements of the digital divide.

In discussing the lack of access to the Internet, studies show some communities experience a huge gap in the use of computer technologies. According to Bissell (2004), access in Native American communities continues to lag behind that of all other Americans. While 94 percent of Native Americans living in urban areas have access to Internet technologies, only 39 percent of those in rural areas have access to the Internet and hence are excluded from the benefits of e-government (Bissell, 2004, p. 129). The assumption of NPM advocates is that increased use of information and communication technologies helps make public services more market-like and customer-friendly. Customer service initiatives in government emulate those in the private sector by increased usage of "satellite offices in shopping centers for renewing driver's licenses and vehicle registration" (Rosenbloom & Kravchuk, 2005, p. 21). The range of services provided through e-government initiatives is quite expansive. For illustration, let us consider two popular examples: motor vehicle registration programs and the e-filing of taxes. Motor vehicle registration divisions across the United States are responsible for a variety of services including issuance of licenses and vehicle credentials, revenue collection and management, and compliance with legislative mandates. In all states, motor vehicle registration is also the primary source of motor vehicle information for law enforcement agencies and identity information for government generally. Currently all states provide an online portal with interactive, easy-to-use facilities. In Arizona, the Motor Vehicle Division (MVD) is a part of the Arizona Department of Transportation (ADOT) and plays an important part in managing vehicle records for government use. The MVD accepts credit card payments and provides online vehicle registration services to members of the public.

The e-file tax system began in the 1980s. In 1987, electronic filing of individual income tax returns with refunds was successfully operationalized. By 2000, more than 40 million Americans filed their taxes electronically each year. This was two million short of the initial Internal Revenue Service (IRS) goal, but this shortfall eventually disappeared. The decision to permit e-filing was a part of IRS modernization efforts. Electronic filing of taxes proved extremely successful for both members of the public and the business sector. Congress, through enactment of the IRS Restructuring and Reform Act (RRA) of 1998, which also created the Electronic Tax Administration, had challenged the IRS to have over 80 percent of all tax returns filed electronically by 2007. This has been achieved, and most taxes are now filed electronically, making the IRS the world's most efficient tax collection organization. Through e-filing, the IRS collects more than three trillion dollars annually at a cost of less than 39 cents per 100 dollars collected. Thus it is a very efficient system. Members of the public benefit from e-filing because of the additional advantage that tax refunds are processed much more quickly.

Broadly speaking, studies in e-government are an outgrowth of information and communication technologies. ICTs largely differentiate the end of the 20th and beginning of the 21st centuries from the "modern" era gone by. E-government is in a large part a measure of the applications of the Internet and other technologies in bureaucratic settings. As Northrop (1999) noted, the National Association of Schools of Public Affairs and Administration (NASPAA) recognized that computing ought to be an essential skill for students in Master's of Public Administration (MPA) programs. Understanding computerization in government is an important component in educating for public service and a first step in e-government education.

E-government education has the potential to provide skills for emerging administrators. It is now an examinable area in public administration programs all over the globe. E-government is taught to midcareer and young scholars alike. It forms part of the MPA curriculum at several universities. Syracuse University, a leader in MPA programs, offers a certificate in e-government as well. Hundreds of NASPAA member universities have accredited MPA programs offering courses in e-government. These courses are increasingly popular and prestigious, drawing a large number of students from other disciplines including communications, engineering, and sociology. E-government now joins administrative law, budgeting, local government, federalism, human resource administration, organizational behavior, and other areas of public administration in mosaic discipline of public administration.

Subfield Identity and Research Outlets

E-government as a subfield has established its own identity through the emergence of networks within the American Society for Public Administration (ASPA) and an increasing acceptance of work in the field's premier journals, especially *Public Administration Review* and *Journal of Public Administration and Research and Theory*. The *International Journal of Public Administration* also issued an entire volume dedicated to e-government scholarship. There are a growing number of legitimate e-government journals that reinforce its salience. Among the list of important periodicals dedicated to e-government scholarship are:

- *The Electronic Journal of e-Government*
- *The Journal of E-Government*
- *eGovernment Quarterly*
- *e-Service Journal*
- *Public Technology.Net*
- *eGovernment and Public Sector*
- *GovExec.Com*
- *Federal Computer Week*
- *e-Gov Bulletin*
- *Electronic Government*

Articles on e-government have also appeared in other field-specific journals including:

- *Electronic Commerce Research and Applications*
- *E-Learning*
- *Government Information Quarterly*
- *International Journal of Electronic Government Research*

- *International Journal of Law and Information Technology*
- *Journal of Electronic Commerce in Organization*
- *Journal of Government Information*
- *Journal of Technology in Human Services*
- *Electronic Journal of Communication*

Besides the impressive array of journals, there are several centers of e-government all over the world. Some are virtual centers sponsored by corporations in the industry. Others are academic in nature, focusing on policy dimensions of e-government. One of the field's leading scholars, Darrell M. West, is based at the Taubman Center for Public Policy at Brown University. The Center produces annual reports on the state of e-government globally. There are similar well funded e-government centers in Europe and a few in the developing world. These centers often share policy documents and conduct cross-cultural studies in issues pertaining to e-government. Examples of these centers can be viewed in box 2.1.

Currently there is little cohesion in the scholarship of e-government, because of the field's relative immaturity and unclear theoretical formulations. A small consensus is the acknowledgement that the e-government movement crystallized with the emergence of the Internet as a primary medium of communications with wide applications in public service delivery systems.

Why is e-Government Taught?

Courses in e-government aim for several objectives. The first objective is to enable students to understand the issues and policies pertaining to e-democracy and articulate the business model of empowering the customer. Courses also aim to develop a body of knowledge to help students understand the history and legislation within which e-government occurs. Other stated objectives of e-government courses include:

- To introduce basic concepts of e-government and the use of information systems in public agencies, including comparative e-government aspects

Box 2.1. *Examples of Multidisciplinary e-Government Centers.*

Center	Website
The Taubman Center	http://www.brown.edu/Departments/Taubman_Center/
Center for Technology in Government	http://www.nysl.nysed.gov/edocs/ctg/ctgdir.htm
Center for Digital Government	http://www.centerdigitalgov.com/
Center for Technology and Information Policy	http://www.maxwell.syr.edu/ctip/ctip.htm
National Center for Digital Government Research and Practice	http://www.ksg.harvard.edu/digitalcenter/
The Center for Information Policy and Electronic Government (CIPEG)	http://cipeg.umd.edu/
E-Governance Lab, School of Policy, Planning and Development	http://www.usc.edu/
Center for Information Protection; Information Assurance Center (IAC)	http://www.iac.iastate.edu/
The Berkeley Center for the Information Society	http://www.icsi.berkeley.edu/BCIS/
Center for Information & Society	http://cis.washington.edu/
The Centre of Information Society Technologies (CIST), Sofia University, "St. Kliment Ohridski"	http://www-it.fmi.uni-sofia.bg/cist/
Center for the Information Society	http://cis.ist.psu.edu/

- To review select strategic management models used to develop e-government projects and to offer students skills and best practices for the employment of e-government tools
- To aid students in obtaining proficiency in areas of government utilizing ICTs
- To address the economic, political, and social implications of implementing e-government
- To understand the application and design of technologies used in e-government

These five learning outcomes are neither mutually exclusive nor an exhaustive list of all the objectives in most e-government courses. The general trend is to provide awareness of why ICTs are changing the ways government interacts with citizens. In studying e-government, emerging managers and students typically respond to questions such as:

- What are the costs and benefits of e-government?
- Should digital democracy be promoted?
- What are the tools of e-government?
- What problems are associated with the digital divide?
- Who gets access to ICTs?
- What kinds of services lend themselves to provision via e-government?
- What barriers do public officials encounter in the application of e-government technologies?

Essentially, e-government courses rely on both students and educators keeping abreast of the fast-paced technological innovation that informs this area of study. Therefore, e-government students must continuously find Internet resources to build their vocabulary and gain insights on the products in use in various public service settings. Among the most popular sites visited are those that identify technologies used in government. For example, the State University of New York at Albany manages the Center for Technology in Government, which provides continuous updates on the ICT arena through various links to useful sites. The Executive Office of the President, through the Office of Management and Budget, plays an important role in building a data bank of executive e-government strategies at the federal level.

A second dimension of pedagogically sound practices in the e-government subfield is the use of interactive online teaching technologies including Blackboard and Sakai. These offer better opportunities for the development of a robust Internet community by linking consumers of ICTs with active learners.

E-government offers interesting assessment opportunities for learners. Most profound are techniques that help learners identify a prospective client for whom they then develop an e-project. E-government, much like budgeting, has great potential for hands-on learning, such as simulations in which students build strategies for planning and implementing e-government techniques. There are several opportunities for learners to assess web design for government departments utilizing ICTs in areas such as procurement, applications for services, customer satisfaction evaluation, taxation, and training. Learners, as participant observers, have a greater opportunity for developing and testing what works, as well as how and why it works. Student feedback has enormous potential for refining principles of government website design.

There are also many opportunities for integrating e-government studies into a policy studies curriculum. For example, courses in environmental policy and politics often refer to the roles played by e-government in rulemaking. No doubt, the existence of ICTs has changed the manner by which rulemaking in the management of natural resources and the wider environment is accomplished. Likewise, the growing area of studies in homeland security is now paying attention to issues in digital government. Learners in the homeland security track integrate topics in e-government to enhance their understanding of safety in the age of terrorism. The challenge has been to provide learners with best practices in managing information technologies. Moreover, the widespread use of the Internet to spread ideologies that enhance global terrorism adds content to issues presented in such endeavors. Such learning experiences have to grapple with issues of cyberterrorism and the potential disruption banking and e-commerce services that are now at the core of advanced civilizations.

In brief, e-government has been integrated in a wide variety of policy areas. The example of the Department of Homeland Security (DHS) exemplifies a new and emergent organization that relies heavily on information technologies for its daily operations. One can hardly imagine the DHS managing its critical tasks without the possibilities of e-government. In addition to the DHS, an emerging trend in the study of e-government policies and the practice of e-government is the proliferation of initiatives that address specific practitioner-driven agendas. While these are technically inseparable from traditional academic centers, they are primarily associated with specific cities, counties, and collaborating private ventures and ICT corporations, demonstrating aspects of interagency cooperation. These agencies contribute by providing useful discussion agendas on methodologies for implementing e-government programs within the public sector. The organizational divisions take into account specific technological, institutional, and organizational factors that affect the application of ICTs as well the experiences of information technology officials and perceptions of the public. Most of these organizations have excellent analyses of e-readiness and hundreds of documented case studies of various jurisdictions, as well as websites that include links to their publications and opportunities for networking. Interagency partnerships can be seen in box 2.2.

Finally, the study of e-government is not devoid of comparative studies. Comparative aspects are an exciting addendum to the core curriculum. Perhaps this is promising because technology is considered more neutral than politics, at least in terms of emerging paradigms. To illustrate this point, one can focus on the applications of e-government globally, as shown in box 2.3.

Developed countries have more technological resources and hence data for comparative studies is most plausible within the West. For example, much like the Executive Office of the President, the Deputy Prime

Box 2.2. *e-Government Interagency (Government and Private Partnerships) Centers.*

Center	Website
IBM Institute for Electronic Government	http://www.01.ibm.com/industries/government/ieg/
The National Business Center (NBC)	http://www.nbc.gov/egov/index.html
Americans for Less Secrecy, More Democracy	http://www.openthegovernment.org

Box 2.3. *e-Government International Centers (Examples).*

Center	Website
The Commonwealth Center for E-Government (British Commonwealth of Nations)	http://www.thecommonwealth.org/Internal/151842/
The eGovernment Resource Centre (Victoria, Australia)	http://www.egov.vic.gov.au/
Center for E-Governance (United Nations University)	http://www.egov.iist.unu.edu
The Fraunhofer eGovernment Center (Germany)	http://www.fraunhofer.de/EN/institutes/
Center for e-Governance (Ahmedabad, India)	http://www.iimahd.ernet.in/egov/
Center for International Research on Communication and Information Technologies (Melbourne, Australia)	http://www.rmit.edu.au/

Minister's Office in the UK has an elaborate infrastructure to coordinate the issues emerging from the fast changing technological world.

In the UK and European Union (EU) numerous information technology management forums have been created for various levels of government. For example, the eEurope 2005 project, initiated in 1999, aimed to get European citizens online by the 2005. The eEurope Action Plan sought to establish a competitive and knowledge-based society through the provision of secure broadband access at affordable and competitive prices. These goals have been achieved, for the most part. The E-Government Unit was highly successful in steering e-government programs in Great Britain. By 2005, for example, nearly all government departments, agencies, and local governments had fully functional websites. As an industry, British e-government accounted to over 1 percent of the country's GDP (Parliamentary Affairs, 2006).

There are numerous other Internet resources devoted to e-governments in countries such as India, Japan, China, and South Africa. The United

Nations reported in 2003 that more than 91 percent of member countries had embraced e-government strategies (United Nations, 2003). Studies from Brown University and the United Nations present observations that non-western countries including South Korea and Chile are among the best performers in e-government generally. Numerous studies show that Western developed countries have much to learn from each other. For instance, a study of best practices in e-government commissioned by the UK Cabinet Office found that a number of governments were moving "beyond e-government toward a much more powerful approach to technology-enabled government, or 't-government'" (Hamilton, 2005). The study looked into the level of sophistication of and scope of e-government across nine countries: Australia, Canada, France, Germany, Italy, Japan, Sweden, the United Kingdom, and the United States. The important point to note is that there are merits as well as problems with comparisons.

Comparative Analysis and Challenges

Hamilton (2005) summarized the challenges to comparative examination of e-government as follows:

> Country contexts, comprising, for example, the legal and market environment, government e-government structure, and the attitudes of citizens toward e-government, vary considerably even amongst our international benchmark group of nine.
>
> Priorities and overall strategies for e-government are different worldwide, with some governments giving greater weight to improving customer service (effectiveness) and others to streamlining processes or reducing costs to serve (efficiency).

Hamilton (2005) further observed that the

> bulk of existing studies of "e-Government" take a rather narrow view, focusing heavily on the provision of electronic services to citizens and businesses. There is less coverage of the impact that

> these services have had, in part because impact is harder than provision to measure. Very little has been published on the intra-governmental aspects of e-Government, especially at the level of individual public services like health and education. (p. 6)

CONCLUSIONS

During the 1990s, e-government was new among the subfields of public administration. Research and teaching has been mostly confined to the examination of how governments around the world deploy e-government strategies. The field is growing and continues to address a broad spectrum of applications and impacts of ICTs on the delivery of public services. While these applications have offered innovative possibilities in the practice of public administration, much ground remains to be covered in building a coherent theoretical base. Theory building must appreciate diverse approaches and be based on recognizable practices. Only good theory can influence administrative actions. Building good theory will eliminate the potential for confusion and chaos in the emerging field.

The potential for chaos is real, especially as best practices, now popular in the literature, begin to look more like principles of administration. Since e-government is still evolving and is increasingly interdisciplinary in method, scholars and practitioners in the field should not lose sight of the possibility that interdisciplinary lenses can lead to ambiguity and fuzziness in theory building. Although studying e-government lends itself to various approaches, the introduction of ICTs, upon which e-government is organized, was largely influenced by prevailing paradigmatic shifts, foremost of which was the drive for reinvention and reengineering government. Common to the reform approaches has been the centrality of attaining core administrative values such as accountability, efficiency and effectiveness in service delivery. The construction of research questions based on a wider pool of cases and practitioner examples drawn from different countries is promising. Therefore, to the extent that case studies of implementation of e-government policies offer useful lessons, their inclusion in contemporary studies is a worthwhile endeavor. In summary, studying e-government requires an inclusion of cases and best practices from local as well as international sources and must focus on understanding the social, economic and political contexts of new ICTs.

Best Practices Examples

Case 1: Comparing e-government Benefits using Practical Examples: Focus on Transparency

The World Bank documented had documented global e-government case studies that illustrate the benefits derived from use of ICTs in providing government services (World Bank, 2011). The benefits can be categorized in five areas:

- Better Service Delivery to Citizens
- Improved Services for Businesses
- Empowerment through Information
- Transparency and Anti-Corruption
- Efficient Government Purchasing

Using this scheme, it is possible to examine any case of e-government at the state or local level to determine the benefits derived. For example, completing road and motor vehicle license renewal forms, filing taxes, and being able to track the status of an application online provide citizens with an avenue through which they have become more service oriented. When customers go online, there are clearly notable efficiencies. For example, online transactions eliminate the amount of time needed to respond to most queries. There are certainly other efficiencies associated with reduced time that are frequently lost when customers go from office to office or wait in long lines to be served.

Another advantage is the possibility that provision of online services promotes trust and confidence in government. This is especially so when a government's objective is to promote the core value of transparency and probity in its management of scare public resources. When government publishes its transactions online, everyone with access to the information can be made aware of that government's activities. Integrity is preserved in this process when online transactions are in traceable electronic formats.

Case 2: The American Recovery and Reinvestment Act of 2009 and Transparency

The following application of ICTs for the promotion of transparency illustrates the importance of the study of e-government. President Barack Obama was elected in 2008 amidst an economic recession that economists of all ideological strides described as the worst economic recession since the Great Depression. The response to this economic crisis was immediate and partisan, for the most part. Congress passed the American Recovery and Reinvestment Act of 2009, which President Obama signed into law in early 2009 just a month after his historic inauguration. This legislative initiative aimed to create new jobs and save citizens from rising unemployment. An additional goal of the act was to "foster unprecedented levels of accountability and transparency in government spending" (Internal Revenue Service, 2009). The government went on to employ Keynesian economics in an attempt to spur economic activity and provide funds for long-term growth, injecting 787 billion dollars into the struggling economy.

With the provision for transparency, the Obama administration sought to calm the public and instill confidence that public funds were being used in a transparent manner. It created a website (Recovery.gov) to provide easy access to data related to Recovery Act spending and allow members of the public to report any cases of potential fraud, abuse, and waste of funds. The site contained links to information about where the money was going, together with images of projects, and even information about grants and job opportunities.

As with other government programs, there were mixed reactions to the entire stimulus package. While the White House claimed that it had saved or created about three million jobs, the Republican opposition dismissed the intervention as more "big government" spending that would only expand the already crippling national debt. Literally thousands of online conservative news outlets and blogs rejected government claims that the stimulus funds were helpful in stemming an economic free fall into depression.

In the ensuing national debate, different assessments pointed to the sharp political divisions in the country. *Time* argued that the "Recovery Act is the most ambitious energy legislation in history, converting the Energy Department into the world's largest venture-capital fund" (Grunwald, 2010).

Key Concepts

Access to ICT technologies
Application Strategies
Business Model
E-Commerce
Information and Communication Technologies (ICTs)
Network theories
New Public Management
Privacy
Reinvention of Government
Refounding Period
Security
Stakeholder approaches
Studying E-Government

Discussion Questions

1. What are the pros and cons of studying e-government?
2. Select any two journals that publish articles on e-government and describe some of the major themes addressed in any given issue. What are some of the questions being raised in the lead articles?
3. To what extent is e-government a theme in the study of bureaucratic reforms?
4. What are networks? Are there network theories that you are aware of in other fields of political science?
5. What are the merits of comparative studies in e-government?

INTERNET ACTIVITIES

1. Visit at least three U.S.-based e-government center websites and provide a list of their current research activities and publications. Identify common research agendas, if present. 2. Visit at least two non-American or international e-government center websites and provide a list of their current research activities and publications. Compare and contrast the research agendas of the two organizations.

Chapter 3

Policy Foundations of e-Government

While the term "policy" is imprecise or contested, there is agreement that it concerns laws, plans, behaviors, and the actions of governments and their ramifications. In most democracies, government, through the political establishment, initiates public policy. As Peters (2009) noted, public policy is the sum of government activities that have observable influences on the lives of a given society. In many cases, the choices taken or not taken by government become policies (Dye, 2010). In other words, policy is associated with decision making.

Lindblom (1959) and other leading scholars of public administration are credited with developing the theoretical frameworks that best describe this important connection. In his seminal work "The Science of 'Muddling Through,'" Lindblom (1959) described the policymaking process as disjointed and incremental. Because politicians seek to make changes with the lowest political risk and engage in "satisficing" implementing radical reforms requires considerable political tact and skill. It follows, then, that making policy decisions that change the way government works is a daunting endeavor.

The emergence of e-government, which is nothing short of a revolution, elicits greater public focus on the policymaking process. However, the policies that govern application of ICTs in government are constantly evolving because the capabilities of ICTs are changing all the time. It is unusual to have consistent policy in the area of e-government. For example, policy governing the design of single portals, based on long-held American beliefs regarding information policy, did not envisage the full potential of ICTs. As such, its portal model, exemplified in First-Gov (now USA.gov), has had mixed successes and is subject to periodic reviews (Fletcher, 2002; 2003a). Therefore, as in other areas, some policies written for short-term applicability become irrelevant when technology changes. Other policies on ICTs have long staying power and serve to address critical problems in society.

A singular e-government policy would raise more questions than answers. While operational definitions of e-government are fuzzy, given the range of options presented earlier in the book, policies on e-government are even less clear. Almost every organization in government has its own policy toward conducting government business through electronic media. One agency might wish to accept only public petitions through its websites, while another might require all payments for services be paid through the Internet. Many of these decisions are a result of policy initiatives to promote cost savings and efficiency in government. Manuals and handbooks now exist to help policymakers at different levels of government design and implement effective e-mail and Internet policies (Flynn, 2001). In advising organizations, Flynn (2001) pointed out that the first step is to assess the risks of introducing any policy change. Public organizations have to take extra measures to prevent their websites from carrying offensive content that could result in expensive lawsuits. Thus a city's e-government policy might have the attributes described in box 3.1.

All public agencies have a host of policies to govern their information systems' management. A series of policies are put in place to retrieve

Box 3.1. *City Government Policy Attributes and Features.*

Attribute	Common Elements
Purpose of City website	To provide information of the city's choosing to the public to conduct the city's business and promote the city's goals as guided by the city council.
Scope of Application	Website function is mandated by policy, for example, to direct citizens to appropriate service outlets or facilitate services such as tax payments or Freedom of Information requests.
Content Issues Guidelines	Policy regarding freedom of speech, commercial speech, media contacts and linkages to other sites
Privacy and Disclosure	Issues concerning personally identifiable information (PII), URL (Uniform Resource Locator) or domain and IP address, Public Records Act and e-mail addresses, policy regarding cookies, security
Contractual Services and Online Services	Compliance with city e-government policies.
Authentication	Protection of data and prevention of abuse of personal data via electronic signatures, PINs, SSL.
Liability and disclaimer	Protection from liability resulting from information posted on city websites, delays, inaccuracies, errors, or omissions arising out of use of the site
Direction to other services and information sources	Links to city departments and non-city websites
Access to information	Statement on administrative staff directories and electronic reading rooms.
Disabled access	Statement on compliance to regulations governing access by persons with disabilities

and save data (data mining and warehousing), acquire and process information, locate contractors and service providers, and provide wireless security. In this chapter, we will consider e-government policy in terms of key players, especially at the federal level. The questions that we tackle are: Who are the policy makers? Which macro-policies are employed? What are some of the critical policy management issues in the field?

Our focus is on federal institutions whose actions have fundamental consequences in how e-government is conducted in the United States. Similar to other policy areas, the connection between different actors is notable. E-government has witnessed the proliferation of issue networks in all segments of government. Issue networks, as Heclo (1995) stated, are webs of individuals who guide national debates in areas of specific interest. Network members hold similar ideas on how to proceed with key areas of policy implementation. Interestingly, issue networks in the e-government policy environment are members of a growing virtual community of linked websites. Unlike issue networks of the pre-electronic era, e-government issue networks are actively sharing information about the frontiers of the ICT revolution, often utilizing the very technologies debated. The debate on regulation or non-regulation of certain e-government capabilities is shaped by economic and practical concerns.

Who then are the actors in the e-government policy web? It is relatively easy to pinpoint stakeholders in the issue networks, such as government procurement administrators, systems administrators, government IT managers, communication and information officers, digital management firms, business interests, and politicians in legislative bodies including appointees to the White House support staff. While all these groups mix with one another in deliberations on e-government, the public does not have serious opinions on technical and practical aspects of e-government. This is in sharp contrast to e-commerce, where public surveys show that members of the public support government regulation of telemarketing as one aspect of the electronic revolution.

Yet this is not the full story. In areas of security and public key infrastructure, the public has some concern about identity theft and intrusion into individuals' private lives. Opinions on Internet safety and disclosure of private information are key concerns that have been well articulated in public policy. At a more general level, e-government applications and impacts of e-government technologies also matter to the public. Therefore, policy agenda setting in those areas elicits the strongest reactions. Agenda setting of e-government issues is driven by widespread public use of computer-based interactive communication systems such as blogs and e-mails.

Let us now examine some of the key players in the policy-making machinery and describe each of their functions. We first briefly describe some of the roles taken by the Office of the President in setting the policy agenda for e-government. Then we turn to roles played by two independent regulatory commissions whose leadership is appointed by the president. These commissions are designed to be more independent than other administrative agencies and have more legal protection than Cabinet members against dismissal by the president. As Milakovich and Gordon (2004) pointed out, these organizations include the FCC and the FTC, which represent a "major type of administrative entity" (p. 15). Lastly, we examine the role of Congress and a few private vendors with key roles in policy networks.

The first widespread emergence of an e-government agenda was in the early 1990s. After that, the evolution of information management systems became an integral part of federal administration (Holden, 2003). The Clinton/Gore administration took advantage of advances in the ICTs to call for reinvention of government during the promotion of their signature National Performance Review program. The NPR, which many argue "was the longest-running reform effort in the history of the Federal Government" (NPRG, 2001), was based on the vision that the federal government could be less expensive more efficient. It promoted an entrepreneurial spirit that encompassed the increased use of ICTs (Kamensky, 1996; Kamensky, 2001; Kettl, 1998). Vice President Al Gore ably led the NPR process by providing the political force required for successful implementation. One of the review's critical recommendations was the adoption of ICTs in government management practices. As Chadwick and May (2003) observed, government in the information age must adapt in the way that large, vertically organized corporate bureaucracies have been forced to adapt. The NPR planned to create "entrepreneurial organizations" built upon new working practices derived from the proliferation of ICTs. No doubt, Gore's NPR aimed to create customer-focused public bureaucracies.

Although the Clinton administration is credited with the introduction of e-government services, the vice president received much criticism from those who felt he had politicized efforts to reform government through the introduction of new technologies. Political pundits mocked alleged statements made by Al Gore in Congressional debates about the invention of the Internet. While he was campaigning for the office of president, Gore told CNN's Wolf Blitzer on March 9, 1999, "During my service in Congress, I took the initiative in creating the Internet." (CNN 1999) This was plainly a statement about his work as a congressman on the Internet, and not a claim that he had invented networking research. One bill he later introduced was the Information Infrastructure and Technology Act of 1993, which opened the Internet to commercial traffic" (Brock & Waldman, 2008).

A huge part of NPR initiatives involved widespread use of ICTs in the provision of government services to cut costs and promote efficiency and effectiveness in service delivery. President Clinton also signed into law in 1995 the Paperwork Reduction Act, requiring federal agencies to become more responsible and publicly accountable for reducing the burden of federal paperwork on the public and to increase efficiency generally (Fletcher, 2002b).

Expansion of the Internet and other revolutionary ICT developments became more obvious during Clinton's watch. Concerns with the digital divide continued to receive the attention of the executive branch. Although more than half of the U.S. population is connected to the Internet and has access to computer-based communication systems, minority groups fare poorly in terms of access and usage. Several reports show that Hispanics and African Americans lag behind other groups in Internet penetration. Additionally, the elderly, the demographic most strongly associated with voting and civic engagement, across all population categories are the least likely to use the Internet. By some indications, individuals 50 years of age and older were among the least likely to be Internet users, with an Internet use rate of 29% in 2000. Other disadvantaged groups such as the disabled also had not at that time been avid consumers of ICTs and the Internet in particular. (NTIA, 2000).

Addressing the digital divide in 2000, President Clinton announced new budget measures to lessen the gap between Internet haves and have-nots. He proposed funding for an FCC-mandated e-rate program to provide a 20 to 90 percent discount on telecommunications services and guaranteed Internet access to public and private schools and libraries. Tax relief was given to companies that donated computers to libraries, schools, and community technology centers to aid in this effort.

Similar relief was recommended for corporations that sponsored programs in support of these initiatives. The Clinton administration designated deprived areas as empowerment zones and enterprise communities that would be targeted for these programs. The Clinton administration created up to 1,000 Community Technology Centers in low-income urban and rural areas and provided funds for teacher training in the use of new ICTs in classrooms. Other monies were allocated to promote innovative applications of information technology for underserved communities under the Technology Opportunities Program (TOP). The program targeted Native Americans for training for careers in information technology. Clinton's overall strategy embraced the New Public Management and government reinvention circles' value of encouraging public/private sector partnerships. The march toward e-government initiatives continued under George W. Bush and Barack Obama.

The Executive Office of the President

The Office of Science and Technology plays the primary role in advising the president on technology matters. Based on its advice, President George W. Bush accomplished a series of initiatives. For example, he signed into law the Controlling the Assault of Non-Solicited Pornography and Marketing Act of 2003 (CAN-SPAM Act), which established a framework of administrative, civil, and law enforcement tools to help consumers, businesses, and families combat unsolicited commercial e-mail known as spam.

The law allows consumers to stop spam and protects against spam containing explicit sexual material. The law is an outcome of widespread public frustration resulting from continued presence of spam in e-mails. Spam accounts for half of all e-mail traffic and grossly interferes with the smooth running of personal and e-government communication. Spam imposes significant costs on Internet Service Providers (ISPs), government agencies, and other partners in governance. ISPs and government agencies use enormous resources to contain spam. Moreover, some spam is fraudulent or criminal, thereby putting pressure on law enforcement agencies as well.

The law imposes stiff penalties including fines or imprisonment for those who knowingly send spam containing unmarked, unsolicited sexually oriented material to the public at large. There are also penalties for spammers who use misleading or false identification in sending spam. Senders of e-mail are required to place warning labels on messages containing pornographic material. The CAN-SPAM Act established important ground rules for civil enforcement by the FTC, other federal agencies, state attorneys general, and ISPs. The law is framed within traditional American beliefs concerning consumer empowerment, which have been given further prominence by reinvention of government rhetoric. Thus, consumers are provided with the choice not to receive further unsolicited e-mail messages. Senders that do not honor consumers' requests are subject to civil penalties. The law capped statutory damages for civil violations and set federal standards to guide how additional state laws on spam might be shaped.

President Bush gave prominent public support to engineers and other innovators who develop ICTs. In speeches at various forums, he announced his administration's support for technological innovations including ICTs. In April 2004, President Bush announced a series of measures to inspire American innovations in the area of technology. Innovations included technologies to assure better delivery of health care and access to high-speed Internet. In his 2006 State of the Union Address, Bush announced his administration's proposal to increase funds for technological innovation. "The American Competitiveness Initiative would commit $5.9 billion in FY 2007, and more than $136 billion over ten years, to increase investments in research and development (R&D),

strengthen education, and encourage entrepreneurship and innovation" (Bush, 2006).

The American Competitiveness Initiative was the banner theme of Bush's address. The president's primary goal in all these measures was to improve productivity in public service delivery and improve and advance America's competitiveness in the global economy.

"Ask the White House"

Another important Bush administration initiative was its increased use of computer moderated communications, especially through the White House website, to exchange ideas and encourage dialogue between staffers and the public. Through the administration's Ask the White House forum, members of the public could submit questions to administration officials. By this symbolic act, the White House provides leadership in at least three areas:

a. Sensitivity to public concerns
b. Transparency in how it addresses some of the issues of the day
c. Appreciation of e-government

The issuance of executive orders with implications for e-government is another area of presidential leadership. Though these continue to grow in number, President Clinton's 1996 Executive Order 13011, titled Federal Information Technology, is among the most significant executive orders touching on e-government policymaking and strategizing.

The Chief Information Officers (CIO) Council was established by Executive Order 13011 on July 16, 1996. A charter for the council was adopted on February 20, 1997, and later codified by the E-government Act of 2002. The CIO Council serves as the principal interagency forum for improving practices in the design, modernization, use, sharing, and performance of federal agency information resources. The council's role includes developing recommendations for information technology management policies, procedures, and standards; identifying opportunities to share information resources; and assessing and addressing the needs of the federal government's IT workforce. The chair of the CIO Council is the deputy director for management of the Office of Management and Budget (OMB), and the vice chair is elected by the CIO Council from its membership. The council's membership comprises CIOs and deputy CIOs from the following federal agencies (CIO, n.d.):

- Agency for International Development
- Central Intelligence Agency
- Department of Agriculture
- Department of the Air Force
- Department of the Army
- Department of Commerce
- Department of Defense (DoD)
- Department of Education
- Department of Energy
- Department of Health and Human Services
- Department of Housing and Urban Development
- Department of the Interior
- Department of Justice
- Department of Labor
- Department of the Navy
- Department of State
- Department of Transportation
- Department of the Treasury
- Department of Veterans Affairs
- Environmental Protection Agency
- Federal Emergency Management Agency
- General Services Administration
- National Aeronautics and Space Administration
- National Science Foundation
- Nuclear Regulatory Commission
- Office of Personnel Management
- Small Business Administration
- Social Security Administration

President Bush continued to support the work of the President's Information Technology Advisory Committee (PITAC). The existence of this committee demonstrates the importance of ICTs at the highest level of government and the complex mix of actors in the broad policy area. There have been other important executive branch circulars, especially OMB Circular A-130 (Office of Management and Budget, 2000) and GAO-02-1083T (Government Accountability Office, 2001) that provide foundations for policy makers. The OMB circular established policy for the management of federal information resources. It included procedural and analytic guidelines for implementing specific aspects of policies, including guidelines on providing public access to records, electronic information collection, records management, and training procedures.

Federal Communications Commission

The FCC is an independent agency of the United States government. It was created and is directed by the congressional Communications Act of 1934. Although the FCC is a child of the New Deal, presidents of all ideological persuasions have embraced it. The FCC regulates all non-government use of radio and television (TV) broadcasting spectrums, including interstate telecommunications ranging from wire and satellite to cable transmissions. Previously, wired communication regulation was under the purview of the Interstate Commerce Commission (ICC). The FCC's mandate includes the regulation of all international communications to and from the United States, and thus it is one of the most important actors in U.S. telecommunication policy.

Every year, the FCC examines market changes in ICTs and issues advisory reports for policy making. The FCC examines and scrutinizes factors that facilitate or impede competition among rival providers of ICTs. FCC reports are authoritative documents taken seriously by the body politic. For example, in its 2006 report on video competition the FCC observed:

> Americans are voracious consumers of media services. On average, we spend close to 30 percent of our day engaged in some

> activity involving media, with television viewing the dominant media activity. For the September 2004–September 2005 television season, the average household tuned into TV for 8 hours, 11 minutes a day. This is almost 3 percent higher than the previous season, more than 12 percent higher than 10 years ago, and the highest level observed since television viewing was first measured by Nielsen Media Research in the 1950s. Within the same period, the average person watched 4 hours, 32 minutes each day, again a record high. (Federal Communications Commission, 2006)

These data are important inputs in the policymaking processes.

Administratively, the FCC has five commissioners appointed by the President to direct the affairs of the agency. The Senate must confirm the appointments, whose term is for five years, except when an unexpired term is filled. The president designates one of the commissioners to serve as chairperson and chief executive. The chair delegates management and administrative responsibility to a managing director whose supervisory purview includes several staff units and bureaus. Only three commissioners may be members of the same political party. Furthermore, none of them can have a financial interest in any commission-related business.

FEDERAL TRADE COMMISSION

The FTC predates the FCC. President Woodrow Wilson signed the enabling FTC Act into law on September 26, 1914. The FTC's predecessor was the Bureau of Corporations (BOC), created in 1903 under legislation encouraged by President Theodore Roosevelt. The original function of the Bureau of Corporations was to collect information, conduct industry and policy research, and prepare reports at the request of Congress and the president. The FTC's mandate is to manage the antitrust policy concerns with corporate concentration, cooperation, and competition. Much like the FCC, it issues annual reports for policy makers. Its administrative machinery resembles that of the FCC.

Congress and Commercial Interests

Congress has enacted important pieces of legislation to support e-government strategies. The first major law was the Paperwork Reduction Acts signed into law in 1980 by President Carter and amended in 1995. The amendments were introduced by Senators Sam Nunn (D-GA) and John Danforth (R-MO), and Representatives William Clinger (R-PA) and Norman Sisisky (D-VA). The Paperwork Reduction Act was initially premised on the notion of cutting red tape and achieving savings in time and money. Specifically, the law seeks to minimize the paperwork burden for individuals, businesses, tribal governments, educational and nonprofit organizations, and federal contractors. Another stated objective is to ensure the public maximizes its benefits from information created, collected, maintained, shared, and disseminated by or for the government. Its larger goal is to strengthen decision making, accountability, and openness in government and society. The law established the Office of Information and Regulatory Affairs (OIRA) within the OMB. The act gives the OMB authority to approve activities which eliminate paper trails. It established the Federal Information Locator System (FILS) to provide an index of information sources in the federal government. The system is designed to encourage information sharing between federal agencies. In 1989, Congress did not reauthorize OIRA and the Paperwork Reduction Act (PRA) because of disputes between the executive branch and the Chairmen of the House and Senate Government Affairs Committees, among other reasons. These differences revolved around ideological issues such as executive regulatory power and drew the attention of groups such as the Chamber of Commerce, trade and citizen organizations, and the National Governor's Association.

The Clinger-Cohen Act of 1996, previously known as the Information Technology Management Reform Act, amended the Paperwork Reduction Act of 1995(PRA). The act, named after its first co-sponsors, Rep. William Clinger (R-PA) and Senator William Cohen (R-Maine), is aimed at reforming acquisition laws and information technology management within the federal government. The law updates the conceptualization of information technology and regards interconnected systems and subsystems of equipment as an essential core of ICTs in e-government.

> The PRA gives the director of the OMB significant leadership responsibilities in supporting public agencies' improvement of their information technology management practices. But the performance of the OMB led many to call for more attention to strategic planning and clarification of operational tasks and roles (Fletcher, 2003b).

As a result, the OMB in 2000 released one of its most important executive circulars to provide agencies with guidance necessary for implementing provisions of the Clinger-Cohen Act. OMB Circular A-130, titled "Management of Federal Information Resources," clarifies some of the policy issues emanating from the legislation. For example, the circular provides procedural and analytical guidelines for implementing specific aspects of information technology policies at the federal level. Subsequent memoranda defined the technical and administrative terms that would help administrators implement the law. Box 3.2, adapted from the OMB's circular, is a simplification of the key operational terms.

Therefore, in sum, the PRA and Clinger-Cohen Act require agencies to better link their ICT planning and investment decisions (Fletcher, 2003b). They built on the original 1980 Paperwork Reduction Act by establishing a more comprehensive approach for executive agencies to "improve the acquisition and management of information resources" by:

- focusing information resource planning to support their strategic missions,
- implementing a capital planning and investment control process that links budget formulation to execution, and
- rethinking and restructuring the way they do their work before investing in information systems. (OMB, 2011)

Additionally, the two statutes require public bureaus to establish policies for ensuring that ICTs are reliable and secure. The OMB directs that

Box 3.2. *Examples of OMB Circular Abridged Operational and Administrative Terms.*

Agency	Any executive department, military department, government corporation, government controlled corporation, or other establishment in the executive branch of the federal government, or any independent regulatory agency. Within the Executive Office of the President, the term includes only the OMB and the Office of Administration
Capital planning and investment control process	A management process for ongoing identification, selection, control, and evaluation of investments in information resources. The process links budget formulation and execution and is focused on agency missions and achieving specific program outcomes
Government information	Information created, collected, processed, disseminated, or disposed of by or for the federal government
Information technology	Any equipment or interconnected system or subsystem of equipment that is used in the automatic acquisition, storage, manipulation, management, movement, control, display, switching, interchange, transmission, or reception of data or information by an executive agency. The term "information technology" includes computers, ancillary equipment, software, firmware and similar procedures, services (including support services), and related resources. The term "information technology" does not include national security systems as defined in the Clinger-Cohen Act of 1996 (40 U.S.C. 1452)
Information Technology Resources Board	The board established by Section 5 of Executive Order 13011
Major information system	An information system that requires special management attention because of its importance to an agency mission; its high development, operating, or maintenance costs; or its significant role in the administration of agency programs, finances, property, or other resources
Records management	The planning, controlling, directing, organizing, training, promoting, and other managerial activities involved with respect to records creation, records maintenance and use, and records disposition to achieve adequate and proper documentation of the policies and transactions of the federal government and effective and economical management of agency operations

(continued on next page)

Box 3.2. *(continued)*

Service recipient	An agency organizational unit, programmatic entity, or chargeable account that receives information processing services from an information processing service organization (IPSO). A service recipient may be either internal or external to the organization responsible for providing information resources services, but normally does not report either to the manager or director of the IPSO or to the same immediate supervisor.

Note. Adapted from Office of Management and Budget Circular no. A-130, 2011.

information classified for national security purposes should be handled in accordance with Executive Order No. 12472 (OMB, 2011). Executive Order No. 12472 required organizations to ensure that all national telecommunications infrastructures were secure in all conditions of crisis or emergency.

Other major pieces of legislation that form the foundations of e-government policy are found in box 3.3.

High Performance Computing Act of 1991

The High Performance Computing Act of 1991 aims at maintaining the U.S. lead in the field of ICTs. The law set forth many provisions, including (1) setting goals and priorities for federal high-performance computing research, development, and networking; (2) providing for interagency coordination; (3) providing for the creation, oversight, and evolution of the National Research and Education Network; (4) improving software; (5) accelerating high-performance computer system development; (6) providing technical support and research and development of software and hardware needed to address fundamental problems in science and engineering (Grand Challenges); (7) educating undergraduate and graduate students; and (8) providing for security. The law also establishes an advisory committee on high-performance computing.

Box 3.3. *Summary of Relevant Legislation.*

Legislation	Key Highlights
Federal Acquisition Streamlining Act of 1994, Title V (FASA V)	Enacted to revise and streamline the acquisition laws of the federal government, and for other purposes. Amended the Competition in Contracting Act of 1984 (CICA) and other federal procurement law with respect to subject agency (National Aeronautics and Space Administration [NASA], Coast Guard, DoD, and respective military departments)
The Government Performance Results Act of 1993 (GPRA)	Provides for the establishment of strategic planning and performance measurement in the federal government. The GPRA requires executive agency heads to submit to the director of the OMB and Congress a strategic plan and performance goals for their agencies' program activities and requires such plan to cover at least a five-year period and to be updated at least every three years.
Clinger-Cohen Act of 1996 (Division E-Information Technology Management Reform Act)	Reforms acquisition laws and information technology management of the federal government; authorizes DoD appropriations for fiscal year 1996 military activities and military construction projects; prescribes personnel strengths for such fiscal year for the armed forces
Government Paperwork Elimination Act of 1998 (GPEA)	Reduces the amount of paperwork required for federal programs
The E-government Act of 2002	Enhances the management and promotion of electronic government services and processes by establishing a federal CIO within the OMB and by establishing a broad framework of measures that require using Internet-based information technology to enhance citizen access to government information and services. The Act defines "electronic government" as the use by government of web based Internet applications and other information technologies, combined with processes that implement these technologies, to (1) enhance the access to and delivery of government information and services or (2) bring about improvements in government operations.

Source. Library of Congress, n.d.

Next Generation Internet Research Act (1998)

The Next Generation Internet Research Act of 1998, passed by the 105th Congress, amends the High Performance Computing Act of 1991. The law authorized appropriations for fiscal years 1999 and 2000 for next-generation Internet programs. It requires the PITAC to monitor and give advice concerning the development and implementation of these programs and report to the president and Congress on its activities.

The major purposes of the law are twofold: (1) authorize research programs related to high-end computing and computation, human-centered systems, high-confidence systems, and education, training, and human resources; and (2) provide for the development and coordination of a comprehensive, integrated U.S. research program focused on a computer network infrastructure to promote interoperability among advanced federal computer networks, economical high-speed data access that does not impose a geographic penalty, and flexible and extensive networking technology.

E-government Act of 2002

The most important law governing the management of e-government is the E-government Act of 2002. The law was sponsored by Senators Joseph Lieberman (D-CT) and Conrad Burns (R-Mont.) in May 2001. The two served on the Governmental Affairs Committee with ranking member Fred Thompson (R-TN). During the hearings leading up to enactment of the bill, there was full consensus, as Lieberman put it, that "the government takes full advantage of the Internet and other information technologies to maximize efficiency and provide the public with seamless, secure online information and services" (Lieberman, 2002b). In addition to providing for better information services for the public, the legislation makes permanent the Government Information Security Reform Act (2000) that Senators Lieberman and Thompson co-sponsored. The information reform initiative was a part of the larger government plan to protect the country's security infrastructure. This 90-page e-government bill was the most comprehensive piece of legislation on e-government up to that time and the only piece of legislation to focus access and accountability in government management of information.

By creating a new Office of Information Policy in the OMB, the law raises the visibility and importance of information policy and information management in the federal government. Another milestone is that the bill establishes an Office of Electronic Government, whose head is a Senate-confirmed administrator. Additionally, the legislation mandates the federal courts to post opinions online. The primary intent of the bill is to make the government more accessible and government information more accessible and usable.

The law received widespread bipartisan support. Congressman Tom Davis (R-VA) and Congressman Jim Turner (D-TX), chairman of both the House Government Reform Committee and its Subcommittee on Technology and Procurement Policy, were instrumental in the passage of the act in the House of Representatives. The bill was fully supported by the White House staff. Its intent coincided with the president's broad agenda of enhancing productivity and efficiency in government. The E-government Act codified much of the strategy the administration was already implementing. Perhaps the most important point is that Congress institutionalized that strategy. The E-government Act is important because it forms the framework for all future administrations' engagement in the new public administration paradigm.

Other actors in the passing of the E-government Act of 2002 included large-scale corporate vendors such as America Time Warner and Microsoft. Stakeholders in the tax preparation industry supported the bill. Each group had vested interests which led to areas of conflict. For example, a consortium of tax preparers that included H&R Block and Intuit inked a deal with the IRS that would preclude its entry into the marketplace for online tax preparation services. The tax preparation firms did not wish to see the IRS become a consultant to taxpayers. They preferred that the IRS provide links to tax preparation services. The bill was signed into law in December as the E-government Act of 2002. Its highlights are available in 3.4.

Box 3.4. *Highlights of the e-Government Act (2002).*

Title	Highlighted Provisions
Title I Office of Management and Budget Electronic Government Services	Establishes a powerful Office of Electronic Government within OMB, enacts a modest e-government fund, formalizes the status of the Chief Information Officers Council, encourages innovative government-wide solutions, authorizes the GSA to advise the OMB Office of Electronic Government, and requires an annual E-government Report to Congress.
Title II Federal Management and Promotion of Electronic Government Services	Implements e-government on a multi-agency basis by identifying the responsibilities of each executive branch agency and requiring GSA to establish an interoperable framework for electronic signatures.
Title III Information Security	Defines a framework for ensuring the effectiveness of federal information security. Agency heads are responsible for assuring the security of their information systems. The director of OMB is responsible for developing and overseeing the implementation of policies, principles, standards, and guidelines on information security, including through ensuring timely agency adoption and compliance. Charges the National Institute of Standards and Technology (NIST) to play a stronger role in advising OMB and developing security standards and guidelines.
Title IV Authorization of Appropriations and Effective Dates	The E-government Act took effect 120 days after its December 17th enactment. Congress was authorized to make appropriations for fiscal years 2003 through 2007.
Title V Confidential Information Protection and Statistical Efficiency	The Director of OMB was authorized to oversee confidentiality and disclosure of policies and to ensure that information provided by individuals and organizations for statistical purposes is held in confidence and not used as the basis for adverse actions. Breach of confidentiality is a felony. The title also reduces paperwork imposed on the public and improves data collection and sharing between the Census Bureau, Bureau of Economic Analysis, and the Bureau of Labor Statistics.

Source. Extrapolated from the White House OMB resources, http://www.whitehouse.gov/sites/default/files/omb/memoranda/m03-18.pdf.

Senators Joseph Lieberman and Fred Thompson also initiated an exciting experiment in e-government by establishing their own interactive website. Their plan was to engage citizens as partners in the legislative processes. Citizens posted comments on how Congress could help promote the cause of e-government. The initiative also solicited comments from civil servants. While the initiative attracted several posts, its impact remains unclear.

Compliance Issues

The OMB issues progress reports on the implementation of the E-government Act. OMB sees the act in the context of savings and high productivity. For the most part, specific government departments and units also conduct their own audits on e-government to comply with the provisions of the E-government Act. For example, the U.S. Department of Labor Employment Standards' Administration Office of Federal Contract Compliance is required to develop an inventory of website contents by Section 207(f)(2) of the act.

Periodic reports on e-government are now widely available from large centers of e-government studies such as at Brown University in Providence, Rhode Island, and from numerous think tank organizations. A report issued in 2006 states that although the United States lags behind small Asian countries in implementation of e-government strategies, it is still a world leader. Of 198 countries studied that use digital government forms, only 19% of government agencies around the world offered online services in 2005. Taiwan is ranked first, Singapore second, the United States third, Hong Kong fourth, and China fifth (West, 2006). The review indicated a progressive decline by the United States since 2001 when it had been the global leader in e-government. By 2004, the United States had fallen behind Canada and tied with Singapore (Atkinson, 2004).

In another important policy evaluation report, leading e-government scholar Darrell West concludes that the U.S. government was responding to the serious concern of making online services available to the broad public regardless of individuals' abilities, skills, and economic situations. In 2003 a large percentage of local, state, and national government agencies complied with minimal web accessibility standards. There were relatively few investigations into incidences of unconstitutional discrimination in online service provision. In *Achieving E-government for All*, West (2003) identified as problematic the fact that most government websites provide online information that was mostly written to the educated public. Low literate or illiterate Americans, whose numbers are in the tens of millions, continue to struggle with websites that don't address their needs.

According to West (2003), critical policy concerns included disability access, readability, non-English language accessibility, interactivity, equity of access across agencies, and user fees and premium sites. Design of Internet communication delivery systems should generally be sensitive to different kinds of disabilities and strive toward universality.

Readability refers to the use of sentences and words devoid of jargon. In particular, reports posted on government websites must be consistently readable. The content must be translated into other languages commonly used in the country as well. Policy in the area of interactivity should continue to place a high premium on provision of contact information to those who visit government sites and wish to contact public service providers. Another policy area of interest is for government agencies to tailor their online delivery systems to client needs rather than striving for generic variants in Internet web design. Finally, access fee requirements pose a challenge to poor members of society. These are policy areas that are receiving keen attention in policy-making bodies at the national, state, and local levels.

President Obama and e-Government

The Obama administration is addressing some of the concerns previously raised. In terms of policy outlook, his campaign applied more cutting edge ICTs than candidates in previous presidential campaigns (Hendricks & Denton, 2010). While campaigning, Obama (2007) stated:

> Let us be the generation that reshapes our economy to compete in the digital age. Let's set high standards for our schools and

> give them the resources they need to succeed. Let's recruit a new army of teachers, and give them better pay and more support in exchange for more accountability. Let's make college more affordable, and let's invest in scientific research, and let's lay down broadband lines through the heart of inner cities and rural towns all across America.

His campaign issued a comprehensive technology and innovation plan that promised to ensure full and free exchange of information among Americans through an open Internet and diverse media outlets, create a transparent and connected democracy, encourage the deployment of a modern communications infrastructure, and enhance America's competitiveness. (Obama, 2007)

The Obama White House continues to employ new information technologies in reaching out to the public. For example, the administration established a website to report how it was responding to economic recovery plans as embodied in the American Recovery and Reinvestment Act of 2009. The administration also issued a memo to allow members of the public to provide feedback on efforts to revive the economy by contacting the government directly through the e-mail address recovery@omb.eop.gov.

Under the banner of promoting transparency and connected democracy, the Obama administration promotes application of technologies in government service. The administration places restrictions on how its staff interacts and communicates with lobbyists. Key measures include reiterating the importance of scientific inquiry in the national psyche. The administration argued that the previous administration had sidelined science and in some cases privileged ideology in finding solutions to national problems. Obama's administration, however, gives much rhetorical support to science and the place of scientific inquiry in the 21st century.

From the outset, the administration considered use of best-in-class technologies a means of bringing American government into the 21st century. The administration appointed the nation's first chief technology officer (CTO) to ensure the safety of government networks and lead interagency coordinative efforts by working with chief technology and information officers in federal agencies. But the administration continues most of the policies established under the Clinton and Bush administrations, especially in supporting the continuation of the mandate and leadership of the OMB in overseeing e-government infrastructure.

CONCLUSIONS

In sum, despite the rapid growth in e-government, public policy remains relatively stable and engrained in several key pieces of legislation including the E-government Act of 2002, the Paperwork Reduction Act of 1995, and a series of presidential executive orders and circulars. With the exception of the appointment of a new technology czar, the CTO under the Obama administration, the policy-making and advisory organs remain unchanged and include PITAC, the FTC, and the FCC.

Although policy will continue to address issues such as the regulatory framework and the digital divide in certain communities, for example by providing broadband access to rural communities that continue to lag behind in accessing Internet and digital technologies, the policy community considers improvement in e-government an essential component of promoting an efficient and democratic government. In this age of cyber-insecurity and terrorism, the administration is likely to build on previous efforts at securing the information technologies infrastructure.

KEY CONCEPTS

American Competitiveness Initiative
Clinger-Cohen Act of 1996
Chief Information Officers (CIO)
Community Technology Centers (CTC)
Data Mining and Warehousing
Digital Divide
Digital Management
E-citizens
Empowerment Zones
Executive Order, OMB Circular A-130, GAO-02-1083T
Government IT Managers
High Performance Computing Act (1991)

ICT Revolution
Information Systems Management
Internet Service Providers (ISPs)
Issue Networks
Next Generation Internet Research Act (1998)
Policy Agenda Setting
Policy Management
Policy Networks
President's Information Technology Advisory Committee (PITAC)
Software Systems
Technology Opportunities Program (TOP)

Discussion Questions

1. Why is the E-government Act important? Who were the key players in pushing for the enactment of the E-government Act?
2. Although Congress and the President strongly supported e-government, the funding resources are finite. What are the key considerations when funding these initiatives, including planning, management, governing regulations, and cost accounting requirements? Are there alternative ways of funding the implementation of e-government projects?
3. Can you suggest reasons why the United States has fallen behind Singapore in implementing e-government strategies?
4. Discuss the assertion that the problems associated with spam may not be "solved by federal legislation alone, but require the development and adoption of new technologies."
   Does the law provide a well balanced approach that will help to address some of the harmful impacts of spam?
5. How is your local government addressing the issue of accessibility of Internet services?

Internet Activity

Use search engines such as Google, Hotbot, Yahoo, MSN, Lycos and draw a list of empowerment zones and community technology centers in your area. Discuss how they have fared, the progress they are making, and problems encountered in meeting their objectives.

Chapter 4

Design of e-Government

From the previous discussions we have identified that the design of e-government systems based on computer-mediated communication must consider client types. Issues of accessibility and cost are at the core of any meaningful e-government system. In this chapter, we explore generic design concerns as well as steps in the e-government design process and include a brief discussion on e-procurements. We first provide an organizational context and reiterate the promise of e-government.

An organization is a group of people intentionally arranged to accomplish a common goal or set of goals. Public organizations range in size from those with a few commissioners to departments of tens of thousands of individuals such as Homeland Security and Health and Human Services.

Organizational Context

There are several important aspects to the goals of public organizations. These features are explicit and well recognized. Most public organizations are creatures of political processes established to provide services that the market might not provide optimally. All organizations operate according to systemic values or priorities established in these political processes. These values are the personality or culture of the organization.

Virtual organizations are the essence of e-government. A virtual public organization is a temporary network of independent agencies that come together to exploit opportunities for providing services in e-government. Virtual organizations are theoretically similar to regular organizations in the sense that they transform inputs into outputs. They emerge from generic organizational structures and seek to create entities that generate public goods and services. The services they provide are not substitutes for regular work but are continuations of public organization.

Similar to other organizational forms, virtual organizations exist as subsystems to promote specific programs. They aim at implementing policy goals written in laws and executive decrees. They do not change the aims and functions of government. The reality is that e-government is not a panacea to bureaupathology. There are limits on how much government can effectively embrace the e-government culture. Still, any e-government agency or virtual organization is a part of public service. As such, e-government cannot be a replica of e-commerce or any private sector enterprise. By law, a public service agency cannot discriminate along socioeconomic lines. E-governments must be prepared to provide public information and work to enhance efficiency in government (Stiglitz, 2000). But e-governments are not just entities designed to create efficiencies and cost savings for the taxpayer. E-government is also a means to connect the government to its stakeholders.

E-government systems are similar to traditional bureaucracies in all important aspects. For example, they share both open and closed system properties. As social systems, they consist of patterned activities and are driven by individuals or groups with values and motivations. In other words, they are not independent from social, economic, and political influences. Therefore, e-government designs are not devoid of control by power elites who have influence on whether to establish single or multiple portal systems (Danziger, Dutton, Kling, & Kraemer, 1982). By definition, designs that serve as one-stop centers for accessing government services are popular in most government systems.

South Carolina Business One Stop (SCBOS) presents a classic successful e-government project undertaken by several of the state's regulatory agencies. We consider it here because it has received numerous recognitions including the Government Management Information Sciences Elite Achievers award in 2005. The project was also awarded the Network World Magazine Top 50 Enterprise All-Star Award in 2005 in addition to the Federation of Tax Administrators Taxpayer Service and Education Award and the John F. Kennedy School of Government Top 50 Government Innovations Award for 2006 (*South Carolina Business Journal*, 2006).

The original participants of the project were South Carolina's secretary of state; Department of Revenue; Department of Commerce; Department of Labor, Licensing, and Regulation; and Department of Health and Environmental Control. Other participants were the Employment Security Commission and the State Budget and Control Board (TiBA, 2005). Participants from these agencies constituted an executive steering committee to oversee the implementation of the project (Davis, 2005). Each of these agencies had a large role in the regulation of businesses and the licensing, permitting, and registration of new businesses (TiBA, 2005). Originally, the Department of Revenue and a few select agencies played the lead role in the SCBOS project (Brown & Lee, 2002).

Aware of the potential savings in establishing a one-stop portal, the political leadership in South Carolina pulled together resources to imagine and design a system that would increase government efficiency and customer satisfaction and reduce the time for applying, processing, and receiving permits, licenses, and registration. It was also in the interest of both business and government to design a system that would make it easy to start a business in the state of South Carolina. The leadership is aware that the old system was riddled with vague, cumbersome, and time-consuming regulations that caused much delay in business start up time. The case in the state of South Carolina was consistent with findings in a study sponsored by Microsoft that showed businesses wasted an estimated 47 hours annually in the pursuit of obtaining required licenses, permits and registrations (Microsoft, 2008).

Perhaps Friedline (n.d.), a channel development manager with TiBA Solutions, illustrated this frustration best by observing that the paper trail did not serve the "public interest" and was hampering the entrepreneurial spirit (p. 2). He painted a picture of an entrepreneur making endless journeys through the dark, asking paid professionals, family, and friends and visiting bureaucratic offices for information. As is the case in other bureaucratic transactions, applications and licenses sought must be paid for and processed, paperwork reviewed, approved, and responded to, and licenses mailed. Even after the paperwork is complete, the process is repeated ad infinitum until all known paperwork is assembled. The main challenge is to find a solution that would make it more efficient for all the concerned government agencies to provide effective services to members of the public.

SCBOS Design Process

SCBOS started as an initiative called DORBOS by the South Carolina Department of Revenue in 2001. It originated as a set of hyperlinks in the South Carolina state government portal. The project then received its own page in August 2001 and was updated with new web addresses in November. Originally, the links pointed to the Revenue Department and other state agencies. In December 2001, one year after its debut, SCBOS was enhanced on the state web portal to include business information. September 2002 saw the addition of web-accessible services from the SC Employment Security Commission (Davis, 2005). In 2005, the governor of South Carolina signed bill H3768 to provide funding for SCBOS. The total development cost of SCBOS was \$3.6 million, of which \$1.5 million went toward analysis and design costs and \$2.1 million toward construction (Davis, 2005). The analysis phase was begun in January 2003 and was followed by the design project in February 2004. The initial "go-live date" was March 5, 2005 that was moved to May 24, 2005 (Davis, 2005).

The original mission of SCBOS was the creation of a web-based system that allowed new businesses to register for specific taxes and update certain taxpayer data. Before DORBOS was initiated, businesses could only apply for registrations and permits via manually completed paper forms, each requiring common data that was repetitively provided (Brown & Lee, 2002).

The processes used in the 2001/2002 version of the SCBOS structure were relatively simple and straightforward. The system gathered data from applicants through the use of a Q & A wizard that followed an 11-step process flow and stored the data on an SQL server (Brown & Lee, 2002). Any fees that were due for licenses/registrations were collected by the Department of Revenue via an online payment system that accepted credit cards. The data collected were loaded into the mainframe system. ID and license numbers were assigned, records of accounting transactions were created, and then licenses and reports were "generated out of the mainframe process" (Brown & Lee, 2002).

The first phase of SCBOS allowed users to create new business accounts, add different types of taxes to their existing accounts, and update their business information, addresses for example (Brown & Lee, 2002). The Department of Revenue used this online interface to allow businesses to register for up to seven different tax types including sales and use, withholding, and corporate taxes. This phase also established a "maintenance module" that allowed internal users to monitor the system, process address changes, and generate a number of reports. Between August 2001 and July 2002 the SCBOS system received 3,500 applications, collected nearly $88,000 for 12,200 retail license registrations, registered over 1,500 corporate accounts, and created over 1,500 withholding tax accounts (Brown & Lee, 2002).

The second phase of SCBOS, which emerged after 2003, saw the organization of a joint registration system for the Department of Revenue and the Employment Security Commission. There were other goals for the 2002–2003 fiscal year. SCBOS added more functionality to the payment system to accept payment by electronic fund transfers (EFT) in addition to credit cards. The system was also updated to conduct a search of bankruptcies before allowing registration completion.

Originally, the team managing the SCBOS project was broken down into two workgroups. One team worked on developing data collection standards and another group focused on content improvement. The project management was later divided into nine teams: "main, website, marketing, training, featured business, legislation, system maintenance, enhancements, [and] new development" (Davis, 2005).

The SCBOS system has many components. The four major components are "security services, messaging, workflow definition and execution, [and] custom controls" (Davis, 2005). The major components are reusable throughout the system. A general system is used at the agency level and builds around each agency's existing infrastructures (TiBA, 2005). A core structure was also built to handle the inquiries and requests from the SCBOS website. The core system is composed of a workflow maintenance module, an electronic shopping cart, an e-payment module, and a SCBOS accounting module. The core also contains a messaging module. The messaging module communicates with the agency system to pass along work requests. The core SCBOS accounting module communicates with the agency level accounting modules (Davis, 2005).

The overall infrastructure is broken down into 15 environments. The agency environment accounts for five of these environments. The remaining environments are grouped under administration applications, consumer applications, and content management systems. The administration environment houses an application server, web server, and reporting server. The consumer environment is composed of an application server, web server, and SCBOS core database. The consumer application server also communicates with the e-payment and accounting systems (Davis, 2005).

The goals of the 2005 launch of SCBOS were numerous. The overall purpose was to allow new businesses to register for all necessary licenses based upon data collected by an expanded wizard module. The data collected were dispatched to the appropriate agencies for consideration and issuance. The total charges were calculated and collected, and copies of receipts and all licenses, permits, and registrations are accessible online (Davis, 2005).

As of August 2005, SCBOS had nearly 3,400 users who applied for 3,465 licenses, permits, and registrations and paid $67,370 in fees. The Department of Revenue estimates that between May and August 2005 new businesses saved around $267,000, and also estimated an annual savings $1.33 million (Davis, 2005). The SCBOS team also touts the benefits to government entities. Among these benefits are a reduction in operating costs, mainly from decreases in printing and postage costs, reduced data entry and review responsibilities, increased and immediate collection of fees, improved customer service, and the stability and standardization of data across several different agencies.

E-government's organizational entities are lean public agencies that perform specific tasks. They are not free from regular bureaucratic problems such as excessive adherence to rules, overspecialization, informal versus formal communication lines, and unclear authority structures. These virtual forms of organization encourage networking and are interdependent with traditional bureaucracies to reduce uncertainty and share knowledge based on best practices. While virtual organizations have specific goals to achieve, their means to this end is through differentiated technological structures and avenues.

To illustrate some of the claims made here, laws such as the E-government Act (2002), the Paper Reduction Act (1980; 1995), and the Clinger-Cohen Act (1996) all call for implementation of e-government agencies that will share information and adhere to a set of prescribed federal rules. Engagement in virtual public organizations is conditioned by legislative and executive mandates and control through funding and oversight. Linkages to non-governmental agencies are managed through service contracts and formal agreements. Of course, the starting point is the establishment of units within public agencies to coordinate implementation of e-government strategies. Although not referred to as virtual organizations in the enabling statutes, these entities are the bedrock organizations.

Work in this area is still embryonic in the sense that certain technological capabilities are being further developed and refined. More specifically, issues of accountability and privacy are at present not completely in the hands of administrators. Private software engineers and management teams play an important role in the implementation of effective security strategies. Therefore, as we shall demonstrate, the design of e-governments is a collaborative opportunity with risks as well as benefits.

Having established the premises for designing e-government, it is important to recognize that e-governments are probably best conceptualized from a rational choice perspective. These organizations are reactions to new challenges emerging from the desire to enhance rationality, efficiency, and effectiveness in public service delivery systems. In a nutshell, the promises of e-government include increased efficiency, integration, and quality in service production. E-governments also contribute to enhancing transparency in government and limiting corruption opportunities. E-governments are an important asset in the building of democratic interactions between members of the public and officialdom.

THE PHASES OR STAGES OF e-GOVERNMENT

The literature identifies different perspectives on the phases or stages of e-government. The various stages are all elements in the rational design of e-governments. For our purposes, at least two perspectives merit attention. Consider the scheme in box 4.1. At the micro level, at least three discrete stages that mirror traditional implementation phases can be identified. In the second perspective, five discrete stages are presented and shown in box 4.2. The second framework is the most popular and is well developed in works done by international agencies such as the World Bank, United Nations, and consultant firms including Gartner Inc. InfoDev, another development firm that works in developing countries and consults with donor agencies to help their clients become sensitive to the impacts of ICTs on poverty reduction, has a three phase presentation as shown in box 4.3. These phases are abstractions of the objective reality of e-government development. The point is that design projects

Box 4.1. *The Three-Phase Model of e-Government.*

Phases of e-Government	Actions
Planning	The first phase is the planning process in which management tests an e-government blueprint. The agency acquires relevant hardware and energizes staff working in the ICT units. The first phase also involves installation of background networks and collaboration with other governmental agencies through a virtual organization network. This is the phase in which new clients are added into the network. This might mean developing strategies for data collaboration and agreeing on network server domains. It is a pilot experimental stage as well.
Post-planning and post-pilot implementation and reconfiguration of hardware and software	Phase two includes all those processes that ensure backup services are provided. It entails reconfiguring hardware and installing additional hardware. At this time, logical connectivity issues are examined and incorporated into the post-planning stage.
Full implementation and periodic evaluation and system maintenance	The third and final phase involves full implementation of system capacity. All relevant hardware and software are installed as the system capacity is put to full use. It is the stage for providing basic electronic services. It involves training as well as demonstration of basic feature of the e-government system. At this time, an elaborate infrastructure that includes centers of e-government is in place.

occur within the various stages of e-government development. These three designs are basic frameworks that are not mutually exclusive but simply reinforce each other and help us recognize how administrators design e-governments.

Design Challenges for Public Administrators

The assumption is that upon establishment of organizational entities to manage e-government everything else falls in shape. The reality is quite contrary. The processes of designing and implementing e-governments confront numerous challenges. First is the issue of cost of ICTs; the

Box 4.2. *The Second Model of e-Government.*

Phase/Stage of Development	Description and Actions
Emerging	An official government online presence is established. Content is predominately static and not necessarily in response to citizen expectations. Static information source.
Enhanced	Government sites increase; information becomes more dynamic. Regularly updated, downloadable forms and documents; features like site search and e-mail.
Interactive	Users can download forms, e-mail officials, and interact through web. Portal with links to related sites, specialized databases, online forms submission, user log-in.
Transactional	Users can pay for services and other transactions online. Secure access for online payments, e-mail confirmation and acknowledgement receipt.
Seamless, Integrated	Full integration of e-services across administrative boundaries. All services and links accessed through single central portal, all transactional services offered through single integrated site, customizable user pages.

Source. Asia Oceanic Electronic Marketplace Association, 2007.

upstart costs are extremely heavy. These costs not only include hardware and software infrastructure but periodic updates and maintenance as well. The maintenance requirement is a function of user needs. Management might wish to maintain a variety of e-services including e-mail, Full Text Search, Wireless Area Network, and Palm database. E-governments require adequate funding mechanisms for both acquisition and maintenance of their systems. It is important to note that maintenance staff minimally include a systems administrator, maintenance engineers, help desk officers, and software support officers. These are new positions that must be adequately compensated.

Box 4.3. *Additional Alternative View: Phases of e-Government.*

Phases	Actions
Publish	"Publish" websites seek to disseminate information *about* government and information compiled *by* government to as wide an audience as possible. In doing so, publish sites serve as the leading edge of e-government.
Interact	Interactive e-government involves two-way communications, starting with basic functions like e-mail contact information for government officials or feedback forms that allow users to submit comments on legislative or policy proposals.
Transact	A "transact" website offers a direct link to government services, available at any time. In the past, government services such as land registration or the renewal of ID cards required long waits, confrontation with stifling bureaucracy, and the occasional bribe. Innovations such as citizen service kiosks located in shopping centers in Brazil or portable government computers that can be carried into rural pockets of India bring e-government directly to the citizens of developing nations.

Source. InfoDev, n.d.

Training and Enterprise Architecture

There are numerous costs associated with training this manpower. Users must be trained in basic use, copyrights, and equipment safety rules. The Digital Millennium Copyright Act, signed into law October 28, 1998, covers most of the copyright concerns in the electronic media. As experts advise, nearly all the information in electronic form has copyright protection (Reddick & King 1997).

Besides being aware of copyright issues, administrators need to be competent in basic web development techniques and operational systems including the use of HTML, software such as Dreamweaver, FrontPage, and other packages such as JavaScript. Design modalities and enterprise architectures have a profound impact in service provision in new ways of providing electronic government (McCracken & Wolfe, 2004).

Concern about potential inefficiencies and inefficacies in operation of e-government systems is well documented, especially at the federal government level. Congressional studies show that federal IT spending has grown beyond $60 billion annually, forcing decision makers to rethink enterprise planning across federal government units (Office of Management and Budget, 2006b). Enterprise planning is essential in the design of e-government and has been an important feature of federal e-government since 2002 when the OMB mapped its basic features. OMB's guidelines were developed to enable departments and agencies to share organization and technological solutions to existing common design problems. The idea entails designing a framework to serve as an architecture that would facilitate the integration of IT systems. This enterprise views government organizations in a holistic way. The federal enterprise has established benchmarks and a blueprint for IT management and provides guidelines for future approaches to system operability and information sharing. From a budgetary point of view, the idea is to ensure that IT investments support the functions of government. Administrators seek to prevent a situation where technology drives the agenda of government operations.

In OMB Circular A-11, *Preparation and Submission of Budget Estimates*, released in June 2006, federal agencies and departments are required to demonstrate that their information technology investments are aligned with the guidelines provided in the federal enterprise architecture (FEA) standards (OMB, 2006a). OMB announced that it would not approve funding without agency adherence to these standards. The administrative circular echoes some of the principles in the enabling statutes. For example, the language in the enabling Clinger-Cohen Act is specific about what is expected of administrators and defines information technology architecture as an integrated framework for maintaining and acquiring existing information. Briefly, the expectation is that the federal system is to be integrated for purposes of meeting agency strategic goals. Design work revolves around streamlining and updating operations, especially in the areas of finances, human resources, health and security, and technology optimization. In other words, departments and agencies design systems that achieve greater efficiencies through better planning. At the federal level, advances in planning have been achieved through FEA initiatives. We conceptualize FEAs as the primary planning system used by the OMB for critical management purposes. It is a logical structure for classifying complex information.

According to an OMB report (2005) entitled *Enabling Citizen-Centered Electronic Government*, the main goals are:

- To improve the utilization of information resources to achieve a citizen-centered government,
- To increase enterprise architecture practice and techniques and to enable government to better align its IT investments, and
- To increase cross-agency, private-public sector partnerships, and encourage intergovernmental collaborations in finding common solutions to lowering costs.

FEAs are organized around five reference models: performance, business, service, data, and technical. Each of these reference models represents the common framework for departments and agencies to find and develop collective solutions to IT applications and services relevant to e-government. The Clinger-Cohen Act provided the incentive for FEAs by requiring that CIOs adopt these strategies to integrate agency goals and promote business processes with IT. The brief descriptions of the reference models derived from the OMB are presented and summarized in box 4.4.

The task of ensuring that design is integrated and meets the objectives outlined previously falls with agency CIOs. According to the Clinger-Cohen Act (1996), CIOs are tasked with "developing, maintaining, and facilitating the implementation of sound and integrated information technology architecture for the executive agency." Of course, CIOs have other executive-level duties, which we describe later.

In addition, administrators working in e-government systems must receive adequate training in evaluation techniques. Periodic evaluations that disaggregate by gender, area, education and other variables help identify equity problems that might result in costly litigation. Other specific barriers to serving the public better through e-government include understaffing in qualified project managers and IT architects needed

Box 4.4. *Federal Enterprise Architecture Reference Models.*

Performance Reference Model	A framework that measures the output of major technology investments
Business Reference Model	A framework that describes government business operations independent of the agencies that perform them
Service Reference Model	A framework that identifies information technology service applications
Data Reference Model	A framework that describes data and information used to support government delivery of service applications and components
Technical Reference Model	A framework that describes the standards, specifications, and technologies that support government and facilitate service applications

Source. OMB, 2007.

to successfully manage federal IT investments. E-government requires committed leadership, especially at the political end of the spectrum. This is because the objectives behind e-government require broad, well-defined policy framing.

A related area of concern is overcoming the turf wars between agencies, especially when a central coordinating government agency finds it difficult to integrate different services across subagencies. It is not uncommon to find coordination problems resulting from lack of budgetary commitments by cooperating bureaus. Just as with managerial issues, the design and implementation of e-government programs suffer if policy guidelines are too ambiguous.

Security Concerns

A perennial source of concern relates to IT security. First, security refers to property security from hackers and other malicious individuals. Second, it is about the integrity of e-government systems. They must be secure from system obstructers and disruptions. Any organization's critical applications, services, and databases rely heavily upon its server infrastructure. The effectiveness of any critical e-government application or software solution depends upon a secure and optimized network infrastructure. Managerial concerns tend to focus on assessment of these concerns and remedial measures. Assessment includes examining network configuration to determine that every device works optimally and meets security specifications. Contracting out through e-procurement helps ensure that the communications infrastructures meet the required standards. Other benefits of contracting out are short-term capital issues, lower control and maintenance costs, higher service levels, and deeper concentration and access to technical expertise. Experts in local area network (LAN), wide area network (WAN), and other network infrastructures can determine if the design is in compliance with best practices and make appropriate recommendations for review and upgrades. Upgrades have been known to save money and improve efficiency.

Security encompasses respect for privacy as well. If personal data are transmitted through computer-based systems, the data must not be used for unauthorized purposes. Related to the existence of secure operational environments is the fact that e-government design cannot succeed without trust from all stakeholders. Trust remains one of the key priorities in the design of e-government systems much as it is in the area of e-commerce. Gronlund's (2002) argument is that e-commerce has incorporated more complete mechanisms for ensuring trust in systemic operations than are available in e-government. Gronlund (2002) named TRUSTe, BBBOnLine, and WebTrust as examples in design that establish trust in e-commerce. Similar trust providers are less developed in e-government. This requires the government to invest in a variety of security management solutions including protocol and performance analysis. Other solutions require technical means of establishing client and consumer confidence in the electronic environment.

For public agencies, compliance with mandates such as the Health Insurance Portability and Accountability Act (HIPAA), Federal Information Processing Standards (FIPS) and Federal Information Security Management Act of 2002 (FISMA) is required. Most experts in ICT security recommend a layered approach to this security. This includes coming to terms with the reality that firewalls, Intrusion Detection Prevention (IDP) systems solutions, and other strategies sometimes fail. In an era of increasingly sophisticated attacks, other, deeper intrusion and inspection technologies and new integrative products are essential. The challenge is always to put in place systems that limit the chances of facing litigation and breaches to national security in today's world of cyberterrorism. This can be assured through elaborate security policy reviews and development.

The third source of concern is the perennial question of the digital divide. Can designers go beyond the questions of affordability and lack of access by lower income groups? The central design question is, whom do public administrators want to serve? The next question is, what are the needs of members of the public? Designers must consider involvement of all stakeholders. E-government can only be successful when stakeholders are consulted at the policy formulation stage.

Finally, because all policy documents speak of integrating systems, the challenge is to ensure that government organizations are committed to this policy. Moreover, sharing of data between virtual organizations is conditioned upon a commitment to similar data formats for all organizations. This means creating common standards of technological interoperability. Risks associated with designing systems that have connections outside the government are real and include the introduction of malicious software by irresponsible individuals who might post viruses and worms including Trojan software or employ maneuvers to deny services to qualified persons. A second risk is that another user of an outside but connected domain can lure a user of an e-government service to export classified materials.

The challenge is to overcome these risks. Although there are possible countermeasures, including screening, firewalls, and PKIs, these countermeasures have other associated implementation problems as well.

CONCLUSIONS

In conclusion, this chapter has examined the design of e-government by focusing on the stages and phases of development and the idea of FEA. By presenting various discussions on stages of e-government we note the lack of congruence in the evolution of e-government. However, these phases provide a rubric by which to gauge a country's informational and technological changes. On the other hand, by looking at organizational dynamics we discern that e-government creates new organizational forms that need to be understood. This section has also discussed problem areas in the design of e-government.

Key Concepts

Bureaupathology
Contracting Out
E-government Design Stages and Phases
E-procurement
Federal Enterprise Architecture (FEA)
HIPAA security and privacy mandates
IDP solutions
Organizational Structures
Protocol and Performance Analysis
Technological Interoperability
Virtual Organization

Discussion Questions

1. List at least two barriers to serving the citizen better through e-government.
2. Discuss the various strategies that public administrators employ in ensuring e-government safety, especially over the Internet. What is the role of help desk attendants in an organization you work for or are familiar with?
3. You have been contracted to design a secure e-government system in the Department of Aging. What are some of the ideas you would incorporate in your planning session?
4. Comment on the claim that when government officials evaluate security solutions, cost is always an important consideration. Does proven reliability of the technology matter? If so, how?

5. Which phase in the design of e-government is most critical? Explain why you think so.

INTERNET ACTIVITY

Identify and visit websites of at least ten local government agencies and rank them according to their aesthetic attraction, quality of services provided, levels of interaction opportunities, and overall design. State if the suite designs meet the standards for a well-designed communication tool for e-government. Decide your own evaluation criteria.

Chapter 5

e-Government and Administrative Law

In this chapter, we explore legal issues that encompass e-government. We do so within a broad framework of administrative law. We begin with the premise that administrative law in the United States is founded on the principles of judicial fairness, the rule of law, and basic constitutionalism. Enmeshed in constitutionalism is the principle of federalism, which establishes local, state, and federal jurisdictions and their limitations. Public administration continues to search for approaches that lead to better and more efficient, effective, responsive, and lean government. As noted previously, e-government is a part of this broad goal. The administrative state, especially its agencies as they function within the bounds of enabling acts and their own broad rules, must be constitutionally competent. Briefly, such is the preamble for e-government environments.

This chapter probes the legal environments of e-government. Specifically, the chapter addresses two questions: has e-government changed the way administrative law is conducted and what are the fundamental legal and quasi-legal issues in e-government environments?

ADMINISTRATIVE LAW

Our first task is to define administrative law. Administrative law is an amorphous body of law that defies positivist definitions. For practical purposes, it is a body of law "concerned with actions by administrative agencies" (Cooper, 2000, p. 5). It is an aspect of public law concerned with procedures by which public organizations engage in rulemaking. Rulemaking essentially is quasi-legislative power delegated by Congress to bureaucratic agencies. A rule issued under this authority is an agency statement that has the full force and effect of law.

Administrative agencies issue at least three types of rules: (1) substantive rules, for example, safety rules on computer information integrity; (2) procedural rules, for example, the ones that agencies follow in the conduct of e-government business that may include rules about maintaining domain names for a given time or the qualifications for a systems administrator; and (3) interpretive rules, for example, advisory opinions about qualifications for availability of a service (Cooper, 2000). These categories notwithstanding, the e-government framework provides an opportunity to have a functional typology of rules as identified in box 5.1.

Rulemaking involves complex procedures outlined in the Administrative Procedure Act of 1946 (APA) and other statutes. Rulemaking

Box 5.1. *Different Types of Rules.*

Basic Format and Types of Rules in the ICT Arena

- Rules that regulate aspects of information processing
- Rules that regulate information transmission
- Rules that relate to the information itself—the content
- Rules that govern secrecy protocols and personal data protection
- Rules about the form of information, for example, message signatures to give legal validity to messages in ICTs.

requires public participation and must be seen as a fair process with room for judicial review. The APA has detailed guidelines for advance notice and public participation. APA amendments and other rules and regulations permit the use of electronic communication to a large degree. For example, transmission of mandatory data for planning has been widely accepted. Under the APA, rules must also be transmitted to the concerned parties in a manner that is both equitable and fair, essentially through publication in the *Federal Register*, now available online. Research in the area of e-rulemaking has grown tremendously (Shulman, 2005; Schlosberg & Dryzek, 2002). In this chapter, we shall briefly illuminate some of the key aspects of rulemaking in an electronic age.

Administrative law is also about the enabling statutes that pronounce policy actions in any given public program or activity. Since some scholars consider the implementation of public policy to be the core of public administration, we have already considered aspects of public law in the coverage of policy foundations of e-government. However, there is an argument that the fundamental principles of cyberlaw (e-law) are not clearly identified (Klotz, 2004). Cyberlaw is the overarching law that establishes the parameters by which e-commerce and e-government are aligned. Federal and respective state laws guide cyberlaw. For example, state laws may prohibit advertising commercial activities on government websites. However, there may be permissible advertisements if community websites fulfill much broader public interest functions. In cases where community websites advertise commercial activities, there must be a justifiable public purpose. Like all other laws, rules must, of necessity, be premised on constitutional fundamentals. This is because by practice the constitution provides the overarching guidance upon which competent administration occurs (Rosenbloom & Lee, 2005; Rosenbloom, Carroll, & Carroll, 2000).

Since the advent of the use of ICTs, concerns for "big brother" activity have never ceased to exist in the public psyche (Lyon, 1988). "Big brother" is an affront to citizen privacy, especially when private information held in trust by public bureaucrats is compromised in the emerging ICT media. Of course, privacy is not the only constitutional issue.

Government secrecy is also troublesome, particularly for democratic governance. The expectation is that ICTs can help enrich the avenues and processes for disseminating governmental information (Raab, 1997). A pictorial representation of these constitutionally based arguments, found in Figure 5.1, shows the connections that establish the legal frameworks.

Many of the earlier frameworks are based on the application of legal frameworks established prior to the Internet (Klotz, 2004). Lawmakers continue to fall behind in providing new laws to address emerging e-government regimes. While this is a valid concern, it does not necessarily mean that the introduction of new "e-laws" is an answer to all e-governance issues. Too many new information laws can be an impediment to successful development of e-government programs. In the past, these laws "addressed traditional problems of social and political power

FIGURE 5.1. *Basis for Cyberlaw.*

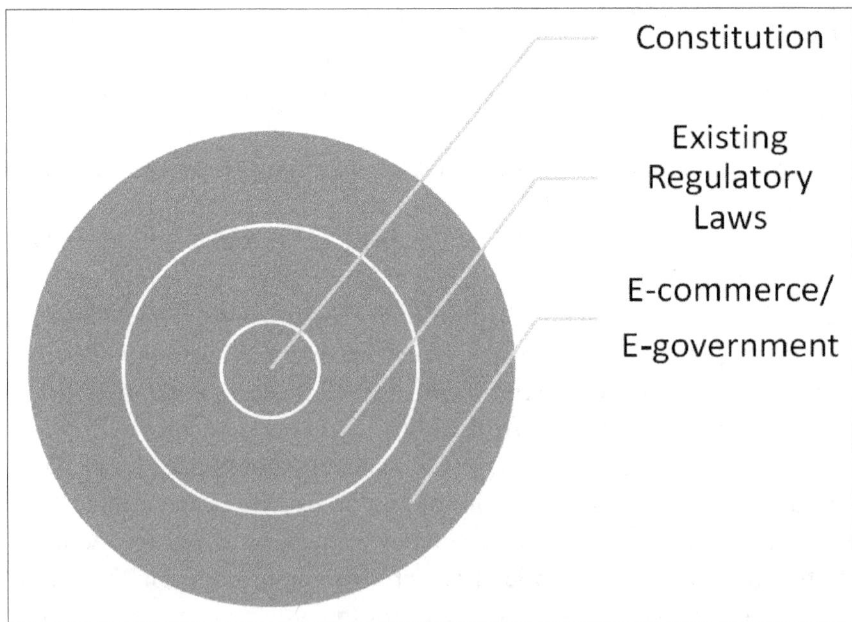

and conflicts in terms of information handling and communication" (Burkert, 1985, p. 119).

Among the important areas of concern is the question of how government agencies *use* their power in the emerging e-government environment. Cyberspace is replete with fundamental uncertainties of identity and location. Advances have been made in the area of locating origins of Internet sites, but anonymity, encryption, and shifting domain bases complicate cyberlegalities. For example, it is not clear whether ISPs are responsible for communication problems associated with their customers. Legally, though, the principle of analogy has been applied. That is, courts and bureaucrats assume that ISPs are analogous to telephone companies and therefore can be required to provide information about their customers. Policymakers and administration officials therefore visualize and understand Internet activities as similar to telephone operations. For example, if wiretaps by bureaucrats are authorized in the telephone media, so could be some forms of data mining in cybertechnologies. This is an aspect of Kenneth Warren's authoritative detailing of important points to consider when delegating power to public bureaucracies (Warren, 1997).

Role of Government

Philosophically, issues of regulation of e-government, business, and communication technologies attract the attention of 21st century public administrators. The question of regulation is best understood in the context of what the public construes to be the role of government in a digital age. The digital era brings new challenges to how we understand government. In the 20th century, the Sherman and Clayton Antitrust Acts gave the government power to regulate industry because monopoly proved to be contrary to the public interest. In addition, the creation of the federal reserve system and the 16th amendment to the U.S. Constitution, permitting federal income taxation, gave government the authority to regulate both behavior of private industry and public consumption of products of the now mature American capitalist economy. Regulation in the Internet age hinges upon the same principles of protecting the public interest.

New ICTs dictate that government acts to regulate e-commerce by employing the same logic as it did during the early antitrust regulatory regimes. Conversely, e-government opportunities challenge government to act decisively in the determination of what services should or should not be provided to the public online. In the current economic structures, public presence in online activities is complicated by the overlapping needs of ensuring both security and privacy. Government also has to provide guidelines in matters that transcend jurisdictions. As Stiglitz et al. (2000) stated, the appropriate role of government in the economy should not be static but must evolve as the economy and technology evolve. Their study outlined principles for online informational government activity. They devised a set of twelve principles for government action in a digital economy to be used when evaluating new government activities generally. These principles are delineated in box 5.2.

Stiglitz et al. (2000) divided the activities into three categories according to how the activities affect the public as follows: "green light" activities raised few concerns, "yellow light" activities raised increased levels of concern; and "red light" activities signaled significant concerns and hence required proportional attention and action. While these principles are not a grand theory for conceptualizing the perceived role of government regulation and action in the digital age, they provided a platform from which e-government scholarship engages the underlying question of how public administration interacts with industry in the age of the Internet.

Government action involves regulation and is an area that continues to be a major arena for policy disputes that pit two sides against each other. Those who argue for regulation of any kind traditionally emphasize that government regulation increases fairness and democratic accountability. In addition, supporters contend that regulation protects citizens from excessive profit making and other vices of industry (Gellhorn, 1982). In some cases, regulation is a preemptive strategy for preventing the occurrence of major social problems. For example, through regulation private

Box 5.2. *Principles for Online and Informational Governmental Activity.*

"Green Light" for online and informational government activity	"Yellow Light" for online and informational government activity	"Red Light" for online and informational government activity
• Providing public date and information is a proper governmental role • Improving the efficiency with which governmental services are provided is a proper governmental role • The support of basic research is a proper governmental role	• The government should exercise caution in adding specialized value to public data and information • The government should only provide private goods, even if private sector firms are not providing them, under limited circumstances • The government should only provide a service online if private provision with regulation or appropriate taxation would not be more efficient • The government should ensure that mechanisms exist to protect privacy, security, and consumer protection online • The government should promote network externalities only with great deliberation and care • The government should be allowed to maintain proprietary information or exercise rights under patents and/or copyrights only under special conditions (including national security)	• The government should exercise substantial caution in entering markets in which private sector firms are active • The government, as well as corporations, should generally not aim to maximize net revenues or take actions that would reduce competition • The government should only be allowed to provide goods or services for which appropriate privacy and conflict of interest protections have been erected

Source. Stiglitz et al., 2000.

companies can be forced to release information that would otherwise be hidden from the public. Another related argument has been that regulation helps control monopolistic power and keeps prices and profits reasonable. In the context of social policy, some regulation is necessary for societal order. In recent times, supporters of regulation point to the financial meltdowns in 2007 and 2008 as examples of what can go wrong in the absence of regulation.

The opponents of regulation have argued that private property should not be regulated. In many instances they cite constitutional provisions, especially the 4th and 5th amendments, which protect individuals from unreasonable searches and guarantee due process in matters of dispute respectively. Many of those in the antiregulation arena contend that markets are the most efficient allocator of resources and that government has no right to meddle in the affairs of business. This idea is premised on the ideological belief that markets are self-adjusting entities and that the role of the government must be minimal. Another variation of the same argument is that regulations promote only special interests by allowing capture of various policy interests. In some policy areas, those against regulation present economically derived cost-benefit data to support their arguments (Lipsey & Courant, 1996).

Administrative law in the context of e-government is also managed within the same regulatory and institutional structures as any other government forms. For example, the regulation of Internet activities and issuance of morality standards and access ratings are both still under the purview of the FCC. Consumer privacy, fairness, and systemic safety are still at the core of the FCC's "bounded social regulation" mission. However, much still relies on self-regulation on the part of industry stakeholders and members of the public at large. The legislative initiatives addressed, including the E-government Act of 2002, constitute the legal framework for electronic administrative communication. We have already discussed these issues in the previous chapters.

In sum, administrative law controls both traditional bureaucratic and e-government bureaucratic systems. Both systems, as we saw in chapter 4, have one central goal: to deliver government services to citizens.

E-RULEMAKING

Administrative rulemaking in all spheres of government follows a well-prescribed path (Kerwin, 2003). The normal trajectory is that the legislature passes a law stating the objectives to be met. Public agencies are delegated responsibility to interpret the law and create rules and regulations for policy implementers. The general sequence at this stage is well known: advanced notice of proposed rulemaking and the proposed rule is publicized and offered for public comment before being published in the *Federal Register* and codified in the *Code of Federal Regulations*. It is at the level of public comment and participation that ICTs come into play. As Schlosberg, Zavestoski, and Shulman (2007) observed, the United States federal government is, by design, facilitating the electronic submission of citizen comments during federal regulatory comment periods. Although the genesis of public comment is the Administrative Procedure Act of 1946, advances in ICTs have enabled increased deliberation and resulted in an increase in substantive information on various changes in agency rules.

The first major significant cases of using ICTs in rulemaking were at the Nuclear Regulatory Commission, which began using electronic bulletin boards to solicit public comment on proposed changes in its business in the early 1990s (Kerwin, 2003). Other examples of successful e-rulemaking endeavors include Environmental Protection Agency (EPA) institution of programs that enabled members of the public to comment on the rules it was amending. The agency also created a Listserve for feedback purposes. Most public agencies have since the early 1990s instituted e-programs that include chat rooms and electronic conferences to enable participation and dialogue in rulemaking decisions (Kerwin, 2003).

These efforts have considerable merit. For instance, e-rulemaking is unique in the sense that it allows citizens commenting on agency rules to see the comments of others sending posts. The e-rulemaking system is also highly structured, unlike the mass political blogs that might attract less substantive comments. While those are also common in e-rulemaking endeavors, the high level of structure confines some of the negatives associated with computer-based communication tools.

At least four problems can be discerned from attempts at expanding e-rulemaking in public agencies. First, there is a tendency in certain agencies for an agency to receive numerous comments that it may not be able to sift through in a timely and accurate manner. Studies indicate that inviting public participation in e-rulemaking tends to yield thousands of unmanageable documents. For example, participants in the United States Department of Agriculture's (USDA) National Organic Program provided over 300,000 public comments (Shulman, 2005).

Second, although there are studies that show e-rulemaking can be deliberative, in the sense that commentators can post rejoinders to other participants in online deliberative forums, the actual content is not significantly superior to that provided in traditional fax- and paper-based avenues. Moreover, the "click and send" activism permitted by government websites must confront malicious mail from those whose intent is not to contribute to the rulemaking process. Electronic interactive forms might be clogged with material that is irrelevant to the deliberative process, such as mass mailings of pornography. Yet administrators have to go through it all to discern the relevant information.

A third problem evident from the growing e-rulemaking industry is that a number of government websites are poorly designed and do not necessarily garner sufficient visits to the web pages with "click and send" function keys. Poorly designed comment submittal forms are a hindrance to meaningful deliberation in the e-rulemaking format.

The fourth drawback is the question of access associated with the digital divide (Kerwin, 2003). Agencies cannot receive comments from members of the public who are functionally illiterate in computer-based communication systems. Additionally there remain social issues of poverty that deny millions of people access to convenient computers except at the public library.

ACCESS TO PUBLIC DOCUMENTS

The United States is among the leading countries in terms of transparency in government operations (Otenyo & Lind, 2004). The adoption of advanced ICTs has not in a significant way altered the rules governing openness in the conduct of government work. Essentially, openness is an administrative principle that successive administrations seek to retain. The onslaught of e-government did not fundamentally change administrative behavior in terms of conducting government service. More significantly, access to public documents is, perhaps, made easier in the e-government structures. Freedom of Information Acts (FOIA) at the federal and state levels encourage disclosure of certain types of information by government agencies. These statutes and "sunshine laws" mandate public officials to conduct public business in transparent ways. They have in large measure created opportunities for greater scrutiny of official decision-making processes.

Interpretations regarding which documents are to be declassified or the various document classifications remain the prerogative of executive officials. However, for the most part, under various clauses of the federal FOIA, certain non–security sensitive material can be made available to the public and posted on websites. Court orders can confirm the principle of open government by directing government agencies to release for circulation documents requested by interested members of the public. But, before public documents are released, specific rules and regulations must be followed.

The Electronic Freedom of Information Act (E-FOIA)

The E-FOIA was a product of intense lobbying and activism from citizen groups who were concerned about administrative decision making and demanded to have greater access to hard-to-get information. The law mandates federal government agencies to make public information on agency rules, opinions, orders, records, and proceedings. Agencies are required by law to establish places where employees and members of the public as well as law enforcement personnel can obtain and make submittals or requests to obtain information. Moreover, each agency is required, in accordance with published rules, to make available for public inspection and copying (a) final opinions, including concurring and dissenting opinions, as well as orders, made in the adjudication of cases; and (b) those statements of policy and interpretations which have been adopted by the agency that are not published in the *Federal Register*. The E-FOIA is seen as an instrument for citizen empowerment and as a check on bureaucratic mismanagement.

Enacted in early October 1966, the original FOIA was the first law to establish an effective legal right of access to government information, underscoring the crucial need in a democracy for open access to government information by citizens. Then, information was hard and costly to access. Computers were in limited use and no substantial cross-referencing existed. President Bill Clinton worked to update the law to bring it to the contemporary realities of the ICTs. In 1996, he signed into law the Electronic Freedom of Information Act Amendments. The legislation brought the FOIA into the information and electronic age by clarifying that it applied to records maintained in electronic format. Although these amendments broadened public access, they do not necessarily provide sufficient protections from political partisan misuse.

Public disclosure rules in the age of ICTs have changed for better or worse. Witness the public circulation of excerpts from phone conversations regarding an alleged sexual affair between President Clinton and White House intern Monica Lewinsky reported on various Internet sites following morally damaging release of Independent Counsel Kenneth W. Starr's report. The Starr Report led to a House impeachment of President Bill Clinton on December 19, 1998, on the grounds of perjury.

Another incident was the release of e-mail excerpts depicting Michael Brown, former director of FEMA, as not being serious in his actions in the wake of the agency's failure to provide satisfactory response to Hurricane Katrina. Louisiana Congressman Charlie Melançon (D-LA) argued that e-mails written by Michael Brown showed a lack of concern for the unfolding tragedy and a failure in leadership. In one e-mail, after being prompted for action, Brown remarked: "Thanks for the update. Anything specific I need to do or tweak?" (CNN, 2005). There was widespread disappointment with the manner in which the disaster that devastated sections of Louisiana, Mississippi, and Alabama in late 2005 was handled (CNN, 2005).

The fact that e-mail messages and logs are considered public records leaves administrators with very limited options on what to communicate in the free cyber-superhighway of the e-mail media. While the use and abuse of e-mail reinforces the salience of transparency as a value, transparency and disclosure must be managed responsibly. This brings us to the central question of privacy and its place in ICTs.

Without doubt the conflict between access to public documents and individual privacy is real. The challenge for administrators is to strike a balance between these opposites. The key to achieving an optimal outcome has always been to manage privacy regulation using a model of accountability and responsibility which encourages internal self-regulation while embracing externally determined regulatory structures. Public trust in e-government and its ability to manage personal data, sensitive and otherwise, is likely to wane without assurance that certain types of data will not fall into the hands of malicious individuals.

The two most important legal frameworks for understanding privacy issues are the Privacy Act of 1974 and the Family Educational Rights and Privacy Act. These statutes apply to both public and private agencies to protect privacy. By law, federal websites are required to have privacy policies and other protocols that contribute to the protection of personal data.

However, recent occurrences in the political realm, conditioned by security concerns, have changed the balance between privacy and disclosure. There is more tension between open access and national security than in the pre–September 2001 era (Chiger, 2002). There has also been an upsurge in terms of making e-government a tool for monitoring activities of groups and individuals deemed to be security risks in addition to the preexisting trend of building systems for promoting accountability and access to information.

In the current shift in the security environment, e-government is being transformed. More specifically, since the terrorist attacks of September 11, 2001, in New York, Washington D.C., and Pennsylvania, some government agencies have become more security conscious and have removed from the realm of public knowledge certain pieces of information that can provide terrorist groups added advantages in their dangerous and harmful activities. For example, NASA now limits public access to some of its programs previously covered online. Another example is the Department of Transportation, which has removed contents of its pipeline mapping websites. Likewise, the EPA has eliminated information in reports with guidelines on how to expose hazardous materials. A more dramatic example is the removal of specific content on enforcement issues from the Federal Aviation Administration's official website. There are numerous other examples from departments including the Department of Energy and the Nuclear Regulatory Commission, both of which have a security import. In a nutshell, access to certain types of security information has been restricted (Harris, 2002).

Since September 11, 2001, Congress has passed far-reaching legislative measures to intercept electronic communications of individuals of interest in the war against terror. The argument behind 2001 passage of the "Uniting and Strengthening America by Providing Appropriate Tools Required to Intercept and Obstruct Terrorism Act" (Patriot Act) is that it allows law enforcement agencies to protect liberty by providing security. One of the main provisions of the Patriot Act creates a new crime, domestic terrorism, and grants the National Security Agency, the FBI, and the CIA greater access to private communications, including the rights to wiretap phones, monitor e-mail, and survey medical and financial records. In fact, President Bush authorized secret wiretapping of phones, monitoring of e-mails, and surveying of medical and financial records of individuals using software such as Carnivore and Echelon. It is argued that Echelon, managed by NSA, sifts through over 90% of e-mail communications and is capable of intercepting personal data. Carnivore programs, which track e-mail activities, were previously only permissible through court orders, but President Bush authorized massive eavesdropping without adhering to the letter of the law, citing executive prerogative.

Although there has been considerable public outcry over the implementation of certain provisions in the Patriot Act, it survived legislative sanction and received new support in terms of program funding.

Additionally, Congress passed the USA PATRIOT Act Improvement and Reauthorization Act of 2005 (H.R. 3199), which was signed into law by President Bush in March 2006. This legislation reauthorizes all expiring provisions of the Patriot Act, adds dozens of additional safeguards to protect Americans' privacy and civil liberties, strengthens port security, and provides tools to combat the spread of methamphetamine drugs.

Electronic Signatures

The final point that merits our attention and discussion is the use of electronic signatures. According to the U.S. Electronic Signatures in Global and National Commerce Act of 2000 (E-sign Act), electronic signatures are "sounds, symbols, or processes attached to or logically associated with a contract or other record and executed or adopted by a person with intent to sign the record." Increasingly, electronic signatures are honored in both e-commerce and e-government. Hundreds of stores often require customers using debit and credit cards to use electronic signatures to validate and complete transactions. In the private sector, the E-sign Act applies broadly to all transactions affecting domestic and international trade. There are several areas of general applicability, for example, in insurance, mortgages, loans, banking, securities, and retirement services. The act establishes the legal validity of electronic signatures and other records. Box 5.3 shows the main points in the enabling law.

Box 5.3. *E-sign Act Key Points.*

The Electronic Signatures in Global and National Commerce Act Key Points
• Applies to commercial transactions affecting interstate and foreign commerce • Established legal validity of e-records, contract, and signatures • Preempted laws and regulations that deny effect and enforceability of an electronic signature • Government activities are covered under the Government Paperwork Elimination Act • E-sign Act (PL 106–229) signed into law June 30, 2000 by 106th Congress; took effect October 1, 2000

Although government activities are not within the broad scope of the E-Sign Act, there are some relevant principles established in its intent. Some are captured in the Government Paperwork Elimination Act, which we have discussed previously. Regardless, in the public sector, agencies such as the U.S. Bureau of Citizenship and Immigration Services (USCIS) require applicants for various types of documents including smart cards, employment authorization, and permanent resident cards to sign electronically in tandem with providing certain biometrics. While electronic signatures are an important validation tool in e-government infrastructures, they raise at least two important legal issues. First, do these signatures have the same force of law as others done on paper? Second, can they be valid at all times and in all places where they are utilized? Technically, the answer to the questions posed should be yes given the legal frameworks for PKI.

PKI is a security architecture introduced to provide an increased level of confidence for exchanging information the Internet. The term PKI can be very confusing. PKI may mean the methods, technologies, and techniques that together provide a secure infrastructure. It also means the use of a public and private key pair for authentication and proof of content. PKI utilizes cryptographic keys to verify the authenticity of senders (signatures) and ensures privacy (through encryption). Cryptography works in a fairly simple way; if one key is used to encrypt information, then only the related key can decrypt that information. Knowing one of the keys does not mean one can easily calculate the other. Public keys can be distributed and seen by all users or simply made private. The main benefits of PKI are summarized in box 5.4.

At the federal government level, PKI meets some security needs but not others. PKI is established as a means to implement electronic signature technology. The federal PKI approach entails the determination of government needs through risk assessments. Administrators have built a PKI infrastructure that places a considerable amount of emphasis on policy and technical interoperability among agencies. Policy interoperability

Box 5.4. *PKI Benefits.*

PKI offers the following benefits:

- certainty of the quality of information sent and received electronically
- certainty of the source and destination of that information
- assurance of the time and timing of that information (providing the origination time is known)
- certainty of the privacy of that information
- assurance that the information may be introduced as evidence in a court or law

Source. ArticSoft, n.d.

involves the determination of trusted PKI domains that meet the standards required by agencies. Conversely, technical interoperability involves the validation of certificates from different domains that interact with government agencies.

The key challenge to PKI interoperability is to find solutions when the number of domains increases. One way has been for the federal government to establish institutional structures that bridge operations. For example, the Federal Bridge Certification Authority simplifies PKI interoperability. It encourages agencies to work together in an economical, effective, and efficient manner. The federal government PKI policy manager in the GSA Office of Government issues specific guidelines on digital identity credential issues and manages the overall certification process. The policy manager also issues Access Certificates for Electronic Services to e-government users.

An argument can be made that if a large agency such as the IRS accepts tax e-files without these signatures but with Personal Identification Number (PIN) codes, then the level of confidence in e-government infrastructure is reasonable. While the assumption is based on general public trust of government, the unknowns are seldom discussed. Anyone thinking about the Y2K 2000 issue and the numerous disruptive worms and viruses may have a hard time giving full trust to the system.

Box 5.5. *Identity Authentication Systems.*

PIN or Password
Digitized image of a handwritten signature
Knowledge-based authentication
Biometric profile
Click-through on software program's dialogue box
Digital signature or other encrypted authentication system

The main identity authentication attributes are shown in box 5.5. Trusting electronic signatures, even if they are in encrypted authentication systems, may also be affected by traditional habits. Signing a document on paper has over the years been regarded as a definitive sign of affirmation. One can hardly think of a situation where a check is honored or a driver's license issued without a signature. Important official documents are considered authoritative only under a signature. Therefore, signatures are a serious issue, especially if communication is to be considered serious. The electronic signature version suffers from the traditional bias in favor of ink and paper-based versions, especially in the realm of public service. Public administrators may find it challenging to accept electronic signatures in instances where huge public monies are in play, for example, in contracts. This is where administrative law and e-governments confront each other.

Agency rules or statutory provisions have to be explicit in determining cases where electronic signatures have to be valid instruments of communications. For example, in the case of the USCIS, rules posted on its website indicate this possibility. Those receiving certain services from the agency are required to adhere to specific provisions posted in USCIS centers across the nation. Generally, there is no hard legal restriction on use of electronic signatures in the e-government infrastructure. From a technological standpoint, electronic signatures are not any more or less secure than ink and paper ones. What is important is to establish and adhere to validation and data authentication rules.

Key Concepts

Administrative Law
Administrative Procedure Act
Authentication
Carnivore
Certification of Authority (CA)
Data Integrity
E-rulemaking
Echelon
Electronic Conference
Electronic FOIA Amendments of 1996
Electronic Signatures
Federal Register
Freedom of Information Act
Patriot Act
Personal Data Act
Personal Identification Number (PIN) codes
Privacy Act
Public Key Infrastructures (PKI)
Regulation
Rules
Secrecy Act
Transparency

Discussion Questions

1. Identify some of the methods by which e-governments facilitate public participation in agency rulemaking.
2. Identify electronic signatures. Discuss the limitations, if any, of electronic signatures.
3. Discuss the advantages and disadvantages of e-rulemaking. Select an example of a public agency and outline its strategies for e-rulemaking.
4. Does e-government enhance the quality of public participation in rulemaking? Explain your point.
5. How have developments following September 11, 2001, affected public information disclosure rules in e-government?
6. Should government regulate all Internet activity? What do you perceive to be the role of government in the era of digital technologies?

INTERNET ACTIVITY

Visit any political blog and examine the nature and quality of discussions that are posted there. Then visit any regulatory government agency and click on the area provided for public comment on its rulemaking mandates. Critically evaluate some of the comments posted in the area. Some sites may not show these, so you may have to find government sites that have ongoing discussions. Compare the quality of discussions on the government site and those on the more popular public or commercial blogs. For a start, visit http://www.blogsearchengine.com/ and the government regulation site http://www.regulations.gov/fdmspublic/component/main.

CHAPTER 6

THE e-PUBLIC MANAGER AND THE CIO

We can hardly comprehend e-government without speaking about the e-manager. Although much has been written about the role of the manager in public service, the literature on e-managers is scant. We conceptualize the e-manager as focused on managing employees remotely. Managing people remotely is a feature of today's workplace because many organizations have introduced new ways of working (e-work) and employees have embraced telecommuting.

To begin, we must understand how a number of authors have described the emerging computer-driven business management strategies and associated public sector leadership efforts. The task of the e-manager goes beyond managing e-work. It is also about spotting inefficiencies and uncovering IT-based problems in the workplace. The e-manager analyzes and identifies opportunities for the entire agency. E-management entails recognition of threats and abnormalities and the optimization of operations, especially through strategic planning and efficient use of organizational resources. It is about engaging the world through cyberspace. Plenert (2001) stated that an e-manager is "a world class manager who makes change happen rather than one who is just affected by change" (p. ix). Although his work focused on the emerging regime of e-commerce, it is quite relevant to e-government. Here is why: The current environment is a globalized world (Luke & Caiden, 1999). In March 2006, American newspapers reported ferocious public opinion opposing the contracting out of the operations of key U.S. ports to Dubai Ports World (DP World). DP World, a United Arab Emirates state-owned enterprise, was backed by former President George W. Bush but vehemently opposed by members of the public who felt that a foreign-owned enterprise from a region that harbors terrorists should not be trusted to manage operations in U.S. port facilities. The deal was cancelled after Congress brought pressure to the White House. At the same time, DP World announced it would subcontract its U.S. operations to American companies. The fact that another country was being offered an opportunity to manage security-sensitive ports in the United States was perceived as an error in judgment on the part of the executive, particularly because of the existing security-conscious ecology of post–September 11, 2001, public administration. Yet, from a big picture perspective, the decision by the executive to contract out services to a foreign government was an aspect of the realization that we operate in a globalized world. E-commerce functions outside the purview of nationally confined boundaries per se. So does e-government. One-stop portals that are widely used in e-government provide linkages that are global in outreach.

Both e-government and e-commerce are dependent on web-based data and information sharing. Both are also dependent upon strategic partnerships, alliances and efforts at developing interchangeable and transferable models. Because e-commerce preceded e-government, it has a larger base of case studies to inform scholarly discourses and frameworks (Turban, King, Lee, & Viehland, 2004). However, what is important today is that both provide services through the Internet and value the efficiency afforded by the new ICTs. Moreover, both share the ideology of customer friendliness and workforce responsiveness and empowerment. The new values arising from technologies have created a management pattern based on the notions of change in management styles and possibly emergence of an e-manager. The roles of this new type of manager, as Plenert (2001) claimed, are found in box 6.1.

The e-management model is about dramatic change. The idea of "dramatic change" as a key characteristic to leadership is well established in the public management literature. Kotter (1990), in trying to make distinctions between management and leadership, observed that leadership is not just about establishing direction, motivating, and inspiring but also about producing change, often dramatic. In the case of the e-manager the change is so rapid that it is difficult to keep pace. It is about communicating in a high-speed communication era. It provides a new business model for e-commerce and e-government. It is about eliminating steps in reaching the customer or client. The e-manager is a type of superhuman who can manage through high-speed computer-based communication systems. The e-manager needs to know what is technologically new and relevant. Plenert (2001) defined the e-manager as "a leader that optimizes the efficient use of eCommerce and web based technologies in a world-class management environment" (p. 7). Building on Plenert's definition, we define an e-manager in the public sector as a leader that optimizes the efficient use of e-government technologies and ICTs in a networked political environment.

Box 6.1. *E-managerial Roles.*

- Define goals and strategies
- Motivate change in the direction of goals and strategies
- Plan for change
- Incorporate systems that will facilitate change
- Empower employees to make changes
- Reward successful change programs

Source. Plenert, 2001, p. x.

When Plenert (2001) associated management with leadership, he was not making a new point. The literature that describes management in the public sector has long associated the role of the manager with leadership. Denhardt (1993) observed that public managers as leaders "must use power to empower others," "must create a vision of the future that already exists in the minds of others," and "must act as though in charge and be aware that they are not" (p. 129). Gortner, Mahler, and Nicholson (1997) identified leadership as one of the key functions of a manager. In their estimation, the leadership role entails creating conditions for work to be done efficiently and effectively. These authors provide a list of what they consider to be the roles of managers in public sector organizations, which can be seen in box 6.2.

Besides the obvious fact that leadership is common to conceptions of management roles, other variables matter as well. We will only mention here that traits such as the ability to motivate others and communicate well are core roles in the management model. The importance of managerial support for employee motivation programs is well documented and studied in public administration (Milakovich & Gordon, 2004; Nigro, Nigro, & Kellough, 2007). The centrality of good communication was abundantly addressed in Denhardt, Denhardt, and Aristigueta's (2002) work on management in the public and not-for-profit sectors. They provide their

Box 6.2. *Roles for Managers.*

Figurehead
Leader
Liaison
Monitor
Disseminator
Spokesperson
Entrepreneur
Disturbance handler
Resource allocator
Negotiator

Source. Gortner et al., 1997.

readers with many important thoughts on communication between the manager and worker. The key areas in this formulation do not preclude communications as negotiator, resource allocator, agency spokesperson, disturbance handler, and other responsibilities. Robert Denhardt and his collaborators (2002) described how a manager should go about effectively communicating to his subordinates, and warn of the danger in ignoring the significance of how one communicates.

Since e-government is about ICTs, it is in the area of leadership and communications that we must now focus. First, some caveats. Leadership studies in trade and academic literature can be confusing. Most textbooks define leadership as the exercise of authority, whether formal or informal, in directing and coordinating the work of others. While management involves power, leadership cannot be bestowed upon a person by a higher authority. It is also conditioned upon situations. Leadership behavior depends on the situation being faced, and more than one set of behaviors exist and need to be used as the situation evolves. The leader must change his or her style depending on the situation. For example, a leader in a crisis situation uses different techniques than she would in a standard operating procedural situation (Yuki, 1994).

The concepts of situational and transformational leadership that are widely used in public administration textbooks explain the context of e-managers derived from Plenert's (2001) ideas described earlier. The e-manager is a product of the world globalized by ICTs. S/he must be able to transform the way management was previously done for maximum gains in service delivery or profit if one is talking about the private sector. The e-manager exercises strategic leadership, that is, an ability to understand the complexities of the environment, and play the role of a change agent to enhance organizational competitiveness and success.

Bennis (1999), Denhardt (1993), Hyde (1997), Meyerson (1996), and Sittenfeld (1999) among others have moved beyond the traditional ways of studying and understanding leadership in the modern environment. Such leadership takes many forms but is characterized by power sharing and courageous but skillful risk taking. All persons in the organization are encouraged to assume leadership in making improvements in the quality and productivity of the organization. In the public sector, leadership has to be seen in terms of involvement of individuals throughout the organization. Leadership in the traditional view was about the position of a particular person. The leader was expected to develop good ideas about the direction of the agency and set goals. The contemporary view suggests that the leader helps the organization understand its needs and potential. The leader integrates and articulates the group's vision and acts as a trigger or stimulus for group action. As a manager, s/he must also be politically savvy and able to find a fit within the different political ideological orders (Nalbandian, 2000).

Commentators in the leadership area provide scores of reasons for the successes and failures in the implementation of public or private programs. For starters, the ideal leaders are those who can simultaneously exercise both formal and informal leadership. They communicate effectively, are competent and fair, and behave in ethical ways, lead by example, maintain high ethical standards, and hold others to the same standards. They must be accessible to their clients and customers. For instance, business executive Meyerson (1996) described his style in a serious yet refreshing fashion.

> Today I travel with my laptop and get e-mail from all over the company. I get thousands of messages per month, some of them trivial, many important. Everyone in Perot Systems knows they can e-mail me and I'll read it—me, not my secretary. Electronic mail is the single most important tool I have to break through the old organization and the old mindset. E-mail says that I'm accessible to anyone in our company in real time, anywhere. I am an instant participant in any part of the organization. No more dictating memos that get scrubbed before their formal distribution to the corporate hierarchy. Now, when I hear about a win in a hotly contested competition, within an hour of the victory I'm sending out congratulatory e-mails to our team members around the world. The impact from that kind of direct communication is enormous. And I'm accessible on issues and concerns that transcend the traditional boundaries of work and the company. Not long ago, for example, I got an e-mail message from one of our

> new senior associates. The news was urgent: his father-in-law had just been diagnosed as having cancer and he was going off the Net for the next two days. I e-mailed back immediately that the company would stand behind him any way we could. The next day I got another e-mail message: it was worse than they had thought; they were in a small Texas town, and they didn't know who to go to for help. I e-mailed back with the name of a doctor at Southwestern Medical School who referred them to the best help they could find.

Communication with e-government involves two important principles: maintaining a high level of contact and encouraging the flow of communication between members of the public and organizational management. In recent times, managers frequently establish links to social networks such as Twitter, Facebook, and MySpace to monitor work-related commentary on their organizations. Communication, therefore, can have informal components. Another important principle is that of formalizing aspects of the interactions within the vast array of social media. Managers cannot run away from being in touch with employees in some of the new mediums. It does not necessarily mean being a remote manager all the time. It means embracing virtual leadership—that is, leading through effective communication and maintenance of collaborative relationships at a distance. Traditional ways of workforce management are eroding away at a fast pace. The Weberian assumptions about hierarchy have been challenged by the new mediums of communication. New mediums and social networking sites supplement avenues for accomplishing work tasks.

The e-manager adds these tools to her arsenals for building a sense of community, teambuilding, and adding value to information sharing. E-managers are expected to provide leadership to emerging virtual teams. A virtual team is a group of individuals who work across time, space and organizational boundaries to solve problems. Members share common missions and goals. There are examples of virtual teams in the public sector. The U.S. Department of Energy and its contractors and subcontractors are using advanced ICTs to manage a highly complex radioactive waste management project at Yucca Mountain, Nevada.

The Yucca Mountain project has begun to implement "virtual teamwork" as a means to provide more efficient and effective collaboration among employees.

Virtual teams are widely used in the private sector. For example, you have most likely heard of software development teams with members in India, Brazil, Taiwan, and the United States whose only communication is via the Internet, Skype, videoconferencing, and over the phone. As the trade and scholarly literature suggests, the task of an e-manager is to ensure that there is team cohesion in roles and responsibilities (Duarte & Snyder, 2000; Kimball, Noble, & Kennedy, 2002; Lipnack & Stamps, 1997). Experts in the industry argue that there is greater need for role clarification in virtual teams because of the lack of frequent face-to-face contact among team members. This is in addition to the need for each team member to strike a balance between coordination and autonomy. This helps in achieving maximum benefits from the collaboration. In addition, the e-manager establishes the unit's mission, goals, tasks, and framework for achieving results. Like in other managerial tasks, the manager clarifies stakeholder expectations and institutes communication protocols.

Given the many responsibilities of the e-manager, there will be cases where an organization's business does fall into the hands of those without the need to know. In the public sector, this reality is reflected in organizations with public safety and security responsibilities. At any rate, many public organizations manage personal data that must be secured and not exposed on the Internet, unless of course there is a court order to do so. Therefore, the task of the e-manager is to clarify who should be informed about organizational business and how tools can be used effectively. The e-manager also guides all deliberations and establishes guidelines on how and where e-filing mechanisms are appropriate and when a phone is the preferred means to communicate. These guidelines should be a part of the agreements between the employer and employee. For many management tasks, however, the expectation is to be cognizant of the new cultures associated especially with younger workers. Younger workers are most likely to be comfortable with management's application of imaginative virtual motivation strategies and approaches.

The ability to motivate followers is crucial in effective management. Managers must find ways to motivate employees, presently Generation Xers and Generation Yers. Members of Generation X are people that were born in the United States between 1963 and 1981. They are labeled X because they are without a defining moment (Jurkiewicz, 2000). They are computer literate and utilize more e-government and e-commerce than other generations before them. Generation Yers entered the full-time workforce in the 2000s and have lived much of their lives with cell phones, Digital Video Discs (DVDs), and laptops (Robbins & Judge, 2009). Therefore, for example, agencies' providing them with Internet connectivity is an important motivating factor. Most government agencies in the industrialized world provide free Internet service to employees.

Further, it is important for managers to have motivation strategies that embrace values that are intergenerational. At a more abstract level, the ability of a manager to motivate employees while instilling a sense of commitment to the new work structures and technologies is paramount to successful e-government implementations. This may entail the younger generations, such as the Gen Yers, teaching the new technologies to the older generations.

The word commitment is at the core of the new e-government paradigm. A Unites States Agency for International Development (USAID) dossier on "Best Practices in ICT policy" issued as advice to developing countries is unequivocal about the role of commitment from the top. USAID's statement reads: "E-government often means changing how governments do business, which usually requires political leadership, clout and changes in budgeting" (USAID, 2006).

We have already mentioned the policy foundations of e-government in the United States and emphasized the roles played by the nation's chief executives and other managers in the implementation of e-government initiatives. At the organizational level, there is need to encourage commitment to virtual communities. This works best through application of numerous kinds of employee involvement strategies including processes for sharing values (shared governance) and employee involvement processes (EIPs) that are relatively easy to actualize in ICTs environments. EIPs are groups of organizational members who meet to identify, analyze, and solve quality and cost reduction problems (Mercer, 1992). EIPs can be an effective avenue to articulate and reinforce commitment to quality of service issues.

Other forms of employee involvement programs are described in the larger management literature. One of their objectives is to lessen the impact of Weberian hierarchies common in public agencies. For the most part, involvement strategies employ a wide variety of computer software programs that track employee skills and match them to the needs of the organization (Mercer, 1992). E-managers embrace adaptive strategies for a variety of reasons beyond mere involvement of employees. To the extent that employee involvement inculcates a sense of commitment to e-government principles, these strategies are worthwhile. Without committed leadership, no successful e-governments are possible. Commitment must be based on proven principles that have informed best practices in e-government. From a practical standpoint, the e-manager in a government setting can look to parallel principles derived from e-commerce and extrapolated from Plenert's studies (2001), as shown in box 6.3.

Each of the principles can be actualized through a variety of managerial procedures. For example, avoidance of fear of technology is addressed through proactive human resource training and development programs.

Box 6.3. *Principles for the E-manager.*

- Avoid fear of technology and the unknown through education and training
- Commit to change and improvement as opposed to focusing on stability. Change becomes a way of life in bureaus, an important value.
- Focus on systemic problem solving philosophies
- Organize around outcomes and subsuming information processing work into actual work
- Link parallel activities instead of integrating their results
- Embrace process reengineering of government operations
- Be ethical and constitutionally competent

Source. Plenert, 2001.

Commitment to change can be realized through employee inclusion and strategies that inculcate value changes. In the latter case, an e-manager pursues a value-shaping program on top of his or her agenda. S/he places shared values at the center of the manager's agenda. "Often the first step a top manager takes to shape shared values is to begin talking about them with close colleagues" (Mercer, 1992, p. 68). Managers who share information with members of the management team have high chances of succeeding at creating change and enhancing organizational commitment (Sittenfeld, 1999). These conversations could be within the framework of virtual organizations or through online training programs.

Other points of these principles require considerable application of communication skills and embracing high ethical standards generally. Focusing on systemic problem solving implies publishing encouraging quality improvement stories in organizational e-newsletters and mass circulated memos. These are graphic depictions of how improvements in electronic service delivery have changed the organization and affected the general public in a positive way. Beyond that, organizing around outcomes, as well as integrating results, is characteristic of the global new public management framework. The final principle entails including a variety of reengineering processes, especially breakthrough thinking about what the public wants, redesigning systems to meet these desires, and evaluating the use of advanced technologies.

The Place of Leadership and Administrative Ethics

Ethical standards stand out as important variables in all e-government decision-making processes. It is well known that unethical decision making can result in losses and expensive litigation. Ethical issues emerge in all e-government operations ranging from procurement of hardware and software to system design to issues of access. Unethical practices compromise standards and yield poor service. Administrative ethics is about professionalism and ensuring systemic security, safeguarding privacy, promoting honesty and integrity and fairness, respecting freedom of speech, adhering to existing laws (including being constitutionally competent), and protecting intellectual property rights. Ethical leadership also entails providing goals that benefit society and avoid harm to others.

These values are closely aligned with those adopted by the ASPA, the Association for Computing Machinery, and other professional associations. Specific ethical principles written for ICT applications in government are rare, with the exception of one written by govWorks Inc. and Arthur Andersen and American Management Systems Inc. (Anderson, 2003). Their five principles, as reported in Anderson (2003), are:

- To prevent the resale of consumer data,
- Disclose all fees and costs associated with e-government services,
- Accurately represent the number and scope of e-government services offered,
- Accurately represent affiliate relationships relevant to vendor selection and
- Helps to bridge the digital divide.

The link between ethical conduct and professionalism is clearly established. Professionalism assumes that managers strive to achieve the highest quality and effectiveness in providing public services. Quality services are an important attribute of all reform movements in the realm of public administration and must be institutionalized within the context of e-government. Implementers of e-government require leadership as an important component of management. E-managers should at the very least be committed to the integration of services and sharing data and information among various departments. This might mean sharpening their decision-making and persuasion skills and building trust among the participants. E-managers must also be competent constitutionally to guide agencies in implementing designs that do not contravene traditional constitutional civil rights and liberties. This entails providing clear policy and operational guidelines within a legal framework. For example, much has been written about managerial roles in procurement and contracting out issues (Cooper, 2003). We shall consider some aspects of this issue in the discussion on e-procurement. Importantly, the art of contracting out is dependent upon information gathering and communicating with suppliers (Cohen & Eimicke, 2002). Information accumulation and assimilation are important parts of a manager's duties. It is a manager's responsibility to organize information and structure the organization to use the information appropriately, especially through application of appropriate management information systems (Cohen & Eimicke, 2002; Danziger et al., 1993). In the e-government infrastructure the availability of vast networks of service providers and databases presents both a challenge and an opportunity for e-managers.

On the positive side, access to multiple providers is made easier by the availability of huge databases in electronic forms. Security for these databases must, of course, be protected appropriately. The downside is that e-government is in large measure a networked multisectoral venture. Multisectoral trends in public service delivery create several critical and difficult operational problems (Cohen & Eimicke, 2002). As Cooper (2003) asserted, governments "rely on networks of contractors to provide services, some of which are for-profit firms and some of which are nonprofits, [so] the challenges of contract management have grown" (p. 46).

A more daunting challenge is the ability to strike a balance between having too much and too little information. Most managers know that being immersed in details can be good management practice but slows down the decision-making process. If a manager delegates, the chances of his subordinates issuing policy-type statements that might not reflect the organizational leader's visions are heightened. E-managers, therefore, need to anticipate the right amount of information to look for and apply in decision-making processes.

Among the most crucial hurdles to be overcome is finding out what contractors do well and what they do not do well. This is particularly a challenge in cases where there is an obvious dominance of a single contractor. There are many cases in ICTs where outsourcing is limited by the scarcity of providers. As Cooper (2003) advised, the first line of defense is to adhere to state and federal guidelines in statutes such as the Competition in Contracting Act (1984), which pushes agencies away from sole source contracting. E-managers should ordinarily establish mechanisms for solicitation that are open and transparent, and seek to achieve the desired results. E-managers must determine the best possible services as well as provide training and incentives to employees. E-managers in the public sector must also confront the politics of the contracting game.

One of the core concerns in government procurement and outsourcing is the politics of the process. If there is to be a theoretical framework that best captures the political nature of outsourcing, it is the principle-agent theory. Early work in this genre focuses on situations within the business world that encapsulate the relationships between employers and contractors. The major concerns revolve around dilemmas associated with compliance to contracts. On the one hand are contractors (agents), whose task is to meet the needs of the employer or principle. In most cases, the principle provides incentives to the agent, a private company, to provide a service or product. As Sappington (1991) pointed out, in a contracted out or privatized scenario, the agent weighs his or her production and transaction costs and strives to operate at the optimum point where agency costs do not inhibit further engagement in the process. In other words, contracting out is a rational choice in which agency costs equal their marginal benefits. Organizations make decisions based on perceived benefits.

In many public organizations, contracting out for ICT projects is assumed to be the preferred course of action because of the skill deficiencies in the public sector. In addition, public organizations often suffer from risk aversion and choose to outsource ICT projects. The best outcomes emerge whenever there is first, goal congruency, and second, proper communication and accountability channels between principle and agents. One of the most difficult challenges in managing public sector outsourcing is that information costs can be high. In addition, as Simon (1957) recognized, agents (contractors) are limited in their decision making because there is uncertainty about the future. The public sector is rich with examples of such uncertainty that hinders agent decision making. Most students of public administration can find examples to illustrate how uncertain economic and political conditions work to stifle decision making. For example, in April 2011, the Obama administration faced the threat of government shutdown and urged Congress to issue continuing resolutions to permit the government to continue functioning. This occurred against the backdrop of differences between the administration and Congress over levels of budget cuts. Hardly any meaningful planning can occur amidst such uncertainty.

As we mentioned earlier, in the case of DP World's bid to manage strategic U.S. ports such as New Orleans and New York, the policy proved difficult to implement because of political issues rather than substantive technical issues. The company had been in association with reputable European firms and had a previous record of good service. Dubai is considered one of the most well-run ports in a globalizing world. Yet, for practical security and political reasons, Congress, on behalf of the American people, blocked the contract process. The point is, in terms of security-sensitive electronic gadgets used in agencies such as the CIA, NSA, and various units within the DHS, one expects politics to be at the center of the e-procurement process. This point is not new in the literature. A number of authors have previously argued against the idea of wholesale contracting out because it has the potential to damage the fabric of American democracy (Milward, 1996; Milward & Provan, 2000). This assertion does not minimize the role of ethical decision making but rather recognizes the political nature of the administrative state. Beyond security concerns, the public expects procurement of expensive electronic gadgets to conform to high ethical standards. In the growing e-procurement literature, one core discussion underscores the important role of the manager (Neef, 2001). Managers are increasingly aware that Internet applications go beyond the ordinary purchases of goods and services and cannot always be controlled by the original supplier.

E-PROCUREMENT

Much work occurs in various aspects of e-procurement that link suppliers and customers in complex electronic trading communities. These communities include online markets, auctions, reverse auctions, and exchanges. Many argue that e-procurement has saved companies much money. Such is the promise of e-procurement in government as well. Incorporating e-procurement strategies has the potential to vastly improve service delivery in the public sector as well.

Just what is e-procurement? Electronic procurement of goods and services refers to supplier exchanges between business and government agencies through the Internet as well as other electronic data systems. E-procurement can also be conceptualized as the B2B purchasing of goods and services or consumer purchasing and sales through computer-mediated information technologies.

The traditional practice has been for e-managers to establish websites that allow qualified and registered users to search for buyers and sellers of goods and services. In the federal government, contractors are registered in the Central Contractor Registration database (www.ccr.gov). During the George W. Bush administration, if an agency wanted to buy a good or service over $25,000 it was required to list the procurement opportunity with FedBizOpps.gov, a federal portal established for this purpose (Garson, 2006). E-procurement is also available at the state level. In Kentucky, business can be transacted through a web portal available at eProcurement.ky.gov. On this website, transactions are permitted twenty-four hours a day seven days a week. The site includes features such as vendor registration, current bidding opportunity browsing, recent award viewing, and vendor registration when permitted. The website includes links on laws, policies, and procedures for doing business with the state of Kentucky as well as privacy notices.

Cost saving is a consistent advantage cited in all government units that embrace e-procurement. For example, North Carolina's e-procurement website states: "NC E-Procurement provides suppliers with increased access to markets without additional supplier market efforts, a single point of access for North Carolina government organizations, a faster and more efficient method of quoting (e-Quote), and increased order accuracy through receipt of electronic orders with a consistent purchase format. Overall, NC E-Procurement can help realize processing, marketing, and administrative cost savings" (North Carolina, 2009). The North Carolina site has important statistics on purchase orders, vendors, and users.

Most e-procurement, however, is not a simple matter. It involves the use of software for functions including supply management and complex auctions. Bailey (2008) and other authors identified several types of e-procurement activities and applications that managers should be concerned with, as outlined in box 6.4.

E-managers recognize that e-procurement has advantages such as taking supply chain management to a higher level by providing real time information to vendors and informing them about immediate customer needs. E-procurement also saves time. One user describes this experience well: "E-Procurement saves me time. My purchase orders are transmitted via fax or e-mail by E-Procurement and I don't have to stand at the fax machine for hours or depend on U.S. Mail." (Iredell-Statesville County Schools, North Carolina, 2009). E-procurement fundamentally reduces costs in the purchasing of goods and services (Croom, 2000; De Boer et al., 2002) but is also an investment that must be well managed. In fact, the investment is quite substantial. In addition, it often involves restructuring of organizational units.

Several practitioner books offer advice on how to implement e-procurements and identify the pitfalls and risks of this strategy. For example, Neef's (2001) work is a primer for introducing the subject to the business community. While most of the literature is about private sector interactions (e-commerce and e-retailing), the insights are also useful for the public sector. E-managers have to be aware of long-term relationships with suppliers and establish strategic partnerships with the private sector. These are essential to successful leadership in contemporary e-government. E-procurement must be seen as a part of the overall e-government strategy.

Box 6.4. *E-procurement Activities and Applications that Managers Should Be Concerned With.*

Web-based Enterprise Resource Planning (ERP)	Involves the creation and approval of purchase requisitions via Internet technologies. It involves the use of software to manage and coordinate resource planning.
Maintenance, Repair, and Overhaul	Involves ensuring that goods and services ordered are reliable, cost-effective, and do not compromise reliability. It involves managing these processes through one integrated system and includes maintenance execution, warranty management, invoicing, and cost tracking.
E-sourcing	Identification of new supplies for a specific category of purchasing requirements using the Internet. Goods and services may be outsourced from other countries.
E-ordering	The process of creating and approving purchasing requisitions and placing purchase orders as well as receiving goods and services ordered through the Internet.
E-tendering	Sending requests for information and prices to suppliers and receiving feedback regarding quality and appropriateness.
E-reverse auctioning	Inviting a group of pre-qualified suppliers who compete against each other to supply a specified good or service. This is meant to drive the price down.
E-informing	Collection and distribution of information to and from external parties (e.g., exchanging purchasing information between buyers and suppliers).
E-marketing	Opening up value chains and allowing buying communities to access preferred suppliers' products and services.

Reinventing Government and the Roles of CIOs

The e-manager must first recognize that e-government is essentially a continuation of the reform movements that gained much visibility under the umbrella of the reinvention and re-founding paradigms. The reinvention movement associated with President Bill Clinton and Vice President

Al Gore defined the role of managerial heads of IT departments in the federal government. Under the reinvention framework, CIOs are charged with the responsibility of providing managerial leadership in the applications of ICTs in their respective departments. Specifically, at the federal level, the Clinger-Cohen Act (1996) and the E-government Act of 2002 establish that the CIO should play a key role in planning ICT activities in various departments (box 6.5). Furthermore, President Clinton's Executive Order 13011 requires establishment of an Information Technology Resources Board to support ICT systems acquisition processes. CIOs report directly to the head of this department. However, for practical matters, the E-government Act (2002) mandated that the OMB serve as the lead federal ICT planning body. The statute also codifies the existence of the CIO Council, which had been established in Executive Order 13011. CIOs coordinate ICT management activities in all agencies.

The federal CIO directs the policy and strategic planning of federal information technologies and oversees enterprise architecture to ensure system interoperability and information sharing. The CIO works closely with the CTO—a position established by the Obama administration to advance the president's technology agenda. Today, CIOs exist in governments at all levels-federal, state and local.

Thus far, it is possible to contend that the role of the CIO has matured and changed significantly. Because technological innovations have continued to flourish, CIOs have adapted to the new world of technological transformations. CIOs not only keep government data centers up and running but also provide a "vision of transformation through an organization where bureaucracy and culture make it difficult to change" (Deloitte, 2004). CIOs have moved from simply being technology stewards to business leaders. As Dawes et al. (2008) observed, In the past decade, the position of CIO… has evolved from chief IT coordinator, chief standards enforcer, and chief IT budgeter, to chief IT strategist, chief IT policy advisor, and, most recently, chief security officer. In short, CIO is not a single role but a combination of roles. It demands a set of competencies that covers more territory than we demand from most other leadership positions.

Box 6.5. *The Role of the Federal CIO.*

The E-government Act of 2002 establishes a Federal Chief Information Officer in the Office of Management and Budget and creates the Office of Electronic Government and Information Technology, which is headed by a presidentially appointed administrator.

The administrator provides overall leadership and direction to the executive branch on electronic government and oversees implementation of IT throughout the federal government, including:

- Overseeing the E-government Fund to support interagency partnerships and innovation in using e-government;
- Directing the activities of the CIO Council, which consists of Federal agency CIOs, advising on the appointments of agency CIOs, and monitoring and consulting on agency technology efforts;
- Advising the director of OMB on the performance of IT investments, as well as identifying opportunities for joint agency and government-wide IT projects;
- Overseeing the development of enterprise architectures within and across agencies, which is being fulfilled through FEA, the framework for describing the relationship between business functions and the technologies and information that support them;
- Overseeing specific IT reform initiatives, activities, and areas of shared responsibility relating to:
- Capital planning and investment control for IT;
- The development of enterprise architectures;
- Information security;
- Privacy;
- Access to, dissemination of, and preservation of government information;
- Accessibility of IT for persons with disabilities; and
- Other areas of electronic government.

Source. Meskell, 2008.

In discussions of what makes a successful CIO, Dawes et al. (2008) suggested that there are at least five competencies that must be learned. These are categorized as (1) strategic thinking and evaluation which emphasizes knowledge of program and policy goals that drive the selection and use of ITs; (2) systems orientation or the relationship between IT and the fully fleshed-out functioning of an agency, program, or policy initiative; (3) appreciation for complexity, which translates into "appreciation for the special requirements of large space scale high-risk, high-visibility projects whose participants seldom hold exactly the same values and expectations and often report to different leaders" (Deloitte, 2004)

(4) information stewardship providing leadership in government information and data management, and (5) technical leadership or basic leadership in all matters pertaining to e-government. These attributes are summarized in box 6.6.

When one compares these competencies with those developed earlier by Deloitte and shown in box 6.7, a leading international consultant, it is evident that the core ingredient is managerial leadership (Deloitte, 2004).

Conclusions

In this chapter, we have conceptualized the e-manager more broadly by building from the premise that public management has responded to the emerging e-government ecology. We observe that while the e-manager

Box 6.6. *Agency CIOs.*

The federal agency CIO's role is established by law in the Clinger-Cohen Act of 1996 and strengthened by the E-government Act of 2002.

The E-government Act calls on CIOs to consult key stakeholders throughout their agencies, including program and project managers, content managers, librarians, public affairs representatives, records managers, and human resources managers.

CIOs are told to consider the following when selecting IT investments:

- Delivering services and information to citizens electronically;
- Reducing burden on citizens and businesses;
- Determining that the investment is part of the agency's modernization blueprint;
- Ensuring interoperability of systems; and
- Simplifying business processes and reusing technology where applicable.

Specific CIO requirements include:

- Participating in the functions of the CIO Council;
- Monitoring implementation of IT standards, including common standards for interconnectivity and interoperability, categorization of federal government electronic information, and computer system efficiency and security;
- Ensuring privacy impact assessments are conducted and reviewed for applicable IT systems; and
- Insuring that agency IT training programs comply with IT development provisions for the federal workforce.

Source. Meskell, 2008.

Box 6.7. *Competencies of Successful CIOs.*

Strategic Thinking and Evaluation	• Business and policy reasoning • IT investment for value creation • Performance assessment • Evaluation and adjustment
Systems Orientation	• Environmental awareness • System and social dynamics • Stakeholders and users • Business processes • Information flow and work flow
Appreciation for Complexity	• Communication • Negotiation • Cross-boundary relationships • Risk assessment and management • Problem solving
Information Stewardship	• Information policies • Data management • Data quality • Information sharing and integration • Records management • Information preservation
Technical Leadership	• Communication and education • Architecture • Infrastructure • Information and systems security • Support and services • IT workforce investments

Source. Deloitte, 2004.

retains the core values of many public managers, the expectations for a constantly changing technological environment demand attention to a host of new competencies including handling important administrative tasks such as e-procurement. These are described adequately in several practitioner-driven sets of literature. This means going beyond the traditional and classical principles of management and the oversold modern techniques such as Total Quality Management, benchmarking, planning, and privatization (Cohen & Eimicke, 2002). While these are important techniques that must be accommodated, the underlying value system in

Box 6.8. *Deloitte's Primer on the E-management Issues and the Essential Capabilities.*

#	Issue	Essential Capabilities and Tasks
1	Money It's not what you spend— It's how you spend it.	Using money wisely, rightsizing, return on investment (ROI) that includes consistent benefits; structuring projects to deliver cost savings
2	Security and Risk Fast, cheap, or secure. Pick one.	Diagnosis, preparation, and enforcement of actions to prevent hacker, virus and cyberterrorist activities
3	Procurement Big money. Big plans. Big problems.	Fast, rigorous, and innovative approaches to procurement. Taking advantage of best practices in public and private sectors and vendor management
4	Integration and Interoperability Silo-busting.	A common language (IT architecture) and shared services
5	Governance Guiding them in.	A strong CIO, providing stable and ethical governance
6	Performance Measures If it's not worth measuring, it's not worth doing.	Standard performance measures and benchmarking and willingness to make tough decisions
7	Portfolio Management	Use of scenario analysis to plot a rational course and thinking about project goals and anticipation of potential problems
8	Human Capital Employer of choice...	Sound human resource management strategies including rewarding employees
9	Customer Service... Provider of choice.	Maintaining customer focus and satisfaction
10	Enterprise Architecture IT happens.	Architecture design and use of guidelines such as the FEA

Source. Deloitte, 2004.

the e-government environment requires new centers of focus. It requires close attention to the work of CIOs who must be guided by operating legal frameworks and guidelines.

KEY CONCEPTS

E-managers
E-procurement
Electronic trading communities
Employee Involvement Processes
Executive responsibility
Generation Xers
Generation Yers
Globalized world
Leadership
Management Information Systems
Managerial style
Motivation
Situational leadership
Transformational leaders
Virtual leadership

DISCUSSION QUESTIONS

1. How does an e-manager avoid having too much wrong information and not enough right information?
2. Why do e-procurement and contracting-out strategies involve politics?
3. Describe the differences between e-managers in the public and private sectors. Why must bureau executives understand the context of leadership?
4. Does situational theory work at all types of organization? Is there merit in developing literature on the roles of e-managers?
5. Why is communication important as a management task? Why do management experts and practitioners believe "information is power"? Explain how managers can manage information structures suitable for their organizations. How do they employ new social networking websites in their communications strategies?

Internet Activities

1. Search for business and public e-newsletters and compile a list of their different objectives and missions. Use the same newsletters and magazines to provide examples of how managers employ e-procurement strategies to meet the needs of their clients. Finally, write a position paper on the role of these strategies as managerial tools in the specific organizations investigated.
2. Visit at least ten different local government websites and identify common themes in the jobs of the CIOs. Discuss these with the rest of the class.

Chapter 7

e-Democracy and Public Administration

Public administration occurs in a political environment. The starting point of any discourse on the political context of public administration is to probe the tenets of democracy. In a democracy, the people, through elected officials, exercise direct and equal participation in their own governance. In its original Greek meaning, democracy is conceptualized as the rule of the *demos*, the people. Although democracy is one of the single most studied ideas in politics, there is no agreed-upon definition of democracy, but it clearly encompasses the freedoms and rights of all individuals. The question of how to attain the basic freedoms and rights has drawn the attention of some of the most brilliant minds in the social sciences. For instance, work on procedural questions is well developed in countless treatises by such luminaries as Dahl (1965; 1971), Schumpeter (1947), and Huntington (1991). While we need not repeat their now-familiar positions, it is instructive to note that in their formulations, the public interest was best articulated by parties that competed for office in periodic, free, and fair elections.

Parties, as theory suggests, are vehicles for political mobilization and interest articulation and, after winning an election, are expected to form governments to promote specific agendas. What is in dispute is the meaning of national interest, which forms an important part of any political party's overarching manifesto, charter, or contract with the people it represents. Critics of the idea of national interest are quick to point out that it always refers to the oligarchic interests of a few elites, or Plato's *guardians*, if you will.

The literature on elites suggests that a small number of privileged groups possess the ability to rule over the crowds and masses, who in Aristotelian classical thinking are not to be trusted with governance. The general fear of mobs, crowds, and masses is based on the belief that "elites would have to be relied upon to protect democratic procedures from the incompetence" of ordinary masses (Bachrach, 1967). Students of crowd behavior frequently have reservations about the power of the multitudes. Most contend that masses can be susceptible to emotional, irrational, and credulous actions (Allett, 1996). Pioneering scholars like William McDougall, among others, implied that it is not entirely inconceivable for crowds to fall for demagogues and masters of crowd psychology like Adolf Hitler (Allett, 1996).

Conceivably, democratic institutions should moderate these interests and, through consensus, be able to arrive at decisions that yield the greatest utility for the broad majority. However, the idea of consensus is often at odds with liberal pluralism, which is "celebrated as a cornerstone of democracy" in the United States (Dryzeck & Niemeyer, 2006, p. 634). In real life, both pluralism and individualism are celebrated in American society. Seminal work on pluralism points to the importance of interest groups in organizing American political life (Dahl, 1961; Truman, 1951). Interest groups collaborate and find allies in their bids to influence policymaking. Public administrators are not left out of the equation, for they serve within "iron triangles" (Heclo, 1977) in policy formation and articulation. As Heclo (1977) explained, iron triangles unite one or more interest groups with congressional committees and executives or administrators to produce actionable policies in all areas, including e-government. Although the general assumption is that civil servants and other administrators should be neutral, Truman (1951) and other scholars felt that was hardly the case. The notion of the administrator without conflicting motivations remains an illusion (Truman, 1951).

Pluralism celebrates those aspects of national diversity that strengthen the body politic. American pluralism is manifest in several ways; first is in the concept of federalism. Thus, for example, each city has its own administrative modus operandi and will follow different protocols in snow removal schedules. Each state has its own laws and each school district has its own governance structure. Pluralism is evident in party diversity as well. The Republican Party is home to millions of religious conservatives and gun-loving second amendment rights enthusiasts. Within the Democratic Party are millions of social liberals and "tax and spend" "big government" supporters. While ideological cleavages exist, Democrats and Republicans, as well as Libertarians, do not see individualism as a threat to group or collective interests. Instead, for practical reasons, they all see individualism as the building block for many democratic traditions (Allett, 1996). Arguably, therefore, society taps into the collective wisdom of members of the public to produce public policy. Democracy makes this happen in a clear way.

It is democracy that informs the selection of the nation's political elite, which aggregates the society's collective wisdom and general will through democratic institutions. Beyond political management, public officials also organize and manage the processes that recruit and select bureaucrats.

In our traditions, the Constitution provides the framework upon which democratic institutions are organized. The concern for rights and freedoms is as old as the nation. After all, the rights to representation and self-determination were at the core of the struggle against British rule in the 18th century. Keen students of public administration are aware that to be effective, one must have a good grasp of the Bill of Rights. The Bill of Rights refers to the first ten amendments to the Constitution of the United States. James Madison initiated most of these amendments to limit the power of government. The amendments seek to protect the natural rights of liberty and property. Central among these rights are the freedom of speech, free assembly, free association, a free press, and the right to bear arms. In legal terms, the rights not specified in the Constitution are reserved for the people and cannot be taken away by the government. In theory, the government should protect the rights of all individuals and enforce majority rule and minority rights. While governments work to protect these basic rights, millions of people in other cultures are often victims of state-sponsored violence and have limited rights.

Democratic theory suggests that all people have inalienable rights and should hold their governments accountable. Since government is expected to represent the will of the people, citizens of any polity should, therefore, have access to most information on government activities that affect them. Perhaps, on a global scale, no other story captures the contradictions and complexities of the role of ICTs in the cause of democratic reform than the story of WikiLeaks. We briefly provide a synopsis of this interesting case before going into further details on the democratic foundations of public administration and why students and practitioners of public administration must study cyberdemocracy.

WikiLeaks and Freedom of Information

Perhaps one of the most fascinating personalities of the 2000–2010 decade is Julian Assange. Many thought he should have been named *Time* magazine's Person of the Year 2010. According to reports, Assange's mother met his biological father at a Vietnam War demonstration in Sydney, Australia, in 1970. She later married theatre owner Brett Assange. Born in 1971 in Townsville, Australia, Assange "describes his childhood as being akin to that of Tom Sawyer" (Strutton, 2010). Assange never met his biological father until the age of 27. As a child, he lived sporadically on Magnetic Island, where he learned to build his own raft, ride a horse, and go fishing. He also loved challenging adventures and went down mine shafts and tunnels. His family moved regularly, causing many friends to describe them as being "very alternative." Others felt the family was borderline hippie.

In October 1991, as a teenager, Assange, known online as "Mendax" was reprimanded for hacking the computer systems of the Australian National University, the Royal Melbourne Institute of Technology, commonly referred to as RMIT, and Telecom Australia. The authorities fined him $2,100 and placed him on a good behavior bond. Assange's interest in hacking did not end, and he collaborated with Suelette Dreyfus and others to write a book titled *Underground*, a treatise about Melbourne hackers (Strutton, 2010).

Although work on the WikiLeaks site began much earlier, during his days as a hacker, Assange's ideas had solidified by December 2006. In 2007, Assange launched an Internet-based whistle-blowing enterprise to leak government documents to the public. Perhaps to conceal his identity, he registered the website in the name of his biological father. The site, WikiLeaks.org, became an instant international sensation and the world's biggest leak in history. Among those infuriated and embarrassed was the British Royal Family (Leigh & Harding, 2011). Leaked cables revealed that a member of the Royal Family had made inappropriate remarks or behaved inappropriately and requested "specific intelligence" about members of Parliament (Cordon, 2010; *Telegraph*, 2010).

Other leaders of world nations were not spared Assange's sharp wit. For example, "Afghan President Hamid Karzai is said to be 'driven by paranoia' while German Chancellor Angela Merkel 'avoids risks and is rarely creative.' Iranian President Mahmoud Ahmadinejad is compared to Hitler" (Cordon, 2010). Libyan leader Muammar Gaddafi's personal nurse is described as a Ukrainian "voluptuous blonde." At the same time, WikiLeaks describes Russian Prime Minister Vladimir Putin as an "alpha dog" (Cordon, 2010).

Records of leaders' private speeches and conversations were now available, thanks to WikiLeaks. This prompted pop culture enthusiasts to conclude that we were in the age of WikiLeaks. The *London Review of Books* expressed this feeling in its assessment of Slavioj Zizek's, *Good Manners in the Age of WikiLeaks* (Koch, 2011). The *London Review* wrote: "In the era of WikiLeaks, the Internet, freedom of information acts and the citizens' claims of the right to know, it is important that we include in university courses attended by our future leaders courses that teach vital life-and-peace-saving lessons in good manners, politeness and tact" (Koch, 2011).

By early 2011, WikiLeaks had released an unprecedented leak of more than 250,000 U.S. military and diplomatic cable reports over the Internet. The military documents included war manuals detailing the military's operations in Guantanamo Bay, Cuba, and other places. WikiLeaks also exposed internal corporate memos about the dumping of toxic material off the African coast.

Thousands of other diplomatic cables found their way into open cyberspace, causing much anxiety and embarrassment in diplomatic circles. Perhaps for the first time, members of the public were exposed to the behind-the-scenes comments from top diplomats, corporate leaders, and world leaders. Out for the public to see were candid comments on some of the world's longest-serving rulers and dictators. Likewise, the leaks revealed some of the most sensitive information about intelligence and counterintelligence among world powers.

The new form of cyberactivism was unprecedented in both scope and magnitude. Some academics felt that the vast amount of classified information released over the Internet constituted a gem of raw data for research. Critics like Drezner (2010) dismissed the notion that the information contained in all the leaks would supplant historical ways of analyzing and researching diplomatic work. For him, WikiLeaks was a short-term boom and long-term drag for international relations scholars. But other critics disagreed and instead saw the release of the diplomatic cables as a vindication of their long-held views that governments all over the world hide important information from the public. After all, as Drezner (2010) pointed out, classified information is hard to come by, thereby leaving foreign policy scholars to "rely on other sources to 'process-trace' decisions on foreign policy, including news reporting, interviews with policymakers, memoirs, and the occasional Bob Woodward book."

Still, the emergence of the Assange factor proved to be fodder for university scholars and legal experts who churned out literally hundreds of presentations on the implications of the leaks on law, politics, and scholarship. The content of the leaks in and of themselves proved to interest members of the public by the scope of their revelations. WikiLeaks, therefore, provided the long-awaited window of opportunity for global publics to expose and debate what it means to enjoy freedom of information.

WikiLeaks caused much agony and embarrassment for the Obama administration, which launched an investigation into the activities of suspected informer Private Bradley Manning, a member of the Army Second Brigade of the 10th Mountain Division based in Baghdad. Military authorities acted on information provided by a convicted computer hacker, Adrian Lamo, who had been exchanging instant messages with Private Manning. Defense authorities believe Private Manning copied thousands of electronic files onto computer discs and shared them with WikiLeaks.

Following publication of sensitive cables, Assange became a wanted man. The CIA and other security organizations closely followed his activities. The U.S. government placed a tactical gag on his website and launched a campaign to explain some of the embarrassing diplomatic cables to its allies abroad. A number of newspaper outlets blocked the publication of the leaks, but Assange's organization was able to enter into a deal with other news outlets to release an unstoppable flood of diplomatic and military documents. Among the newspapers that published WikiLeaks files were the *Guardian*, the *New York Times* and *Der Spiegel* (Leigh & Harding, 2011).

When asked why WikiLeaks.org published online classified field reports about the ongoing war between the U.S. led coalition and the joint forces of the Taliban and Al Qaida in Afghanistan, the site's officials claimed that their goal is to reveal unethical behavior by governments and corporations (Schmitt, 2011). In the case of the war in Afghanistan, Assange claimed the released documents revealed broader and more pervasive levels of violence than have been reported in traditional media outlets. In his vision, the website is providing information to the public in the cause of promoting accountability and transparency. "All governments can benefit from increased scrutiny by the world community, as well as their own people. We believe this scrutiny requires information" (qtd. in Schmitt, 2011).

The fallout and political repercussions of WikiLeaks around the world have been dramatic. For instance, when Dennis Kucinich, Ohio Congressman and chairman of the Domestic Policy Subcommittee of the House Committee on Oversight and Government Reform, sought to reach out to Private Manning he was subjected to much bureaucratic red tape. In his own words, "I put in a request to the Secretary of Defense, who referred me to the Secretary of the Army, who referred me to the Secretary of the Navy, who referred me to the Secretary of Defense, and still not an answer on whether or not I can visit Private Manning" (Horton, 2011). Kucinich and other like-mined politicians feel that the information on the WikiLeaks website is an unprecedented opportunity for the people to be heard. These politicians believe that if the information on the war in Afghanistan is as reported on the WikiLeaks website, then it is time the president removed troops from the war theatre "pursuant to the War Powers Act" (Horton, 2011).

Because the United States is a mature democracy with well-developed institutions, the fallout from the leaks is pale compared to other countries that traditionally thrive on cultures of secrecy and authoritarian control of important information. Arguably, therefore, WikiLeaks had more direct impact on governance in the developing countries. Information leaked over the Internet proved to be fodder for opposition activists in countries where administrative apparatus concentrate on consolidating power of the small ruling elite at the expense of the vast majority of citizens.

Assange claimed that before launching WikiLeaks, he had received inspiration from Chinese dissidents and Internet hackers. These hackers had for decades searched for an alternative means to challenge the excesses of the one-party communist state. The Internet has provided great opportunities for dissidents to speak out against the authorities in Beijing. For Assange, the need to provide voice to all people is not confined to China but as a global issue. As the WikiLeaks site noted, "We believe that transparency in government activities leads to reduced corruption, better government and stronger democracies" (qtd. in Schmitt, 2011).

Assange's efforts are supplementing efforts by people involved in popular struggles for freedom across the globe. Although the "fourth wave" of democratic movements is confined to the Middle East and North Africa, it is largely fueled by the existence of alternative means for political communication and mobilization. Without ICTs and especially new media such as Twitter and Facebook, activists would not be successful at launching successful people's revolutions such as have led to the ouster of Presidents Zine el-Abidine Ben Ali of Tunisia and Hosni Mubarak of Egypt. The events in Tunisia and Egypt triggered other similar uprisings and youth led protests, albeit of different intensity, in Syria, Yemen, Bahrain, Jordan, Sudan, Saudi Arabia, Libya, and the entire Middle East and North Africa. Because the Twitter and Facebook-led revolution is of biblical proportions, it deserves a brief contextual discussion.

To a degree, from the U.S. standpoint, WikiLeaks can be tangentially compared to *The Pentagon Papers* (*The United States–Vietnam Relations, 1945–1967: A Study Prepared by the Department of Defense*) in terms of influencing the nature of political discourse and promoting activism. The papers, then classified "secret," were leaked by the *New York Times* in 1971. The papers revealed that the Lyndon B. Johnson administration had systematically lied to both Congress and the public about the military's activities in Indochina. In other countries, WikiLeaks served to turn around public opinion about authoritarian and corrupt leaders. As Assange himself stated, WikiLeaks deserves credit for revolutions sweeping across the Middle East (Edwards, 2011). Assange claimed that the material published through a Lebanese newspaper, *Al Akhbar*, swayed public opinion about the situation in Tunisia and influenced the course of events. According to WikiLeaks, Tunisians gained confidence to rise up after the site questioned U.S. support for President Ben Ali, ruler for over two decades.

But they were also infuriated with the lavish lifestyles shared among members of the diplomatic corps and covered in the WikiLeaks documents. The American ambassador in Tunisia, Robert F. Godec, described in detail how Ben Ali's family members' lavish lifestyles reminded him of Uday Hussein in Baghdad (Coll, 2011). In early December 2010, WikiLeaks published accounts from the U.S. embassy about the abuse of power among the Tunisian ruling elite.

The published WikiLeaks were not the only trigger mechanism for the revolution in Tunisia. Perhaps more dramatic was the horrific martyrdom of Mohamed Bouazizi, a 26-year-old fruit seller who set himself on fire in the town of Sidi Bouzid to protest police abuse, unemployment, and corruption. Anger spread throughout the country. Activists used Twitter and Facebook to organize meetings and demonstrations. In the end, Ben Ali fled the country on January 14 as mobs battled with security forces that by then had refused to shoot at the peaceful demonstrators.

After Ben Ali was overthrown by a people-led revolution, other regional activists took heed to revolt against dictatorship. As Assange quipped, "And then there's no doubt that Tunisia was the example for Egypt and Yemen and Jordan, and all the protests that have happened there" (Edwards, 2011). As a result, Egypt's President Hosni Mubarak was overthrown in February 2011 after being in power for over three decades. Other Middle Eastern rulers like Muammar Gaddafi, Ali Abdullah Saleh of Yemen, Hamad bin Isa al-Khalifa of Bahrain, and Bashar al-Assad of Syria, among other leaders, were battling popular uprisings or were on their way out.

Although one may argue that the democratic wave affecting the Middle East and North Africa had different sets of motivation, the overwhelming consensus among observers of the relationship between technology and democracy was manifest in the historic events of 2011. Technologies such as the radio, television, cable TV, and computer-mediated communication devices have changed the way politics is done. In some cases, technology has served the cause of democracy by being the vehicle for empowerment of groups that were previously marginalized or had no voice in their own governance. Tunisia, the first country to experience the people-led revolution in the new decade, had been experiencing a rapid annual growth rate of 5.2 percent. Analysts observed that the four key sectors responsible for the high growth rates were the textile/clothing, mechanical/electrical, agrofood, and ICT industries (Jere-Malanda, 2009). In particular, the ICT industry receives substantial investments from the European Union. There is no question, therefore, that expanded opportunities provided by ICT proliferation were a part of the structure for popular uprising in Tunisia that then snowballed across the region. Literally hundreds of media pundits went as far as describing the events as a "Twitter Revolution."

We should point out that *tweeting* politically sensitive images online did not begin in Tunisia. There are suggestions on the blogosphere that the first real heroine in the "Twitter Revolution" was Neda Agha-Soltan, a young Iranian woman killed by state police during demonstrations that followed the disputed elections in Iran in June 2009. Although the Iranian government had shut down national Internet access and allowed limited press coverage of the events, members of the public were able to see the demonstrations in the streets of Tehran through images transmitted via Twitter and YouTube. The video showing Neda's death, which is considered one of the world's most witnessed in human history, became the rallying point for Iranian masses protesting against state oppression. Neda's death (*neda* is the Farsi word for the voice) showed the power of social media for political mobilization in authoritarian countries. According to Nguyen (2011), an award-winning PR professional, social media not only helps people to connect with each other but is also a tool to "mobilize for historical moments and bring about change." Tunisia's case took more than a page from the Iranian protest manual.

The existence of computer-mediated devices and mobile telephony devices has boosted or created opportunities for ordinary citizens to interact with public administrators and other decision makers. The Internet, especially through social networking sites like Twitter and Facebook, contributed to political mobilization in the democratic revolutions underway in the Middle East and North Africa. The dream for a world with more democracy is realizable. Thanks to computers ordinary citizens across the world can push a button, type online, or even talk on a computer to their political leaders and administrators about their priorities (Grossman, 1995).

Although there is a raging debate about the long-term potential of ICTs in enhancing democratic deliberations, the capacity of new technologies for political mobilization in areas that were previously underserved is great. It is these technologies that serve to alter political communication in countries ruled by dictators. In the advanced democratic nations, scholars contend that existing ICTs may not necessarily upset existing power structures (Bimber, 1998; Davis, 1999). In all societies, the ultimate benefit of modern ICTs is to provide greater quality in civic life.

Democracy is about expanding political space by guaranteeing responsible freedoms and limiting irresponsible freedoms. The literature regarding the threats and opportunities enabled by the existence of new ICTs tends to present them as binary opponents, pitting Orwell against Athens. The former position argues that ICTs can lead to big brother government and bureaucratic surveillance and the disappearance of political freedoms. At the opposite end is the school contending that ICTs present a form of Athenian democracy in which the public can engage the ruling elite.

E-democracy: Digital Democracy, Cyberdemocracy or Open Democracy?

From the standpoint of political theory, democracy encompasses processes in which national leaders are recruited through free and fair periodic elections and are empowered by constitutional sanctions to manage the affairs of the polity and to protect freedoms and rights of polity members. Members of a democracy expect citizen participation at all levels of the polity. As leading theorist Habermas (1995) noted, political discourse is a fundamental component of democracy. Members of a democracy expect policy makers to be deliberative and make decisions that broadly reflect the will of their constituencies and the nation at large. The genesis of this assertion is easy to trace. In large measure, Madisonian structures of divided government specify rights and liberties. Though idealistic, theoretical frameworks provide lenses through which the functioning of the political system and its bureaucratic appendages receive legitimacy.

The emergence of e-democracy literature is fairly recent and deserves our attention for various reasons. E-democracy goes under different nomenclatures, including digital democracy, cyberdemocracy, "push-button" democracy, online democracy, and open democracy, and to some extent it is an auxiliary to the emergent e-commons. These terms may conceptually be referring to the same phenomena or issues germane to citizen or public participation in government through ICTs. First, as mentioned, the context of modern public administration is democracy. Without democracy, values such as inclusiveness, representativeness, and accountability are impossible to realize. It is democracy that provides the meaning for the checks and balances that structure administrative behavior.

Second, democracy cannot function without the normal functioning of the civil service bureaucracy. The public bureaucracy is immensely important as a workforce of over 18 million that has an enormous impact on the quality of life of all citizens. Recruitment to the civil service and bureaucracy at large is preconditioned on the notions that these bureaucrats will serve in the public interest and in a non-partisan way. This means that bureaucrats have a significant role in system maintenance, especially during transitions when political guards change offices.

Moreover, civil service bureaucrats have tenure, after a brief probationary period, which ensures continuity in program implementation and other service delivery systems. Bureaucrats implement laws to the extent that these laws uphold America's core values, including freedom, participation, and equality of opportunity. These regime values were upheld in the constitutional debates establishing the nation (Rohr, 1986). The renowned observer of American democracy Tocqueville saw a clear link between participation and the enhancement of quality of life in the country. In his estimation, citizen engagement in democracy generates social relationships that foster progress. Such observations provide the seeds for scholarship focused on social capital. Social capital as articulated in the works of Putman (2000) and Ostrom (1994) has informed our understanding that increased participation in democratic governance through networks of civic engagement is at the core of the vibrancy of any democracy. However, social capital and civic culture can also diminish when communication technologies drive people into habits and practices that lessen engagement to the body polity, the politically organized portion of the population (Putman, 1996; Sennett, 1974). This eventuality was mostly associated with the onset of mass communications systems such as the television. However, in an important empirical study, Katz and Aspden (1995) found no evidence that use of the Internet erodes traditional types of community involvement or lowers civic engagement.

The new Internet technologies have reshaped the outreach of political actors, particularly because of their interactive nature, as well as their ease of access and portability. Internet services are easily accessible on handheld computer devices and afford opportunities to engage in political discourse almost anytime, anywhere, thus rejecting earlier skepticism. Social capital in this case helps to facilitate societal movement toward good governance. As bureaucracy is responsive to political leadership, its use of ICTs in various administrative settings reinforces the drive for good governance.

ICT APPLICATIONS: THE CENTRAL NERVOUS SYSTEM OF OUR DEMOCRACY

As custodians of the state apparatus, civil service bureaucrats play a big role as providers of reliable data and public information. We are familiar with the arguments posited in favor of responsible use of ICTs in that endeavor. For example, one can hardly imagine America without the Library of Congress's digital archives. Furthermore, it is responsible government when public officials maintain information delivery systems to educate and warn the public against threats to their security. For example, the DHS issues online alerts whenever its agencies are alerted to the possibility of attacks to the homeland. Americans are familiar with the increased use of Internet announcements listing names of child molesters and wanted fugitives. The computer-mediated postings reinforce other ICTs such as electronic bracelets and AMBER Alerts posted on highways and now increasingly linked to important information on the Internet.

While electronic ankle bracelets are increasingly being used by the DHS's Bureau of Citizenship and Immigration Services on a limited basis to track movements of immigrants undergoing parole verifications, their use has received considerable negative publicity, especially for its appearance and the selection of who has to wear them. The program, monitored by the Detention and Removal Operations Unit, began a pilot study in Detroit and other cities in December 2003 for the purpose of tracking illegal immigrants facing deportation. One of the programs, the Intensive Supervision Appearance Program, is available to aliens who do not pose a threat to national security and who are awaiting an administrative court hearing or deportation. Case specialists monitor an assigned number of participants using this electronic monitoring device (EMD). The device tracks the movements of the alien, who in most cases is not permitted to move beyond his or her area of residence and work on a 24 hour basis.

Proponents of pilot projects see the bracelets as a cost-efficient and humane alternative to detention. The government's position is that bracelets are a cheaper method than using public funds to detain immigrants slated for deportation but still living in the country. Estimates show that detention space has been in short supply in most government facilities. Additionally, only 14% of potential deportees left the country, putting put tremendous pressure on administrative courts (Eisele, 2006; Zwerdling, 2005). However, widespread application of EMDs in the criminal justice system for tracking rapists and other violent offenders is generally not vigorously scrutinized.

The AMBER Alert system is national in coverage after President George W. Bush signed the legislation in April 2003. States are required to implement the procedures necessary to bring the alerts to the public's attention. Several states have upgraded their emergency broadcast guidelines to conform to national security and emergency management systems. New technologies, especially computer-based communication systems, are incorporated into Code Amber initiatives nationally. For example, Bryant Harper and his collaborators founded BigHits.com Inc. in August 2002 to providing information on crimes committed against children in the United States and Britain. The initiative involves displaying Amber Alerts on websites of willing participants.

By November 2005, the Code Amber Ticker was on over 265,000 associated websites. These tickers are posted on government websites, including those run by sheriffs and police departments all over the country. Moreover, current technologies allow AMBER Alerts to be directly transmitted to citizens on their cell phones, pagers, e-mails, and fax notification systems. The AMBER Alert Portal is also directly linked to the Department of Justice's website. It is arguably the most powerful alert system in child abduction cases.

According to CodeAmber.org, an organization dedicated to providing public awareness programs and information on issues including searches for sex offenders, the origins of the Amber Plan began in Texas. The AMBER Plan was created in 1996 as a powerful legacy to 9-year-old Amber Hagerman, a bright little girl who was kidnapped and brutally murdered while riding her bicycle in Arlington, Texas. The tragedy shocked and outraged the entire community. Residents contacted radio stations in the Dallas area and suggested they broadcast special 'alerts' over the airwaves so that they could help prevent such incidents in the future. In response to the community's concern for the safety of local children, the Dallas/Fort Worth Association of Radio Managers teamed up with local law enforcement agencies in northern Texas and developed this innovative early warning system to help find abducted children. Statistics show that, when abducted, a child's greatest enemy is time. (Code Amber, 2007)

To some extent, also, the Department of State provides risk information to Americans travelling abroad and issues travel alerts to guide their selection of travel destinations. On the local level, authorities maintain websites with excellent links to archives with information on various aspects of city governance such as zoning ordinances, census data, and other facets of municipal government.

Discussions about the increased use of computer-mediated ICTs cannot be complete without referencing applications in municipal policing. Bratton and Knobler's *Turnaround: How America's Top Cop Reversed the Crime Epidemic* (1998) is an excellent illustration of how police instant checks on those stopped for minor crimes help capture large numbers of felons. Bratton is credited for revitalizing Boston and New York City's police departments. As the New York City police commissioner, he oversaw crime rates drop by ten percent per year until he left office in 1996 following disagreements with Mayor Giuliani. Bratton acknowledges the role ICTs played in achieving this success. For instance, the police use computer mapping to zero in on areas with the worst crime records. Using real time statistics (COMPSTAT), the police are able to deploy resources in areas of most need. Through his leadership, the New York Police Department became a national leader in applications of ICTs for crime control. The digital resources have made it possible for government agencies to convey useful information in support of vital public safety operations. These constitute important additions to the understanding of administrative responsiveness to public needs and concerns. Enhancing responsiveness adds value to democratic governance.

Without democracy, civil service value systems are unlikely to reflect the popular will. This affects the quality of services provided through the civil service machinery. The expanding reach of ICTs and especially the growing power and portability of computer-based and broadband (high-speed Internet) communication systems enhances the practice of public participation in governance. Broadband systems with wireless digital "ether" technologies, together with radio, television, cable, cellular phones, podcasts, and online technologies are increasingly becoming the norm in political discourses. These wide variety of public airwaves ICTs and information commons now forms the mosaic of political recruitment, interest articulation, and aggregation strategies by different groups with stakes in the political establishment.

In fact, ICTs are now the "central nervous system of our democracy" (Chen, 2004). ICTs continue to be key tools in political communication and also provide support services to public engagement activities. Although ICTs are central features of the new democratic paradigm, much debate revolves around the ownership of the new enabling media that are within the purview of giant corporations such as Time Warner, Verizon, and others. These corporations continue to exercise much influence over policy choices and frequently come up against FCC guidelines protecting the public interest (Chester, 2007).

The Administrative Role in E-rulemaking

By congressional mandate, agencies write substantive rules that carry the weight of laws (Kerwin, 2003). According to the Administrative Procedure Act of 1946, the main framework through which public participation in rulemaking is endorsed, rulemaking cannot be complete without participation by the informed citizenry. Rulemaking requires the fundamental values of participation and accountability (Kerwin, 2003). In a regulatory framework, rulemaking is often seen as a discussion about the role of corporate power and responsibility. It may well be that the public and corporations see the dialogue in opposing ways. Nonetheless, it is an aspect of democratic governance.

Beyond e-rulemaking, numerous forms of participation merit our attention. Some of the most conspicuous ones include community activism and organizing, advocacy, voting, polling, online public dispute projects, imaging services, and a host of other wireless applications.

Public spaces have been expanded by the increased opportunities afforded by ICTs. In the primitive society, villagers would be called to deliberate issues affecting the commons after hearing drumbeats. Slowly radio and television became important avenues of rallying masses to a specific call. Notwithstanding advances made in digital applications such as moving to digital audio and television broadcasting, discussions of ICTs mostly hinge upon computer-based applications.

Today opportunities for mass rallies have radically changed courtesy of the Internet and other mass communication systems. Multiple wired networks make it possible to deliberate on issues of public interest without necessarily leaving the comfort of one's house. In short, the dot-com era has fragmented and provided an alternative means of public mobilization and activism. They are increasingly becoming important sounding boards in enabling public deliberation of policies (Wilhelm, 2000). E-civics in particular enables citizens to access agency information that helps them make better decisions about quality of life issues. The use of e-civics, which includes components such as websites, electronic bulletin boards, e-mail, and discussion lists, has grown tremendously over the last decade. Applications vary in scope and magnitude. For example, e-civics has increased participation and engagement with local officials in matters such as managing traffic congestion in municipalities. One well-documented example is in Scottsdale, Arizona, where for several years the city's transportation department worked with neighborhoods to address traffic concerns through the Neighborhood Traffic Management Program (NTMP). The NTMP consisted of two processes: the creation of a speed awareness program and a traffic-calming component. The first phase focused on educating the community about traffic concerns, especially speeding issues. In this phase, citizens filled out neighborhood traffic management interest forms to request traffic calming devices such as speed bumps. The subsequent component of the process involved determination of community and neighborhood support for the installation of speed calming devices. In the past, community opinions and views were mostly gathered through public meetings where signatures were obtained from persons most affected by traffic concerns. Organizing for public support for a speed-calming device generally proved to be a tall order. In many communities, Scottsdale among them, citizen participation in e-civics was low until technological tools became more available.

Online public spaces and interactive town halls provide opportunities to engage the municipal government. In the case of Scottsdale, citizens submit comments or questions online directly to the Transportation Commission. This is much more efficient than the previous systems in which time and money were lost through mail, telephone calls, and face-to-face meetings. Principles of e-civics are now readily applied through the NTMP website, which was designed to include information on proposed devices and maps of the affected areas. Similar stories are replicated in other communities as well, and serve to illustrate the emerging power of Internet-based technologies in decision making.

Additionally, wireless connections and portable access devices create fields of presence that go beyond homes. These teletechnologies and networks theoretically rejuvenate the democratic system for those who are in this frame of reference, sometimes known as net citizens. More specifically, the digital-divide frustrates Internet-based mobilization and activism. Of course, efforts at narrowing the divide have increased through availability of connections in public libraries and other low-cost infrastructure support provided by government and private firms. Free-nets and other forms of community services have joined to provide access to low-income groups. Still, there are technical questions to do with uncertainty over who are the actual participants in computer-mediated discursive forums.

With increased Internet accessibility, the level of public access to political information has expanded. There are numerous tools that encourage and advance group formations and advance deliberative processes. Among these tools are simple mailing Listserves organized and managed by traditional interest groups. Other technologies such as blogs provide a useful informal feedback process, especially when expert commentary is posted. Blogs also serve as important instruments for civic education. When read keenly, blogs have the potential for becoming important players in policy agenda setting and meriting the attention of policy implementers. There is also a downside to blogs. Even though blogging provides important informative analyses of events, the danger is that it can be the source for dangerous rumors. Yet, as entities in the growing constellation, blogs facilitate formations of affinity groups relevant for public organizations and collective prioritization of policy relevant information. Interestingly important corporations, including giant retail chain Wal-Mart, contract with public relations consultants to inculcate trust with members of the public via joining public blogs (Barbaro, 2006; Odden, 2006). Most importantly, these consultants seek to influence public opinion by providing their own story directly to bloggers. Wal-Mart has increasingly received negative press coverage on its labor policies.

In addition to blogs, several new software technologies are having an impact on how users access and produce information via the Internet. According to Pew Internet studies, blogging has increased tremendously. A Pew Internet and American Life Project survey established that by the end of 2004 blogs had become a key part of online culture. The survey reported that the blogosphere is now used by at least 8 million Americans who reported having created blogs. The report adds that Internet users who read blogs jumped 58 percent, to 27 percent of total Internet users, in 2004. Five percent of Internet users said they used RSS aggregators or XML readers to get the news and other information posted on blogs and content-rich websites. Interestingly the Pew study recognized that a majority of Internet users (62 percent) did not understand the blog technology.

In tandem with blogging, Really Simple Syndication (RSS) formats are increasingly changing how users access Internet information. RSS is a format for syndicating news and the content of materials derived from news community sites such as Slashdot and news outlets including Wired, the BBC, CNET, CNN, Disney, Forbes, Motley Fool, Wired, Red Herring, Salon, ZDNet, and more. The software breaks down discrete items and is conceptualized as providing headlines or distributing items that one might classify as "new." According to the authoritative technology site WebReference.com, "RSS solves myriad problems webmasters commonly face such as increasing traffic and gathering and distributing news. RSS can be the basis for additional content distribution services" (WebReference.com, 2006). These technologies play an important role in changing public discourse, especially in matters of public policy deliberation.

Community activism, especially through management-of-state apparatus that promote free speech, merits attention. In the first instance, free speech is a core value in constitutional protection of fairness and freedoms. As mentioned previously, the FCC is expected to issue regulatory guidelines on ICTs that take into consideration this important value.

While courts disagree on limits to speech, the principle of guaranteeing and protecting free and diverse speech is at the core of judicious enforcement of e-government policy. The challenge to government is to structure ICT policies to enable it to enhance productive democratic discourses rather than appearing to censor free speech. For example, contemporary community discussion tools such as Scoop, Squishdot, Zope, PHP-Nuke, and Slash are important community-based free speech tools. Functioning similarly, Democracy Design Workshop's Unchat is an Internet chatroom facility that provides opportunities for select members of the public to conduct structured conversations on policy matters. These have enabled ICTs to form important virtual communities in which freedom of expression is embraced.

E-LEGISLATION

E-legislation concerns the use of electronic information and communication technologies to advance the legislative process. Much has been done in this area at all levels of government. For example, the federal web portal Firstgov.gov is an early conveyor of information on all government operations. Additional steps to enhance e-legislation are evident in the publication of the *Federal Register* online. Additionally, nearly all Senators and Congresspersons have websites to present their positions on national and local issues. For example, senior senator from Illinois Dick Durbin's website has sections including "About Dick Durbin, Issues and Public Policy, News and Multimedia, Legislative Agenda," and a link to the Illinois Information Center, to mention a few characteristics. Republican Senator John McCain's website provides a host of links that include his speeches, constituent services, press releases, issues and legislation, and an Arizona map.

Hundreds of elected officials as well as citizens have joined the blogosphere and established contacts with political pundits to state their vision of the country. Further, the proliferation of social networking sites such as Twitter, Facebook, and MySpace, and the self-publishing Internet broadcasting website YouTube.com, have added to this growing arsenal of channels for political communication. YouTube has become an important part of the American political communication culture. President Obama is the first president to post public policy messages directly through this new media. His weekly radio addresses, popularized by earlier presidents on radio and television, are supplemented by YouTube clips of his speeches on various public policy matters. In recent times, heated debates in town halls about the nation's healthcare reform received much coverage in YouTube forums. Concerning the power of YouTube in the health reform policy debates, Congresswoman Debbie Wasserman Schultz (D-FL) lamented, "A lot of those antics at these town halls…have been manufactured…created by the Republican Party…to get themselves on YouTube and spread fear" (Silva, 2009).

YouTube has provided an attractive forum for members of the public to contribute directly to policy discourses. For example, the National Association of Schools of Public Affairs and Administration recognizes the need for civic engagement through this medium and invites the public to contribute to public policy discourses. An example of this innovative means was the NASPAA's attempt to engage public administration students and the public with the new Obama administration through asking the public to "speak truth to power" via YouTube (see boxes 7.1 and 7.2). The organization selected the best entries and displayed them on YouTube for public and official consumption. Hundreds of legislators and their staff, as well as citizens with interests in public administration and policy, are politically engaged in these online discussions.

The legislative process has been greatly enhanced electronically through online archival storage of Congressional Research Service reports. The Legislative Reorganization Act of 1970 created the Congressional Research Office, which serves as the public policy research arm of Congress. This legislative branch agency works exclusively for members of Congress, their committees, and their staffs.

At the federal level of government, the Thomas system operated by the Library of Congress is the premier e-legislating tool for use by lawmakers, the citizenry, and other concerned interests in both the public and private sectors. Thomas.gov offers a plethora of information, including

Box 7.1. *YouTube and Public Policy.*

The Challenge: Speak Truth to Power*

A new President will take office on January 20, 2013. He or she will face a myriad of challenges and choices. Here is your chance to influence the President from Day One.

You choose a public policy problem, current issue, or societal challenge that you believe the new president should tackle as part of his/her first term. You have 90 seconds to frame the issue and to offer your solution on video. The topic you choose may be either domestic or foreign. Your issue should be framed so that it clearly advocates a distinct policy proposal with projected outcomes. Your approach should be non-partisan. You should use evidence and analysis to bolster the persuasive power of your video policy proposal. The overarching idea is for you showcase your MPA/MPP skills and knowledge in your video entry.

* *Speak Truth to Power by Aaron Wildavsky* http://en.wikipedia.org/wiki/Aaron_Wildavsky
Source. National Association of Schools of Public Affairs and Administration.

Box 7.2. *YouTube Contest.*

Whether or not you create a video, you can participate and see who wins by subscribing to the MPA/MPP channel on YouTube.

It takes about 1 minute to sign up and there is no cost. Go to www.youtube.com/signup. Then search for or go to MPA/MPP Channel page and click yellow-colored "Subscribe" box. This way you'll be able to watch (and share) videos created by fellow MPA/MPP students.

Source. NASPAA, n.d.

the ability to search for bill texts and summaries, the status of all bills (including all votes), public laws by law number, roll call vote information, legislation by sponsor, current activity in Congress, access to the full Congressional Record, legislative schedules and calendars, presidential nominations, and treaties. For the average citizen that wants to verify his or her representatives' positions on substantive issues, especially prior to an election, the ability to browse legislation by sponsor is particularly useful. For all learners, the site offers well-developed historiographies on the

Supreme Court, the U.S. Constitution, the Declaration of Independence, and other historical documents.

Throughout the country, state e-legislative forums exist. In Arizona, for example, one useful Arizona State Legislature page lists all current ballot measures (with analyses) for upcoming and previous elections. This site (www.azleg.gov/BallotMeasureAnalyses.asp) contains information on campaigns and measures and analyzes these efforts. In addition, Arizona Governor Jan Brewer took a novel approach to political participation when she launched a website that asks supporters of SB1070, the state's anti-immigrant legislation enacted April 2010, to contribute to its defense. The law requires a police officer to determine the immigration status of any person that makes contact with law enforcement personnel. Critics argue that the law is unconstitutional and would lead to racial and ethnic profiling.

The site (keepazsafe.com) is an innovation in how states can engage members of the public in a matter of both national and state importance. A large number of citizens of Arizona saw the opportunity to contribute as a way of expressing their frustration with the federal government's slow pace of dealing with border issues as well as containing illegal immigration into the country.

In California, a website exists for conveying information on political issues. The website, www.ca.gov, provides access to bill information, assembly and senate sessions, and an e-mail service which notifies the subscribed public of proposed measures and initiative changes. The site also gives information on and access to Governor Arnold Schwarzenegger's state budget. The state's new governor, Jerry Brown, elected in 2011, continues the tradition (www.jerrybrown.org).

Polling and Voting

At the core of e-polling as a widely applied ICT activity is the notion of finding generalizable opinions on matters of public policy. Online newspapers and broadcast media conduct periodic unscientific polls on various aspects of public policy. For example, Cable News Network

(CNN) conducts "mini polls" by posing a question to viewers as a part of presentations in popular shows such as *Lou Dobbs Tonight*, whose main focus has been on immigration and border control issues; *Jack Cafferty's File*, often on homeland security matters, and Howard Kurtz's *Reliable Source*, where viewers post comments on general policy related questions at Reliablesource@CNN.com.

When polling is confined to a relatively homogenous population, it still informs policy debates. The danger of this is that polls represent opinions of only segments of society. The groups consulted can be self-selected through manipulated sampling techniques. The literature now uses the term SLOP, attributed to the University of Chicago, to refer to self-selected listener opinion polls. Recently, other more deliberative forums have been created on the Internet. For example, the National Issues Forum is perhaps more moderately balanced in its polling techniques. Participants meet, often in the form of focus groups, to give opinions on various subjects of policy import. These polls are often at variance with the more reputable Gallup polls or Harris Interactive polls, which have their own interactive websites.

As evident from speeches by major actors in the political system, policy and decision makers pay some attention to these polls regardless of their scientific merits. Polls provide a picture of important areas of governance and in some instances are essential tools for referendums and public juries. They are not, however, tools for citizen participation. Increasingly, deliberative polling tries to gauge the feelings of people. In addition to viewing poll results, citizens can compare candidate strengths and policies by accessing a variety of interactive town halls such as on vote.com and Grassroots.com.

The first experiments in e-voting were at the local level. In 2000, the Democratic Party, reacting to pressure to hold early primaries, contracted with Election.com, a company specializing in Internet elections, to conduct elections in early March. According to Solop (2001), voting instructions and PINs were sent to all 821,000 registered voters in Arizona, along with applications to receive mail ballots. Although it was permissible to send votes through the mail, the vast numbers of voters cast their votes online at 124 Democratic Party primary polling locations (Solop, 2001). Although e-voting led to an increase in turnout of 723 percent, some groups raised concerns that e-voting contravened the Voting Rights Act (Solop, 2001). The case in Arizona became the template for similar primaries in the country.

Something else was happening at the national level. The November 2000 presidential election triggered national debates on the efficacy of existing systems. There were widespread concerns in the State of Florida following the inadequacies of the punch card voting system (Kohno, 2004). State and national voting agencies began more vigorously adopting e-voting machines touted to ensure accuracy in counting. Nationally, experiments on e-voting machines have grown. The federal government, through Congress, passed the Help America Vote Act (HAVA) in October 2002. HAVA provides funds for states to replace punch card voting systems with electronic machines (e-voting) or the use of specific types of voting devices (Garson, 2006). There are different dimensions to e-voting including casting an electronic ballot and counting the votes by electronic means. There is a wide range of direct electronic voting systems, which include touch screen and keyboard based equipments. Other systems, designated as Public Network Direct Electronic Voting, involve the transmission of official vote data from one polling station to another public network. Another way of describing the different variations of e-voting is through Gibson's (2001) lens. Gibson (2001) noted that there are two basic variants of I-voting. In Internet voting at the polling place, votes are cast at official polling stations and transmitted via the Internet to election officials. The second variation is the remote Internet voting option, whereby votes are cast at any location with an Internet connection and transmitted via the Internet to election officials.

Federal and state regulations and reforms target all these different systems. HAVA, in particular, provides more than $2 billion in funding for employing these e-voting systems. In addition, HAVA establishes an Election Assistance Commission to assist in the administration of federal elections.

Most scholars agree that ICTs can help make representative democracy more responsive, but there are also threats to individual freedoms and in some cases disenfranchisement if e-voting machines are hacked. An Associated Press (2006) story reported that Diebold's AccuVote-TS voting machines, used in the United States for all levels of election, are vulnerable to hacking that could alter vote totals or disable machines entirely. The study argued that the e-voting machines fail to prevent attacks from certain viruses and do not meet U.S. federal standards for election machines (Associated Press, 2006). These limitations go beyond hacking vulnerability and include machine failure to boot when appropriately prompted (Barr, 2007).

Critics contend that, contrary to popular attitudes about a more open government, electronic voting machines do not ensure transparency and security (Bishop & Wagner, 2007). Current technology has failed to impress in several trials leading, to several state bans. For example, in California, Secretary of State Kevin Shelley banned the use of all Diebold machines, including 14,000 touch screen e-voting machines, in April 2004. Diebold disputed the claims that the machines lack security and reliability. Following recommendations from a state advisory panel, Shelley also decertified machines from other manufacturers (Associated Press, 2004). Several of the machines failed to function because of low battery power and software flaws, among other technical glitches. The state of California now requires the certification of software and an audit of all e-voting procedures.

There are also additional concerns with the lack of paper trails. California had established a deadline of 2006 for the addition of paper trails into all its e-voting machines. To address this issue the administration in Humboldt County, California, added high-end scanners that produce digital images of all the ballots. The images are transferrable to computers and available on portable devices such as DVDs or Universal Serial Bus (USB) flash memory drives.

A number of arguments for and against Internet voting have been advanced (Gibson, 2001). Opponents contend that the procedure jeopardizes the quality of voting and has the potential for violating voter privacy and security. There is speculation that the quality of participation is reduced in online voting environments. This is especially the case when issues of the digital divide are not adequately resolved (Gibson, 2001). There is a high chance that minorities and the poor can be disenfranchised under such circumstances.

Prospects for vote rigging cannot be dismissed. The high incidence of security violations through hacking and use of viruses poses a serious threat to democracy and cannot be taken lightly. It is conceivable that the quality of participation may be reduced if voters simply rely on online advertisements. The last argument is the weakest, because in a democracy it is the responsibility of citizens to learn about their leaders. Voters need to interact with candidates, and it is not enough to organize political recruitment processes through the online media alone. Responsible citizens have to go beyond online advertisements and know what their candidates stand for beyond the campaign rhetoric and marketing. Proponents of Internet voting see the potential for increasing participation rates. Others argue that online voting is efficient and a rational and logical progression in voting technology (Gibson, 2001). Dunlop (2008) reinforced this point by giving the example of the potential for providing tangible benefits to people with limited physical abilities who are able to participate at their convenience. Another advantage often touted by proponents of online voting point to the economic advantages, especially in terms of saving money and paper. In sum, although there are several hurdles to be overcome, industry analysts believe that in the future, new software will make it harder for the system to be compromised (Gerlach, 2009).

Campaigns and Political Communications

In political communication, there are a wide variety of ICT applications. Applications range from electronic filing systems to electronic billboards used in campaign advertisements. Several states require all candidates, parties, and committees running in their elections to report significant funding sources electronically. North Carolina, for example, imposes this requirement for those that receive more than $5,000 over the campaign period, and the state's electronic office enters all contributions of over $100 to any candidate into an electronic database. The state maintains a website with names and addresses of all registered candidates, political parties, and political action committees. Members of the public can access other voting data on the website.

Besides voting information, state-run websites carry information about lobbying activities, including the names of registered lobbyists. The public can access reports on the activities of lobbyists and the role of money in democracy and send to state officials e-mail correspondence on issues of concern. Other states have set up innovative ways of reporting on campaign finance and other issues relevant to voting.

ICTs became important elements in political campaigns especially after Moveon.Org in 1998 fought against the impeachment of President Clinton and later on formed versatile online communities. Later, online technologies became a key part of the strategy to raise campaign funds for both Democrats and Republicans. For example, in 2000, John McCain raised more than $2 million online to challenge George W. Bush for the Republican Party's nomination. From the Democratic side, Howard Dean's volunteers facilitated his campaign by raising considerable funds over the Internet.

More than any other year, the use of ICTs in political campaigns was advanced by the election of President Obama in 2008. His campaign employed an array of Internet-based technologies, including making use of online social networks such as Facebook and Twitter, to propel him to victory over John McCain (Hendricks & Denton, 2010). Otenyo (2010) described the campaign's innovative ability to reach out beyond the election. Obama's administration went a step further than his predecessors to create websites for members of the public to follow how the administration was handling the economic recession and to elicit contributions from members of the public on how to handle the various challenges facing the nation. In April 2011, the administration announced President Obama's 2012 re-election bid through an online forum on

Barackobama.com, a move that signifies the permanent presence of ICT in political communications.

Online Public Disputes Projects

Online conflict resolution projects are an old form political and civic participation initiative that provides expert consulting and resolution of conflicts to members of the public. Their outreach has expanded with the advent of the information revolution. While the number of national public dispute projects is growing, a number are well established. For example, Raab Associates manages the Online Public Disputes Project in Boston, which provides training to members of the public and civil servants at all levels of government for a fee. The Online Public Disputes Project is an aspect of online deliberation in the sense that it engages the public in important matters concerning health care, the environment, and land use planning. Its outreach has been enhanced by the applications of new ICTs. Online public disputes projects are only an element of growing participatory tools that engage citizens and elected officials in improving the quality of governance.

City Scan Activities

City scan is a democracy-enhancing project by which citizens participate in local governance issues. There are growing numbers of these projects nationwide. It involves the use of mobile and wireless technologies for tracking the performance of public officials. Participants in the scan projects target specific areas of municipal services. Armed with a variety of handheld computer devices, participants of all ages may choose to collect data about neighborhood conditions including graffiti, potholes, broken street lights, fallen sign posts, abandoned cars, uncollected trash bags, litter, or other unsightly and dangerous situations. These computer-based devices have custom-designed software, wireless modems, GPS receivers and digital cameras. Participants take pictures of the conditions and prepare reports and maps using visual databases created from a common computer-based databank. Local government officials use these reports to discuss problems and find solutions. For example, in the city of Hartford, Connecticut, citizens use a variety of scan techniques to participate in the governance of their city. Hartford is considered a model city in this new venture that has spread to other localities. These methods, supported by the local council and city manager, are considered innovative means of citizen empowerment and a considerable boost to democratic government. According to Steele and Holzer (2003), the Connecticut Policy and Economic Council (CPEC) initiated City Scan to "improve communication between the residents of Hartford (especially those in the low income bracket) and City Hall." CPEC aims at providing residents, through neighborhood associations and schools, a means to identify and prioritize problems such as potholes or drug paraphernalia in parks and to pressure the city to take action. Even though no single service is the focus, residents prioritized city cleanliness as their highest goal. The project, partly funded by Microsoft, has yielded tremendous successes in enabling government to take quick action to fix local problems.

CONCLUSIONS

In conclusion, e-government continues to be a fascinating and growing area of research. "The path toward information-age democracy is a deliberate one" (Clift, 2004). Opening processes to greater public participation can be very liberating as ICTs link citizens and/or stakeholder groups directly into government discussions and negotiations. The existing varieties of ICTs have expanded the scope of participation in public policy decision making. In particular, the Internet has empowered a new generation of net-citizens who engage their government and contribute to improving the quality of public services. The trend is global and not confined to advanced countries. Narratives on Internet revolutions are becoming a part of folklore and this can only mean that governments need to use ICTs to promote the cause of democracy. We may add that the United Nations Millennium Declaration calls upon governments to use ICTs to promote "democratic and participatory governance based on the will of the people" (Clift, 2004).

Although there has been an increase in blogging and other participatory activities, much of the interaction is still within the domain of the educated elite (Hindman, 2008). As many authors agree, there is no perfect system, "and there will always be underrepresented interests" (Hiskes & Hiskes, 1986, p. 119). Therefore, much more needs to be done to make the new technologies more viable as instruments of political participation. While currently much of e-government is about these services, the involvement of the citizen as a consumer of public services and as a key member of the body politic or owner of government itself must enhance the ability to communicate and add value to the governance process.

Finally, though the challenges of responsiveness and inclusiveness exist and are a source for concern, communities across the globe and nation are involved in a variety of activities that enhance rather than impede democratic governance. E-democracy is an added framework for shaping the ecology of e-government. It helps reinforce the values embedded in administrative practices—mainly net-citizenship, representativeness, openness, and participatory decision making.

Key Concepts

AMBER Alerts
Blogs
Blogosphere
Broadband
City scan
Democracy
Discussion tools
E-democracy
E-civics
Electronic Bracelets
FreeNets
Free speech
Information Commons
Interactive Town Hall
Net-citizens
Pluralism
Polling
Public Disputes Projects
Public spaces
Really Simple Syndication (RSS)
Rights
Tele-technologies
Twitter Revolution
Virtual communities
WikiLeaks

DISCUSSION QUESTIONS

1. Does e-democracy improve governance structures? Explain your answer.
2. Does the state in which you live embrace e-voting technologies? Write an essay on the politics behind the implementation of this form of political participation. Which other states have similar technologies and how have they faired with implementation?
3. Define the term "blogs." Identify at least three articles in academic journals that speak to the effects of blogging on democratic practices. Should public administrators participate in Internet blogs and YouTube activities? Explain your answer with specific examples from blogs you have visited and observed.
4. What are the implications of programs such as the Intensive Supervision Appearance Program, which targets immigrants, on American democracy and perceptions about the rule of law?
5. Should public administrators pay attention to electronic polling results? Explain your answers.

INTERNET ACTIVITIES

1. Use search engines to differentiate conceptual meanings of the following terms: digital government, cyberdemocracy, online democracy, open democracy, and e-commons. Count the number of hits each phrase yields in Google or Yahoo and report the most widely used phrase. Repeat the exercise after two days and report your findings. Now, attempt a definition for e-democracy.
2. You have been selected to be a member of the board of elections for your county. The board wants to adopt new technologies for its forthcoming county supervisor election. Your task is to compile a list of technologies for democracy. Using search engines, you need to provide an exhaustive list of appropriate technologies that are used in voting worldwide.

Chapter 8

Distribution of ICTs and Limitations to Access

Political scientists conceptualize power relations in terms of who gets what and why and how they get it. These questions are relevant to how we understand questions of Internet access at the local, state, national and international levels. Using the same distributive framework, we ask whether the Internet and by extension e-government is or can be available to all people at all times. Stated differently, is universal access an attainable goal? This chapter looks at the important issue of the distribution of ICTs that carry e-government platforms. The universe of e-government does not end with access to people in advanced countries, and thus we explore questions of the digital divide more generally and make references to international examples as well.

Some people might question why we bother to discuss issues of Internet access at all. In policy studies, considerable weight is given to provision of public services in an equitable fashion. In a democracy, finding an equitable solution to Internet access is as much a technical issue as it is a political and economic issue. In economic terms, people who do not have access to a functioning computer and therefore e-government are disadvantaged because they cannot afford it! Economics recognizes that vertical equity, meaning unequal treatment of people in different ranks, is a reality (Stone, 2002). It is characteristic for analysts to acknowledge at the outset that the economic system in the United States favors a system of distribution of social benefits largely skewed toward those who can attain goods and services from the market. This means that access to Internet services conforms to socioeconomic realities in life.

For the purposes of e-governance, this seems problematic because lack of access to Internet services means being less engaged in the civic community, lacking information vital for full citizenship, and social exclusion. These variables have manifestations that are well understood and can lead to a self-perpetuating cause and effect relationship. The lack of e-services can conceivably lead to low incomes, poor housing, poor health, and inadequate skills and can manifest itself in forms of social exclusion. As a consequence the distribution of e-government services is as much a political issue as is paying taxes. Political scientists need to be concerned about this issue for at least two overlapping reasons. First, a well-informed public has greater potential for civic participation. Without ICT access and skills, individuals are likely to be excluded from the benefits of the information society, including opportunities for telemedicine, access to disaster relief, and medical information. Second, from an economic viewpoint, offline individuals are unlikely to be major consumers of e-commerce. In addition, ICT skills are necessary for full involvement in the modern employment sector. As the table 8.1 shows, availability of Internet resources is growing globally but not uniformly, even among countries with the greatest usage.

The Debate over Equity in Information Access

The debate over equity in information access is about fairness and societal justice. E-government was not an issue when Rawls wrote *A Theory of Justice* (1971). One can assume that today Rawls would consider access to the Internet as an integral part of social primary goods, that is, goods

TABLE 8.1. *Internet Usage Among Leading Nations in 2009.*

Country	Number of Internet Users	% of population
World	1,581,571, 589	23.6
South Korea	36,794,800	76.1
United States	227,190,989	74.7
Japan	94,000,000	73.8
United Kingdom	43,753,600	71.8
Germany	55,221,183	67.0
France	40,858,353	65.7
European Union	308,967,801	63.2
Brazil	67,510,400	34.4
Russia	38,000,000	27.0
People's Republic of China	298,000,000	22.4
India	81,000,000	7.1

Source. Cabrera, 2009.

created by social and political institutions that are important to all people. In the United States at a practical level, the Department of Commerce recognizes that lack of access to the Internet is one of America's leading economic and civil rights issues and has moved forward to address the situation (National Telecommunications, 1995; 1998).

The political argument follows. If we are designing rules for how best to engage citizens in governance, we must certainly question the availability of Internet services to all people. Perhaps most rational people, assumedly utilitarian, would demand that services provided through the Internet be made available to the greatest number of people. But how would that be possible when practitioners and scholars acknowledge that a digital divide exists among people and nations? Indeed, many civil rights groups state that the digital divide "threatens to compound socio-economic and educational gaps by leaving low-income Americans ill-prepared for the 21st century workplace" (Cooper, 2002).

The Digital Divide

Defining the digital divide is controversial in and of itself. The National Telecommunications and Information Administration (NTIA) (NTIA, 2000) defined the digital divide as a disparity between the "haves" and the "have-nots" in the technology revolution. Another definition notes that "...digital divide describes the fact that the world can be divided into people who do and people who don't have access to—and the capability to use—modern information technology, such as the telephone, television, or the Internet" (Midmarket CIO, 1999). The general idea is that the digital divide is between those with access to new ICTs and those without. According to Garson (2006), the literature delineates access into three different but related elements. First is the dichotomous element to the divide, which implies there are groups or places that do not have access to ICTs. Second is the element of continuity in access to computers and other enabling technologies. That is, there are people out there who do not have the convenience of continuous access to ICTs. Third is the broader concept of the divide being a function of digital and computer illiteracy or more accurately the inequality of human capacity and the general lack of skills to use ICTs competently. All of these conceptualizations relate to each other in that they all involve the disparity in access to technology amongst individuals that can lead to a digital divide.

The challenge for administrators is, therefore, to reduce the gap between the haves and have-nots. If computer literacy is not improved, particularly among the technological have-nots, we can expect to see the growth of a technological divide and the attendant expansion of the digital divide. The figures for access show that access remains a problem, even in developed countries such as the United States in the 21st century. The NTIA updated its Internet usage study with the 2003 publication of *A Nation Online: Entering the Broadband Age*, where they noted that only 61.8% of U.S. households had access to the Internet. Data also showed that 65 percent of college graduates had Internet access in their homes, while less than 12 percent of households headed by a person without a high school diploma had access. In 2000, 86.3 percent of households with people earning over $75,000 per year had Internet access, compared to only 12.7 percent of households making less than $15,000 per year. The figures for 2007 showed increased usage among college-educated individuals, with 85 percent of individuals 25 years and older with bachelor's degrees using the Internet. Individuals without high school diplomas had a low usage rate of about 19 percent. In the United States in 2007, home usage among Caucasians was 69 percent; Asians, 73 percent; Blacks, 51 percent; and Hispanics, 48 percent. Many in the Black community believe that the digital divide and the lower usage of new technologies, especially in the "Jim Crow Cyber South," is a structural rather than a cultural issue (Banks, 2006; Walton, 1999). However, other observers, notably the NTIA (2000), rejected the notion of a binary divide and posit instead that African Americans with higher incomes use ICTs as much as other upper-class Americans.

Data from the U.S. Census Bureau indicate that Internet use tripled from 1997 to 2007. 62 percent of American households used the Internet from home by 2007. This was a sharp increase from the 18 percent that used it in 1997. Within the country, the lowest rates of Internet usage in 2007 were in Mississippi and West Virginia, at about 52 percent of the population. In the United States in 2007, 82 percent of all users had high-speed broadband connections compared to only 17 percent using dial-up modem technologies. It should be noted, however, that broadband usage in the United States is lower than that in Western Europe.

According to the *World Broadband Statistics Report* (2010), Western Europe had a usage rate of 27.6 percent compared to 23.2 percent for North America, including Mexico and Central America. The regions of Southeast Asia and Asia-Pacific had usage rates of 20.1 and 18.3 percent respectively. China, the country with the second largest broadband market in the world, had roughly 20 percent of world broadband subscribers, or 51.9 million subscribers. China's *Cun Cun Tong* (Connect all Villages with the Internet) program is rapidly narrowing the country's digital divide (Chook, 2007). According to Internet World Stats statistics, there has been soaring growth across the board. The number of people using broadband in China alone is already over

360 million in 2010 (Internet World Stats, 2011). Globally, broadband technologies are changing connectivity and redefining how we understand the digital divide.

The International Telecommunication Union (ITU) presents some interesting data regarding inequality in access to broadband technologies and its causes: "A broadband connection in a high-income economy costs, on average, around US$16 per 100 kbit/s of data transmission capacity per month (and in Japan and the Republic of Korea, even less at under 10 U.S. cents per month). The average price in low-income economies is more than US$186 per month" (1TU, 2007, p. 27). The FCC defines, as of 2010, Basic Broadband as data transmission speeds of at least 4 megabits per second (Mbps) or 4,000,000 bits per second. A kbit per second is a unit of data transfer rate equal to 1000 bits per second or 125 bytes per second.

In fact, poor countries in Africa have to pay the full costs of connections to the Internet to the advanced countries where most providers are located. Norris (2001) observed that the global divide among countries is a structural problem because "to them that hath shall be given" (p. 5). One of the more popular explanations for the global divide, therefore, is the question of the availability of appropriate educational resources. Warschauer's (2003) research in Egypt cited the limitations of understanding the divide in terms of developmental theories and instead focused on the social embedding of technology, especially its connection with power and educational opportunities.

Norris (2001) associated the rise of digital politics with the knowledge economy and commented that the "knowledge economy is heavily dependent on modern global communications," which are associated with the presence of multinational corporations. This further complicated the questions of accessibility and the need to have international informational equity. However, she disagreed that developmental theories are sufficient in explaining the absorption of ICTs. As has been pointed out, countries such as Taiwan and Brazil have moved rapidly in e-governance, overtaking many postindustrial societies (Norris, 2001). This position was shared by Fink and Kenny (2003) who contended that some developing countries show faster rates of growth in network development than do developed countries. This means that political leadership is also an important variable in narrowing the digital divide.

Even if we set aside the question of lack of high-speed ICT equipment, we still confront the question of skilled access. Not surprisingly, well-paying jobs that require computer understanding and skills generally go to well-educated upper- and middle-class Americans and foreign nationals. The American underclass, stuck in low-wage, low-skill jobs, inevitably does not take advantage of the full benefits of ICTs. As a result, the needs and views of the lower income groups are not often accounted for in the development of technology policies. Thus, new technologies and new applications of existing technologies risk being largely irrelevant to this group, which inevitably falls further and further behind the mainstream. While NTIA's focus has been on traditionally disadvantaged groups, at the micro level, the dimension of income draws more attention; the importance of income disparities among different groups, including ethnic minorities and the elderly, is emphasized in policy prescriptions to narrow the digital divide.

At the macro level, the digital divide manifests itself in agency and national (country) terms. The larger question is therefore whether or not income matters. Of course, a region's relative wealth matters. Box 8.2 shows the two key variables in understanding macro-level dimensions of the digital divide. These disparities are mainly related to issues of dichotomous and skilled access. Low-income individuals cannot afford all the new ICTs. They have to make choices between groceries and healthcare on the one hand and high-speed Internet connections on the other hand.

Studies in lower income countries show that a large proportion of income of the poor is spent on new technologies such as cell phones. One may speculate that lower income individuals often feel the pressure to have these technological devices—even if they can barely afford it. It is often possible to see the poor in places such as Guatemala, Bangladesh, and Ethiopia owning mobile phones but unable to pay for the scratch or pre-paid cards or air time (network charges). For example, Ethiopia, one

Box 8.1. *Micro-Dimensions Frequently Observed.*

- Income-based disparities and gap
- Gender-based disparities and gap
- Age disparities and gap (Senior citizens aged 55 and above)
- Education disparities and gap (Digital illiteracy)
- Location gaps (e.g., Indian Country)
- Ethnicity gap (Hispanics, African Americans and other minorities)

Box 8.2. *Macro-Level Dimensions Frequently Observed.*

- Language (English is the dominant ICT language)
- Country's per capita GDP
- Size and location of country
- Presence of multinational corporations and ICT infrastructure

of the poorest countries in the world, spends nearly one tenth of its GDP on information technologies every year (Dutta & Mia, 2009). The same happens with regard to Internet access charges. These decisions are not always reflected in our analysis of the digital divide but are an important factor to consider.

How to Measure the Digital Divide

In a paper published to counter arguments that the digital divide had been reduced or eradicated, Cooper (2002) noted that:

> Because our society is not a 'café' culture, most personal business is conducted from the home. Searching for information, looking for a job, and entertainment activities (especially TV viewing) are typically done in the privacy of the residence. For this reason, we have measured the digital divide, as we have measured universal telephone service, by the availability of the means of communications (telephone or the Internet) in the home. Stopping by the library to use the Internet or using it at work may be

> transitional steps useful for creating skills in the population, or carrying out specific tasks associated with the activities of those locations, but they are not a replacement for its availability in the home. (p. 3)

Academicians and practitioners alike are divided on how to measure the digital divide. Simplistic criteria, such as determining the number of Internet access points in a location, do little to answer the question of the disparities in ICT usage. It is a matter that continues to draw the interest of stakeholders in the ICT world. Barzilai-Nahon (2006) provided one way to measure the digital divide by advocating the use of different measures that included:

- Social and governmental support and constraining factors, including training, funding, and emphasis on digital empowering,
- Affordability relative to other expenditures and average incomes,
- Use, including frequency, time online, purpose, skill level, and autonomy of use, and
- Socioeconomic factors, including age, education, geography, race, and language, among other factors.

Barzilai-Nahon's (2006) model goes beyond the simple question of whether or not the digital divide has widened or is closing and brings to our attention the questions of income and accessibility.

Another income-based approach to measuring the digital divide demonstrated how the Lorenz curve and Gini coefficient are used to measure inequalities in computer ownership in the United States. The model outlined by Chakraborty and Bosman (2005) was based on data from the U.S. Census Bureau that indicated income inequalities are substantially different among the different ethnic communities in the country. While income inequalities among PC owners decreased between 1994 and 2001 in all states, the magnitude of the inequality was not evenly spread among all ethnic groups. In other words, there is a relationship between PC ownership and the issue of the digital divide.

Narrowing the Digital Divide

Reducing the digital divide is primarily about accessing the Internet. It is to a large degree about the usage of ICTs to create and build knowledge necessary for functioning in the modern economy. In short, the digital divide must be reduced or eliminated to improve quality of life for the majority of citizens. Policy solutions are often designed to ameliorate lack of access to ICTs, especially by wiring schools, training teachers, and providing community access in the less endowed neighborhoods (Norris, 2001). In the United States, the Clinton administration focused on supplying the hardware and enhancing the networks and infrastructures.

In his 1997 State of the Union Address, President Clinton challenged America to connect every classroom and library to the Internet by the year 2000. Several communities attempted to reach this goal with varying degrees of success. The administration followed through on its pledges by providing funding and investing heavily in providing ICT skills to schools and communities. The administration allocated over $100 million to establish hundreds of community centers across the nation (Cullen, 2006, p. 309).

Although both Republican and Democratic Party administrations seek to reduce the digital divide, there have been some marked differences in their approach to the question of access. In 2003, the Bush administration was criticized for seeking to eliminate the TOP and the Community Technology Center (CTC) initiatives, which were aimed at creating equity in access to technology for all Americans. Although the CTC budget was reduced, Congress did not approve eliminating these expenditures (Garson, 2006). On the other hand, President Barack Obama's YouTube address in December 2008 stated that connecting everyone to the Internet was a primary goal of his administration in efforts to place the United States on course for economic recovery. In that address, he promised to install high-speed Internet access in underserved areas and install computers in all public K-12 classrooms. President Obama also promised to provide funding for additional broadband mapping, broadband adoption, and public computing center upgrades. The importance that Obama placed on ICT equity may eventually narrow the ICT equity gaps left by the Bush administration. Obama, widely popular among the technology-savvy college-aged public, was considered more in tune with contemporary digital technologies. This aspect of his savvy was evident during the 2008 presidential election, in which he employed various technologies to win the race to the White House.

Initiatives at the State and Local Levels

Moving from the federal level to the state and local levels, different communities have adopted different approaches to narrowing the gap between those on opposite sides of the divide. In Illinois, the business community and other stakeholders have recognized the need for supporting the federal government's initiatives. The Chamber of Commerce Commission established a community technology fund to provide financial investments to underserved communities. The fund supplements state-level support to the "Connecting my Community" projects in underserved rural and urban areas. Funding has been channeled to improving digital literacy within the communities concerned. In Illinois, the Laboratory for Community and Economic Development at the University of Illinois has been the lead institution in enhancing digital literacy. In a study to identify the ten key skills important to achieving digital literacy, Fesenmaier (2003) provided the information in box 8.3, which can also be applicable to other parts of the United States.

Several programs provided through a statewide network of CTCs are also in place to ensure that all Illinois residents have the greatest possible access to Internet resources. Consortia of educational institutions, states, support programs, and nonprofit organizations aim to enhance, improve, and equalize technical access throughout the state. The "Connecting My Community" program cited previously is one such statewide community initiative. These initiatives work to identify and provide technical services and training resources for residents.

In Arizona, the local efforts to narrow the digital divide have been varied and extensive. Several communities offer computer literacy training through their local libraries. Elderly persons and young children have been beneficiaries of many of these local initiatives. Training opportunities have

Box 8.3. *The Top 10 Skills for Digital Literacy.*

- Send and read e-mail
- Do online research for school or work
- Look for a job online
- Use word processing software
- Read a newspaper or magazine online
- Install software
- Look for a product online
- Use the Internet to look up health or medical information
- Find financial information online
- Use the web to look up local community events (movies, festivals, sports)

Source. Fesenmaier, 2003.

also been extended to non–English speaking residents. City leaders point out that "the library division continues to bridge the digital divide, ensuring that…economic poor do not become information poor" (City of Chandler, 2007). The city of Chandler, Arizona, donated computers to the Chandler Unified School District, including donations to disadvantaged communities. In Scottsdale, Arizona, the city established a proactive approach to providing free access to computers through the senior community center and library programs. These programs are tailored to engage elderly and financially disadvantaged citizens. The reason why the Scottsdale program targets the elderly is because the city has a large number of retired senior citizens. Similarly, in Pima County, Arizona, the CornerStone Campaign recognized the limitations of the tax base and provided funding for hardware to all community libraries. The CornerStone Campaign organization raises funds through donations and community fund drives to help bridge the financial resources gap and encourages volunteerism in the provision of instructional training for members of the community to improve their basic computer skills (Pima County, 2009).

Libraries under Pressure

Even though much is expected from local public library systems, there is considerable evidence that local communities are strained and have difficulties coping with the need to provide the infrastructure for e-government. Bertot, Jaeger, Langa, and McClure (2006) reported, that libraries are increasingly challenged, even as they have stepped up to meet the increasing demand for Internet access and services, as our 2006 biennial Public Libraries and the Internet study shows (www.ii.fsu/edu/plInternet). In the decade between 1994 and 2004, Internet connectivity in U.S. public libraries jumped from 20.9 percent to 99.6 percent, and nearly all offer public access. In 1998, only 3.4 percent of public libraries had ten or more public Internet workstations; now the national average is 10.7 workstations. Therefore, unless local libraries are financially supported, communities will continue to have difficulties reaching their goals of expanding the digital commons.

There are other challenges to reducing the digital divide as well. In areas where citizen participation in e-governance is limited, resources have often been channeled to providing newsletters and web addresses (URLs) with links to important government policy matters to encourage people to be connected to their government. The digital divide is perhaps most conspicuous among the Native American Navajo Nation, where e-governance is very limited.

Native American Country and the Digital Divide

Imagine being in the Grand Canyon. It is an isolated place. The Grand Canyon is a massive landmass situated in the midst of an even more massive desert mosaic that includes the Navajo Reservation. Just like any U.S. municipal division, the Navajo Reservation has public schools. The issue is that children in remote parts of the Navajo Reservation are often not digitally connected. Nationwide there are about 183 schools managed by the Bureau of Indian Affairs. These schools serve over 50,000 students across 23 states on at least 63 reservations. Many Native American children go to schools with limited access to computers. Some schools have inadequate electricity and utility lines hence facing the problem of lack of continuous access. Worse still, many students have no electricity or running water in their homes. For example, in 1998, of the 242 students at the kindergarten-to-eighth grade level in Cottonwood Day School, no one had a computer at home (Mendels, 1998). While the numbers have changed slightly, the problem still exists. There are still areas of the reservation that do not have dial-up access, or even satellite access as is common in other rural areas, because the reservation largely lacks wired telephone service (Fonseca, 2008).

Although the challenge of expanding Internet access in Native American communities received great attention during the Clinton administration, gaps in access still exist. The Clinton-Gore Access Native America initiative was an integral part of the reinvention of government policy. Under this policy, the Clinton administration established reinvention labs across the country to institutionalize new ways of providing a host of services to the people. Through these initiatives several schools across the country were wired in 1998 and 1999. Access Native America did not just cover the Navajo Nation, which by itself covers over 27,000 square miles and is the largest reservation in the United States, but also involved other Native American communities. The list of beneficiaries includes the Pine Ridge Reservation of South Dakota, the Choctaw Reservation in Mississippi, and numerous pueblos in New Mexico (Sweeney, 1998).

On the Navajo Reservation, the Havasupai Day School is connected to the outside world through the Office of Indian Education Programs. Additional program support has come from Native American initiatives, especially from individuals and groups that support the use of Native American languages in the new media. There is a strong feeling that the increased usage of Internet media should go hand in hand with development of content that is indigenous to the people.

Within the expansive Navajo Nation, support for narrowing the digital divide has also come from the local Division of Community Development (DCD). The DCD is part of the executive branch of the Navajo Nation government charged with the responsibility of providing relevant community education for orderly growth of the Navajo Nation. Generally, tribal governments such as that of the Navajo are sovereign nations. As such, each tribal government has its own legal system and laws. The DCD has worked in partnership with nonprofit organizations such as the Bill and Melinda Gates Foundation's Native American Access to Technology Program to fund infrastructure for e-solutions or e-government within its jurisdiction. In 2000, this foundation provided each Navajo chapter a grant for purchasing computers and providing Internet access. But even though the computers were purchased and distributed to the chapters, there were other challenges beyond mere distribution and availability of hardware. Hundreds of Navajo elders who could not use the computers in the local libraries and community centers due to their inability to communicate in English. There were no words in Navajo to explain the new technologies, thereby posing a further challenge in addition to the lack of access occasioned by limitations in infrastructure (Pyrillis, 2007).

One of the priorities of the DCD has been to build and implement a technology infrastructure and support system in the community. The DCD's Information Management team (DCD-IM) has been the key agent in leading the drive to narrow the divide in access to ICTs in the Navajo Nation. Since 2001 much progress has been achieved working through local chapters to develop the foundation for a robust e-government system. The key elements of this initiative are outlined in box 8.4. The DCD-IM plan constitutes the vision for narrowing the digital divide in America's remotest communities.

Considerable progress has been made. DCD has succeeded at providing activities to empower local communities to benefit from e-government, e-voting, and e-commerce services. DCD has received grants from the U.S. Department of Commerce's Technology and Opportunities Program for establishing a regional technology center to provide training and assistance in the development of community.

DCD has also been successful at streamlining e-solutions in partnership with other government agencies. For example, through support of the Department of Housing and Urban Development block grants program, the Woven Information of Navajo Data (WIND) project has been realized. The program is a web-based initiative that displays and archives Native American documents online. The goal of the initiative is to provide a service that helps the community track projects, maintain

Box 8.4. *Navajo Nation Division of Community Development e-Government Vision.*

- To provide a stable telecommunications environment for Navajo chapters and communities
- To provide increased visibility to technology projects in the community
- To serve as a catalyst for increasing technology-related activities throughout the Navajo Nation
- To provide training in technology-related fields and form community information gatherers to begin creating a database of community resources and statistics
- To promote self-sustainability of technology projects at each Navajo community
- To provide an online business site for local entrepreneurs to market and sell their products (e-commerce)

Source. Navajo Nation Community Development, n.d.

data, and generate reports that enhance accountability and information sharing. Currently, accessibility is limited to administrators from participating agencies including project supervisors, chapter officials, and DCD administrators. This demonstrates that e-government has much to do with economic empowerment, community development, and good governance.

Although much progress has been recorded since 1998, the road to full connectivity in the Native American communities, especially in the Navajo Nation, has not been smooth. Due to poorly executed contracting arrangements and the lack of capacity to successfully monitor e-government infrastructures, ICT projects have often failed to function optimally. In 2008, for example, thousands of Navajo Nation residents were unable to reliably use their Internet services for work, study, or communication. At that time the service provider shut down the community's access, citing lack of payments for services rendered, even though the access provided had been provided irregularly. The Navajo Nation, through DCD, had contracted OnSat Network Communications Inc., a company based in Utah, to be the service provider in the tribe's jurisdiction. An earlier audit had revealed that OnSat Network double-billed the tribe, leading to the problem (Fonseca, 2008). The Universal Service

Administration, which administers the service under the FCC's E-rate program, reimbursed 85 to 90 percent of the costs for Internet services to 70 of the Nation's 110 chapters but withheld further funding due to the query (Fonseca, 2008). The Navajo Nation, in turn, was expected to cover 10 to 15 percent of the cost of the service. Many cited mismanagement and poor execution of the contract as a reason for the failure to assure residents continuous access to the Internet.

Since 1998, the E-rate program has provided affordable access to telephone and Internet services to most K-12 schools and public libraries in disadvantaged tribal communities. While most of the Native American communities relied on terrestrial broadband connections, 3 percent of E-rate areas used dial-up networks. Another 3 percent was provided through satellite connections (FCC, 2010). In the Native American school districts, the most widespread usage is in the area of e-mail applications. At the same time, regional libraries depend on the Internet for referencing materials. According to an FCC sponsored study, the greatest challenge in the E-rate–funded projects remains the slow connection speeds in most rural communities and the high cost of installation (FCC, 2010).

The United Nations and the Digital Divide

Local government initiatives have been responsive to the United Nation's readiness report (2005a), which suggested that governments needed to focus on building effective use of ICTs in their development plans. The United Nations vision has been to provide access and equitable inclusion of communities to enable citizens to engage in governance.

The United Nations considers the role of government to be paramount in the reduction of the digital divide across communities. Box 8.5 shows the United Nations' conceptualization of this role. Because these actions involve huge capital outlays, it implies that the market alone cannot end or reduce the digital divide.

The United Nations recognized that income disparities among nations, as well as limitations in developing content in languages used in developing

Box 8.5. *The Role of Government in Addressing Digital Inequalities.*

- Universal access to physical infrastructure
- Universal access to education and ICT skills
- Appropriate access to language tools
- Access to culturally relevant and appropriate content
- A focus on gender access to ICT
- Access to population with disability
- Access to information
- Promoting awareness of the benefits of the information society

Source. United Nations, 2005b.

countries, continue to be a huge barrier to reducing the digital divide among member states. Developing countries also have to add resources to provide an education to women, who have traditionally been discriminated against in receiving educational opportunities. As the U.N. report observes, the digital divide on a global level should be addressed within a framework of social inclusion (United Nations, 2005b). The U.N. framework acknowledges that public participation in governance is only possible if political, economic, and technological barriers are removed from societies. Therefore, without creating opportunities for all, countries will not be able to expand democratic space. The United Nations considers digital inclusiveness as an integral part of democratic governance and hence its support for policies aimed at narrowing the digital divide.

Recent data from the World Bank acknowledge that the intervention of the United Nations helped build the momentum to shrink the digital divide. Currently, the number of people with access to a telephone of some kind, either through a fixed landline or wireless network, stands at about 3.2 billion people. A good number of mobile phone applications have Internet access and will form the future of e-government subsystems. The ITU, which tracks Internet and mobile phone usage, now acknowledges that handheld devices have jumped into the fray to fill the demand for connectivity, especially among citizens of the developing world. More than three-quarters of those people use wireless mobile phones provided through private telecom carriers. According to ITU reports, regular Internet usage has grown from 4.5% in 1999 to 11% in 2003 showing that progress is being made across the nations.

Differential Examples of Narrowing the Digital Divide

At the beginning of this chapter we showed in table 8.1 that South Korea (a country of 48 million people with a land mass the size of the state of Virginia) has done much better than most countries in narrowing the digital divide among its people. How has this been possible?

South Korea's relative success at narrowing the digital divide can be attributed to the country's political leadership. Currently, Internet access is available for nearly 80% of the population. Korea established an agency to specifically deal with issues of the digital divide. This agency is the Korea Agency for Digital Opportunity and Promotion (KADO). KADO has a staff of 142 and an annual budget of approximately $45 million that is fully funded by various branches of the Korean government. KADO was originally established as Korea's Information Telecommunication Training Center in 1982 and has evolved into its current form over the past decade. Since the 1990s, KADO has been working to increase Koreans' access to the Internet. KADO focuses its attention on helping persons with disabilities, senior citizens, rural dwellers and low-income families to get Internet access (Woyke, 2009). Korea adopted various innovative techniques to expand Internet access. For example, KADO now concentrates on offering ICT education to the public. The country offers training in both online and offline courses. The limitations posed by hardware problems are no longer a source of worry, especially with the completion a world-class broadband infrastructure. According to Woyke (2009),

> To reach people in remote areas, [KADO] partners with local governments and civic associations and even holds classes in private homes. Volunteers do most of the teaching.... KADO's education

> efforts have taught 10 million Koreans how to e-mail, search the Web and download files.

The United States does not have an equivalent agency to KADO. Instead, there are multiple players in the e-government regime, including the NTIA, the FCC, and the USDA, often with competing and contradictory goals. As a result the United States lacks a comprehensive, coordinated national Internet policy in 2011.

SHRINKING THE DIGITAL DIVIDE THROUGH CYBER SCHOOLS

The term "cyberschools" refers to online or virtual schools. These distance-learning schools rely on computer-based Internet programs and are popular in developing countries. Many of the cyberschools are run by not for profit groups, often with support from government and international aid agencies. In Africa, cyberschools support efforts by governments to combat the spread of HIV/AIDs. Through cyberschools, age-appropriate digital lessons on HIV/AIDs prevention are transmitted throughout Sub-Saharan Africa.

Cyberschool programs have another broader objective—to narrow the digital divide by enabling early familiarization with ICTs among students in underprivileged communities. Through standardized learning processes, students receive a quality education regardless of their location or station in life. In most of the developing countries, the curriculum is aligned to programs established by local accreditation boards.

Cyberschools are an emerging trend in regions where literacy and education levels are low. In countries such as Bangladesh, which has a population of close to 160 million people with over 40 percent living below the poverty line, there is growing pressure to expand education opportunities at the lowest possible cost. Cyber Schools Bangladesh, founded by Shapir Khosru, seeks to find similar ventures aimed at addressing the perennial problems associated with poverty. The project is organized under the aegis of the Underprivileged Children's Education Programs (UCEP). These programs support more than 25,000 urban children that would have been left behind in the information age (*Bangladesh Observer*, 2005).

With the aid of various nongovernmental organizations and foundations, cyberschools provide educational tools and Internet access to millions of underprivileged schools and communities in Bangladesh and other underdeveloped countries. Their initiatives include offering courses in the English language, to tap the full potential of the Internet. This is because the digital divide is exacerbated by the lack of sufficient content in native languages. One organization that is a leader in the movement is the Cyber Schools Foundation, which started its activities in Bangladesh in 2004 (UCEP, 2011).

Through its initiative, the foundation supports a program that has been relatively successful at providing teachers with ICT training. In addition, the program provides computer labs with Internet connections to children from low-income families. Hundreds of school-age children also benefit from outreach programs that target ICT skill development. Cyberschools, through Internet learning centers physically located at existing secondary and technical schools, supplement other education and training institutions to create a skilled labor force. Graduates of cyberschools in Bangladesh are increasingly finding employment in both government and the private sector.

Conclusions

There are general benefits to reducing the digital divide among communities. The world economy has changed to the degree that ICT skills are essential to participation in governance and also being a full member of the global economy. From an efficiency viewpoint, traditional government structures are proving to be much more costly. For example, when information equity is low and the digital divide is great, agencies are often forced to provide duplicate services, one traditional and one electronic. E-government serves to enhance efficiency in service delivery but administrators all over the world are still confronted with managing the challenge of the digital divide.

KEY CONCEPTS

Broadband Age
Community Technology Center (CTC)
Cyberschools
Digital divide
Digital and computer illiteracy
Digital inclusiveness
E-governance
Korea Agency for Digital Opportunity and Promotion (KADO)
National Telecommunications and Information Administration (NTIA)
Navajo Nation
Social exclusion
Technical divide
Technology Opportunities Program (TOP)
Universal access
United Nations' Readiness

DISCUSSION QUESTIONS

1. What is the digital divide? How is it associated with income inequalities?
2. Discuss the challenges involved in measuring the digital divide.
3. Describe how your community is addressing the digital divide. Can the government be trusted to narrow or end the digital divide?
4. Outline the benefits of narrowing the digital divide among communities in the United States.
5. What problems make the digital divide a major problem in Native American Country?
6. How did South Korea narrow its digital divide? Are there other countries not included in table 8.1 that you believe have achieved comparable success in narrowing the gap between the digital have and have-nots? Share your case with the class.

INTERNET ACTIVITY

Using table 8.1, use Internet resources such as the *CIA Factbook* and the World Bank to explain the relationships between Gross Domestic Product (GDP) and the digital divide. Use the same resources to compile another table to show the Internet usage in the world's poorest countries.

CHAPTER 9

THE IMPLEMENTATION OF ICTs IN e-GOVERNMENT

This chapter examines the factors associated with successful implementation of e-government projects. The implementation process focuses our attention on key players and their tactics, resources, and strategies for producing a successful e-government project. In the context of e-government, it is about fulfilling the promise of ensuring that ICTs are finalized to provide public services. It is a complex process to be managed by both executives and street-level administrators. The former have to deal with the concerns of offering a strategic vision while the latter must respond to operational and tactical issues of making public services available to the public through the Internet and other computer-mediated technologies.

This chapter does not delve into the specifics of technical implementation of e-government projects but attempts to provide broad-brush responses to the question of why e-government projects succeed and who is responsible for their vision. While the how question is reflected upon in a tangential manner, it is important and is raised to understand some of the best practices in e-government implementation. At the end, we also consider administrative elements of evaluation, especially the criteria for evaluating e-government websites and the challenges of meeting stakeholder and public expectations.

Project implementation is a stage in the policy process after problem identification, formulation, and design. Public administrators since Pressman and Wildavsky's (1973) seminal work on implementation have known that the multiplicity of actors and perspectives can be a major challenge to successful implementation of programs and projects. However, their study also demonstrated the significant role of political leadership and partnerships among different stakeholders in promoting successful implementation. Leadership, as the literature suggests, has to be able to play implementation games, to use Bardach's terminology, that include ensuring compliance with rules and regulations and overcoming resistance to project development (Bardach, 1977). Leadership has to work with the lead agency—in the case of e-government the IT department—and be able to manage implementation challenges involving multiple stakeholders.

We study public e-government implementation for at least two reasons; first we do so to understand the consequences and causes of the projects implemented so that we can improve on e-government services. As we shall discuss later, ICT investments are an expensive endeavor, and public monies must serve the public interest. Second, we view implemented e-government and attendant ICT projects as independent variables having an impact on society and the way that government functions. It is commonly assumed that e-government projects are intended to make government work better. However, implementing e-government projects may not always be successful, thereby leading to loss of public funds and other resources. The example of the Bonneville Power Administration (BPA) may help clarify some of the challenges project managers and administrators have to anticipate.

Bonneville Power Administration and Transparency

BPA is a federal agency within the U.S. Department of Energy. Responsible for maintaining over 18,000 miles of high voltage electric capacity, BPA serves a large area in the Pacific Northwest. Congress expects it to raise its own revenues through service charges. BPA's service territory includes 49 federally recognized Indian tribes. BPA supplies inexpensive electricity to a large area that includes Idaho, Oregon, Washington, Western Montana, and small parts of northern Nevada and California. In addition to power transmission, BPA, through the Northwest Power Act of 1980, is required to operate large fish and wildlife mitigation programs and help preserve the environment in the region. BPA has to ensure that its dams are environmentally friendly. Regionally, the agency employs close to 3,000 persons and offers opportunities to several private sector contractors (BPA, 2011).

Administratively, the head of BPA, a political appointee, is answerable to the secretary of energy. Because thousands of high-voltage transmission lines pass through Indian reservation land, BPA's activities are a source of concern for tribal leadership. Although the agency is aware of its responsibilities to the communities, its main customers are the utility companies that serve the individual end-user customers (BPA, 2011).

Although the population of the region has been increasing, BPA, until recently, had not added much to its grid. For BPA to build new power transmission lines, it must conduct feasibility studies and seek certification on environmental impacts from the EPA. This is established in the National Environmental Policy Act. BPA must also consult, in a transparent manner, with members of the public and especially groups representing the Indian tribes. As in other cases, the public prefers that electric rates remain low (BPA, 2011).

In project management, stakeholders must collaborate in a transparent manner. There are several ways through which communications between different stakeholders can be enhanced. One such approach is through online channels. The problem has been a lack of trust between members of the Indian tribes and officials of BPA. Community members charge that BPA has been less than transparent in its expansion of the power grid in tribal areas.

Most of the contentious issues revolve around BPA's power projects, which Indian communities argue contribute negatively to fish and wildlife resources. In an attempt to resolve the issue of trust and transparency, Indian groups asked BPA to develop a website for tribes to read the critical information about the agency's activities in the region. Such a website would enhance accountability and contribute toward achieving transparency in public affairs (BPA, 2011).

BPA agreed to develop a website that would address the community's needs as part of its customer relations and community outreach efforts. The response to the perceived problem of trust and lack of transparency is found in a project titled the "Tribal Matrix" e-government solution. The Tribal Matrix solution emerged after a series of consultations between the administrator of BPA, its vice president for political strategy and public affairs,, senior managers at the transmission services tribal affairs office, its IT department, and its accounts office. The BPA leadership team assumed that its middle level staff was in consultation with Indian tribal leaders. The problem was that no one above the middle level took responsibility for consultations with the key stakeholders, the Indian tribal consumers (BPA, 2011).

There was a lack of executive and staff support for the project. Part of the problem is that the administrators were not familiar with Indian issues and did not go the extra mile to research them. Internal organizational problems were also at play. BPA did not have a proper strategy to work with all the federally recognized tribes in its service territory. In 2002, for example, BPA's agency for tribal affairs was split between business lines, transmission, power, environment and corporate units. Each unit had its own staff, following a federal energy regulation stating that power and transmission operators could not share information that would be injurious to fair competition in the market for electricity. Additionally, tribal leadership was not properly briefed on the details of the project and did not have enough time to internalize BPA's vision as it concerns Indian affairs (BPA, 2011).

Overall, the executive failed to provide enough formal backing, energy, and sponsorship to the project. The lack of support trickled down to the lower levels. Since the project involves developing a simple interactive tool to link customers to BPA's management and staff, much of the work was done in-house using IT staff resources. Most observers noted that the IT staff lacked the necessary skills to manage the project. The technology applied involved providing simple links to search functions, spreadsheets for data entry, opinion boxes, and other interactive applications. The projects failed to work as the IT staff, which had recently been downsized, did not update or make meaningful additions to the website. There was no meaningful maintenance either, leading to files being corrupted and unusable. Tribal Matrix failed to develop a robust database for Indian community affairs that was relevant to understanding BPA's role and activities in the region. Tribal Matrix, as an e-government solution, failed due to lack of commitment from the organization's stakeholders. The goal had been to make all activities in the BPA territory more transparent to the community. This failed to happen, and no one used the tool because it was unusable (BPA, 2011).

A few additional well-documented examples will help illustrate the issue in a brief discussion of a project that failed due to politics, poor communications, lack of organizational maturity, and an inattentive management. Minnesota's Department of Human Services' (MHD) HealthMatch project, which started in 2002, included "three main components: a health care system eligibility rules engine, employee workflow, and a client portal for state residents to initiate cases into the system" (Krigsman, 2011). HealthMatch had an initial budget of \$13 million and was expected to end in 2004. In the end, it cost the government a total of over \$41 million. In addition, \$7.25 million in unsettled lawsuit bills was paid to Affiliated Computer Services (ACS), the software developer hired to implement the project (Krigsman, 2011). From the start, the project faced many problems. There were programming errors stemming from contract performance, which led to blame being shifted to the project's outsourcing to India. There were also problems with income determination errors, MDHS's income estimates not matching actual income, misreported insurance information, and oversight weaknesses (Krigsman, 2011). A Minnesota Legislative Audit Commission report found that the project failed for several reasons, including ACS's technology, management, staffing, and business requirements.

One of the causal factors was that MDHS received free, perpetual license to use the ACS @Vantage Solutions program. According to an ACS @Vantage brochure from before the project fell apart, ACS "is the leading framework for building enterprise MDHS eligibility and case management systems." Although the company customized software to different MDHS needs, the audit disagreed that technology met the client needs and instead contended that the vendor failed to use @Vantage features appropriately (ACS, 2008; Krigsman, 2011). In sum, the failure of HealthMatch after ten years is attributed to poor oversight from the MDHS. The lesson of this brief sketch is that administration matters. With better management, it would have been possible to monitor and correct the inconsistent and poorly tested vendor technologies. Almost all project failures can be understood best by employing different diagnostic approaches. If we look at previous studies, we can arrive at some generalizations.

Studies from scholars and reviews from audits conducted by the OMB showed that IT project failure in the public sector is a source of real concern, mainly because the projects are expensive and high risk (Bartis & Mitev, 2008; Brown, 2000; Fortune & Peters, 2005; Heeks, 2003a; Heeks, 2006). The failure rate of e-government projects in government is estimated to fall between 60 to 80 percent (Heeks, 2006, p. 3). This problem also exists in the private sector where nearly half (43.3 percent) of the respondents in a survey stated that their organizations "killed" an IT-related project before it was fully implemented. Perhaps one of the best academic presentations on researching and understanding this topic is Stanforth's (2010) *iGovernment Working Paper*. She articulated the most current diagnostic approaches to understanding IT project failures.

Stanforth (2010) noted that to "learn lessons from failure require an understanding of both the process of project evaluation and the theoretical viewpoints of those making the judgments" (p. 2). For analytical purposes, she identified three types of diagnostic approaches to understanding IT project failures. These are, in no particular order, the systemic, factor, and interpretive approaches. While all the frameworks have limitations, it is instructive to note that factoral analyses are most popular. Factor analyses have roots in the project management school and focus on recognizing the critical factors responsible for failure. These can range from issues such as the existence of a hostile organizational culture to poor reporting structures to political pressures. Heeks' well-known works capture the key aspects of these factors (2003a; 2003b; 2006).

Heeks' major work in this area focuses on seven dimensions upon which IT project designs are measured against the existing realties. The dimensions are captured in the acronym ITPOSMO, summarized and reinterpreted in an abridged version as follows.

Systems failures occur from a complex interaction of human and technological factors set in a social situation, rather than as the result of the failure of one particular component. The Heeks approach draws much inspiration from works done in the area of disasters and major catastrophes. For example, the September 2001 terrorist attacks on New York City represent a system failure of massive proportions. The different intelligence units constituting the system were unable to work together to prevent the attacks, prompting government reorganization in 2002 (Kettl, 2007). Systemic failure occurs when multiple interacting causal factors are in play. A systems approach adjudges a project to have succeeded if the system achieves what was intended. In addition, the project should be completed at the time and cost that were planned. Finally, the project team and end users should be pleased and "continue to be satisfied afterwards" (Fortune & Peters, 2005).

Interactive approaches derive their theses from the social sciences and focus on describing the normative connections between the specifics of system design and the organizational settings of ICT projects. Thus,

Box 9.1. *Heeks' ITPOSMO Approach.*

Key attribute	Explanation
Information	The formal and informal information held within a system or organization
Technology	Digital ICTs, paper records, and analogue telephones
Processes level	The activities undertaken by stakeholders for whom the e-government system operates, i.e. processes to achieve G2C, G2B, G2G
Objectives and values	Often the most important dimension because the objectives and values establish what stakeholders feel are the right and wrong ways to do things
Staffing and skills	People involved with the e-government system, and the competencies, knowledge, and skills of staff and other users
Management systems and structures	The enabling management systems that organize operation and use of the e-government system and the way in which stakeholder organizations are structured

Source. Heeks, 2006, pp. 5–6.

failure can be attributed to the interaction between officials within an organization resisting a particular ICT and the specific system design. In other words, there is no fit between user needs and system design. To reverse the situation, the system needs to be constructed by individuals within the organization according to their own worldviews. It should be pointed out that the approaches briefly outlined here inform much of our understanding of failures in the ICT world. The material covered here is not exhaustive and barely serves to introduce students of public administration to this very important area of e-government. Students should note that all the approaches have limitations. For example, factor-based models present project implementation as "a static process instead of a dynamic phenomenon, and [ignore] the potential for a factor to have varying levels of importance at different stages of the implementation process" (Larsen & Myers, 1999, p. 398). In addition, much historical reflection is required to understand a project's development and viability. What is important is to recognize that e-government projects are complex and no one linear approach can capture the myriad of variables that inform failure or success.

Toward the Ideal e-Government System

E-government projects have been implemented by all levels of government and therefore should be an area of interest in public administration, especially because strategic planning is also involved. In most cases, the analytical lens through which implementation is studied draws from subsets of rational approaches that look at successful applications of ICTs in terms of weighted values, often measured in terms of efficiency, costs, and citizen satisfaction.

While the discussion is basically confined to federal, state, and local jurisdictions, cross-references to comparative and international experiences also exist and are outlined in, for example, Heeks (2006). Fortunately, as we have shown, there are enough case studies within the United States to provide a coherent body of knowledge on successful institution of e-government services generally. A good starting point is to understand that e-government platforms require much planning and leadership. For example, it is widely believed that successful and mature e-government is a function of innovative and visionary leadership (Grant & Chau, 2005). Leadership is required to establish the vision and set precise goals and priorities. Ambiguous and imprecise goals are not likely to lead to successful project completion. Neither will unrealistic and overly optimistic timetables. Other issues that require organizational leadership are commitment to winning resources for the agency as well as detailed planning. Planning must be based on sufficient and accurate data. Public sector agencies should not shy away from adopting planning strategies used by private sector organizations. Whatever view one takes regarding the transfer of private sector practices to the public, the case of Imagine Pennsylvania (Imagine PA) merits our attention.

The Case of Imagine PA: A Successful Implementation of an ERP Solution for e-Government

Imagine PA was the name given to the Pennsylvania ERP system project. At the time it was implemented, it was by far the most complicated ERP system in the public sector. The project is multidimensional and incorporates political, economic, and social functions. In addition, it encompasses every major agency of the Pennsylvanian state government. Enterprise software systems are designed to manage processes in large organizations. In a government setting, ERP involves influencing and controlling structures of various government divisions.

The decision for the state of Pennsylvania to adopt ERP had several motivations. During the early 1990s, the state's economy drifted away from traditional industrial jobs. During the transition to more service sector jobs, the administration decided to embrace and manage the change by making use of emerging technological solutions. The administration sought to use ICTs to attract new business into the economy and be more responsive to public needs. By 1993 Pennsylvania's government website was up and running in an effort to reduce paper-based bureaucratic services. One of the major limitations of the government website was that the few forms available online were not integrated into the unit information management systems.

A much more integrated system would have provided a more optimal service outcome. Instead, the state's IT system, consisting of 53 different agencies, each with its own IT solutions, produced an expensive and poorly coordinated information management system. In 1992, to support the various agencies, the state required 16 different data centers, each running an autonomous IT solution (Wagner & Antonucci, 2004, p. 4). The existing system produced little by way of economies of scale and inhibited the successful sharing of important information within the government body. Citizen requests requiring multidivisional approvals were cumbersome and time consuming. Worse, government procurement processes were muddled up with challenging complexities and were costly to the taxpayer. There were fears that the system would system could fail the Y2K compliance certification test.

These issues became a subject of concern to the state administrators led by Governor Robert P. Casey that instituted a task force to make recommendations for improvements. The Improve Management Performance and Cost Control Task Force (IMPACCT) produced its report in 1993. Following recommendations from IMPACCT, the governor established a new agency, the Office of Information Technology (OIT), led by a CIO.

OIT initially adopted a "band-aid" approach and merely patched up weaknesses in the existing system. However, as the Y2K compliance deadline was approaching, the administration determined that the patching approach was ineffective. Charlie Gerhart, the newly appointed CIO, had previous experience with ERP systems adopted in the private sector. He successfully provided the leadership that steered OIT into reconfiguring the software for public sector needs. By 1999, the administration was ready to adapt an ERP system to direct e-government solutions in Pennsylvania.

Although Governor Casey initiated the process for reform, his successors, Thomas J. Ridge and Mark S. Schweikert, were equally enthusiastic about the project and gave it the political leadership necessary for success. Governor Ridge "took every opportunity to speak on ICTs" and matched his visible advocacy for the use of ICTs in government service delivery by reorganizing the OIT through the state's secretary of administration, Tom Paese (Hinnant et al., 2003, p. 12). Dawes, Burke and Dadayan (2006) shared Governor Ridge's enthusiasm by quoting the reasons for his support for ICT projects:

> When I became Governor in 1995, I immediately set about changing the business climate and building foundations to make Pennsylvania a global technology leader… Our investments in technology are part of an overall strategy to make Pennsylvania a vigorous competitor for jobs… We also strive to lead by example… New technologies are revolutionizing the way the world does business. Like the private sector, I think government must rethink traditional practices and assumptions or … risk becoming obstacles to opportunity. (p. 4)

Lieutenant Governor Schweikert, who took Ridge's place in 2001, had been one of the executive sponsors for the Imagine PA project while he was a part of the administration and continued his efforts to build on the ERP initiative.

Although the debate about the differences between the private and public sectors has occupied many an excellent mind in the field (Allison, 1994; Kearney, Hisrich, & Roche, 2009; Knott, 1993; Nowell, 2009), the new technologies have provided opportunities for scholars to further tease out the striking similarities in public and private processes of IT project management. The design of the Imagine PA project did not lose sight of the similarities in process and absorbed software that was already widely applicable in the private sector. Systems analysis and program (SAP) strategies make it possible for separately purchased and installed units to extract data from a common database. Available evidence suggest that "designers of the project foresaw a situation whereby at least 80 percent of the commonwealth's needs would be met by SAP R/3 best business practices" (Wagner & Antonucci, 2004, p. 5). The design incorporated systems that would manage a variety of services including procurement, human resources, and payroll. The leadership found that those applications were similar to those in private sector environments.

The interest in embracing practices developed primarily for private sector organizations proved enough motivation for the administration to provide full support for the project. As Bittenbender, former Pennsylvania secretary of administration, stated, "The emphasis was placed on reforming business processes in the agencies...and agency employees were repeatedly told the reason for the ERP implementation was to save money for Pennsylvania, make certain parts of employee's jobs easier and eliminate parts of people's jobs that didn't make sense" (Peterson, 2003). The leadership understood that the existing IT infrastructure was inadequate for bringing about efficient e-government services. Successful implementation is also based on building an efficient team that draws upon expertise from a broad range of state agencies. Bittenbender captured this organizational aspect in these words:

> We set up a very structured leadership team with a good executive committee, and then a steering committee made up of a cross section of deputy secretaries from various agencies so there's senior leadership buy-in on the part of the steering committee. We then asked every agency to set up an agency implementation team, which is comprised of a project manager, a communications person and training liaison, so there's functionality in every agency that's working on Imagine PA. (Peterson, 2003)

Pennsylvania's successful implementation of the ERP system became a model for other projects across the country. This complex but interesting story underscores the ways by which IT solutions developed by and for the private sector can, with relative success, be transplanted to public sector situations. The shortcomings of the previously decentralized and disjointed system proved to be dysfunctional and wasteful. Through centralization, management now had a more efficient structure for monitoring the performance of an entire network and developing a comprehensive strategy for dealing with challenges such as security, data integrity, and information sharing. The new system gives the state e-government infrastructure a common look and functionality of applications and databases. This lowers the costs associated with training and allows different government units to have greater chances to learning from each other. Besides, there are opportunities for developing common approaches to software design and fixing problems that emerge from programming errors. Programming errors are a major cause of network failure.

We have discussed aspects of the essential elements of leadership in IT project development and implementation. All accept that administrators should have an understanding of both political and managerial aspects of IT projects. They should be aware of the need for implementing units to be competent and knowledgeable about the possibilities of IT in government service delivery (Andersen et al., 1994). While these ideas have merit, the definition of success remains a contentious matter, especially if project managers merely focus on completion rates and cost savings. Administrators have to move beyond time and money and embrace some of the broader criteria. Crawford (2011), a keen scholar of the project management office (PMO), broadened the success criteria to include variables such as satisfying stakeholders and achieving measurable outcomes.

Although, as we have pointed out, much research has been done to examine why certain ICT projects have been successful and others have failed, the fact that e-government is a new endeavor precludes our full comprehension of all the issues. In addition, drawing a full list of what constitutes "projects in e-government" can be confusing and a challenge. In most cases, these projects have much to do with developing portals with interactive Internet resources for the delivery of public services. The goal remains to establish an ideal e-government system. Much work on what constitutes the ideal can be drawn from a keen reading into general administrative values. In other words, ideal e-government systems should embrace measurable values such a providing high-quality services in an effective, efficient, and equitable manner. Such values are likely to lead to user satisfaction and therefore constitute a desired e-government outcome. We shall return to this issue later in the chapter.

Much research is drawn from case studies (Andersen & Henriksen, 2005) focused on measuring the efficiency of e-government strategies adopted, and other research (Homburg & Bekkers, 2005) offered perspectives on how e-government should be conceptualized generally. Homburg and Bekkers (2005) examined external and internal perspectives of successful e-government project implementation and contended that success is often a function of the ability of project implementers to have excellent communications and consultations with citizens, business organizations, and actors in government.

The internal perspective focuses on G2G variables, which also imply employee attributes that lead to better decision making and implementation of ICT projects. The internal variables build on known aspects of how bureaucracy works and the ability of organizational leadership to provide a cooperative and efficient framework in agency work relations. The issues concern the nurturing of organizational cultures that support adoption of new ICTs. Homburg and Bekkers' (2005) argument includes the possibility that participating agencies have institutionalized a system of sharing information (virtualization) that is not only decentralized but empowers participating street-level bureaucrats. Other internal factors concern the active involvement of top management in the implementation process (Northrop, 2002; Schelin & Garson, 2004). It is possible that within this framework is an accountable and consultative arrangement directed toward the beneficiaries of e-government services, that is, the citizens.

Therefore, studying implementation must be based on some assumptions about the external factors such as political leadership and the internal organizational settings that have the charge to actualize the political vision. Political leadership must have a commitment to promoting e-government.

In addition, there are initial technical realities that any such discussion must review. The initial assumption in any project management is that some kind of needs assessment and cost and benefit analysis has been concluded and that there are sufficient investment funds for the project to continue. A well-conceived needs assessment involves thorough research and data collection, frequently involving survey techniques, to identify core problems and workable solutions. Data collection may involve other techniques such as issuing subpoenas and conducting structured and open-ended interviews. Importantly, after data are gathered, they should be subjected to rigorous theory-based interpretation. Doing so helps experts arrive at a better understanding of the collected information.

In many cases, a consultant should be hired to conduct an initial feasibility study. If this is not possible, an in-house team or individual can be called upon to perform that task. In-house personnel can have an advantage in understanding organizational culture and security clearance issues over outsourced personnel. However, management must weigh the pros and cons of seeking external consultants, who may be equally competent, cost-effective, and not beholden to the organization.

The literature is replete with examples of some of the pros and cons of outsourcing in general (Barrett & Greene, 2001; Blackstone et al., 2005; Johnson & Heilman 1987; O'Looney, 2002). Outsourcing can be advantageous when in-house expertise is lacking. In addition, ICT entrepreneurs already have pre-packaged software solutions to some of the problems that e-government is meant to resolve. These applications generally cost less when acquired from private vendors. Another advantage of outsourcing is the possibility that not all public agencies have the legal jurisdiction to provide ICT services. In addition, outsourcing serves to shield the government agency from political risk, especially if there are anticipated problems.

Management requires a needs assessment to design areas in need of attention. At this juncture, the distinction between feasibility studies and needs assessments should be reiterated. The rule of thumb is that feasibility studies do not prove that a project is right; rather they serve as estimates to reinforce the cost-benefit analysis of the project. On the other hand, needs assessments are about specifying the job that the administrators want the ICTs to perform and are also vehicles for involving stakeholders in the process of building viable e-government (Garson, 2006). Using case studies from Singapore, one of the best implementers of e-government projects, Tan, Pan, and Lim (2005) observed that it is useful to adopt a stakeholder perspective in implementing projects. This entails being able to identify the stakeholders, recognizing their interests, mapping out proactive strategies for collaboration, and aligning stakeholder interests to those of the administrators.

Not to sound redundant, ICT projects are generally costly endeavors. Gubbins (2004) estimated that over $3 trillion was spent on government ICTs during the first decade of the 21st century. It is, therefore, the role of administrators to ensure that once funds are appropriated a system is established to implement the project in a cost-effective and accountable manner. The initial infrastructural outlay can be challenging and often requires partnership between private investors and government. Partnerships are about sharing risks and responsibilities between the private and public sectors. In large municipalities, it is almost essential that huge projects, such as provision of ICT infrastructures, require partnerships between the different sectors. This exchange of ideas and other resources can also be channeled toward management and organization of e-government projects. In many cases, models developed in the private sector can provide templates for adoption into public sector environments. There is near consensus that the private sector is ahead of most government agencies in matters of technical skill and design and marketing of services. Public administrators and managers often rely on these templates or best practices mainly associated with organizations (including those from the nonprofit community) that have been recognized to be leaders in implementing ICT projects.

The OMB and other government agencies are not oblivious to organizational attempts at finding and employing the best practices, standards, and strategies possible. In collaboration with Congress and state governments, the OMB has continued to identify a number of well-documented best practices. In a policy research project conducted under contract by the University of Texas at Austin's Lyndon B. Johnson School of Public Affairs in 2005–2006, six best practices in e-government were identified. These practices, mainly carried out in state governments, identify some of the best practices in e-government and are shown in a summarized form in box 9.2.

Best practices involve placing the citizen at the center of e-government projects (Daniels, 2001). Much of the advocacy of collaborative practice is based on ideas from the new public management school that assume government agencies must adapt to the changing notion of citizenship and visualize the citizen as a customer. Where possible, government should engage the business world and find means of delivering services in the most cost-efficient way. Much horizontal collaboration within and across government also exists in successful cases of implementing e-government. There is sufficient evidence to suggest that a project will likely be successful if certain critical political and management factors are considered. The main success factors are:

- Internal political factors and the dominant role of politics: the drive from key government officials to institute e-government. They should identify with organizational goals, especially achieving efficiencies. The dominant role of politics, especially the initiatives and will of

Box 9.2. *e-Government Best Practices.*

Strategies are essential to e-government formulation because they provide objectives for state agencies and governments. The report identifies and analyzes numerous types of strategies.

Outsourcing is a controversial issue in many states, with a spectrum of policies represented across the country, ranging from prohibiting outsourcing to near total adoption of outsourcing.

Funding is an important issue because IT projects are costly and success is uncertain. Legislatures must choose between programs and, in many cases, e-government competes with other priorities.

State politics and culture can impede or support e-government development. While IT can alter employee and agency functions, such enhancements do not typically cause agencies to be eliminated.

Strong leadership can support e-government programs and drive IT improvements by encouraging and promoting new projects.

The degree of centralization or decentralization is a key component in e-government management because it affects the level of interaction between agencies. Web portal centralization is a common trend among many states, and it is often separate from agency

organization and decision making. E-government performance measures are essential in evaluating the success of programs, identifying challenges, and addressing specific formulation and implementation challenges.

Source. Seifert and McLoughlin, 2007.

political leaders, must continuously pay attention to e-government issues and adequately market e-government services to the general public and businesses.

- Competent officials: individuals knowledgeable about e-government and its enabling legal frameworks, such as the FOIA. Government ICT officials should be competent at design of e-government projects. They should have sound budgeting skills and innovative ways of handling finances.
- Vision and strategy: the overall vision and master plan for e-government, including using ICTs as a means to an end. Providing vision cannot go far if there is no effort to inculcate trust among the stakeholders.

- Effective project management includes clear definition of responsibilities, good planning and risk management, monitoring of project progress and the ability to establish good government-supplier relations. This includes effective coordination strategies, especially the harmonization of networks and services using available guidelines.
- Strong change management and organizational culture, especially the existence of project champions and stakeholder involvement. Changing organizational culture entails the empowerment of public officials motivated to fulfill goals established in their performance contracts.

Numerous case studies show that the most effective implementation strategies require and involve political and managerial leadership. Implementation successes are largely associated with “push” from an e-government advocate. The presence of a political sponsor to endorse and champion the cause for e-governance helps the implementation process (Fletcher et al., 1992). A few examples can help illustrate this point. The successful launch of the District of Columbia’s Online Business Resource Center was partly attributed to Mayor Anthony A. Williams’s involvement in the project. The mayor had identified e-government as key to turning around the economic condition of Washington D.C. His administration collaborated with the district’s businesses to launch the online resources that now provide a one-stop shop for business networks and resources (www.brc.dc.gov) (Williams, 2005). Similar examples of support from political leaders have been well-documented in New York City, where mayors Rudolph W. Giuliani and Michael R. Bloomberg have been leading supporters of partnerships between ICT companies and government. Successful ICT projects have resulted in the majority of New York City public schools having Internet access and the widespread use of web phones for city residents to access public officials. Through the website NYC.gov members of the public can access statistics on crime control and encourage other aspects of transparency in government. E-government has cut down the cost of doing business in several ways, including allowing small businesses to apply for permits online through a single portal rather than filling out triplicate forms (Giuliani, 2005).

There are similar stories at the state level. Mike Huckabee, as governor of Arkansas, led a public-private partnership to launch a successful e-government project in his state. The project "put together one of the most successful systems of its kind in the country." (Huckabee, 2005, p. 157). The state's Department of Finance and Administration harnessed the ICT resources of several private-sector interests to construct the state's one-stop portal, which made it easier for citizens to download important government documents, renew driver's licenses, and obtain other services. Governor Jeb Bush of Florida supported the development of e-government infrastructures, framing the changes in the context of providing a "smaller and more efficient government" (Bush, 2005, p. 113). He also placed a great deal of emphasis on cybersecurity, citing the need for leadership to protect the state's technology assets and ICT systems (Bush, 2005).

It appears that astute political and executive leadership is inexorably linked to smooth implementation of e-government projects. Not only does the leadership provide the vision and guidance but he or she sets expectations for skilled administrators to interpret and actualize the vision.

EVALUATION OF GOVERNMENT WEBSITES

Evaluation is required at the end of most ICT projects. It is as important as planning and implementation. It must be a continuous endeavor, an essential part of administration in the new information age. If we confine ourselves to evaluation of the government websites that are the major manifestations of e-government projects, we recognize that evaluation serves to reduce errors made in project design and implementation. Evaluation improves the information basis for stakeholder participation in e-governance. Evaluation in the e-government arena is not about economic concepts such as return on investment but rather mostly intangible governance variables including citizen participation and civic duty.

Public involvement is often increased by giving citizens access to more information online and by encouraging participation in live Internet meetings. Government websites are expected to have features that include e-mail and phone contact information and directories for key decision makers; contacts for specific departments; linkages to virtual conferencing sites, and listings of future public meetings (meeting calendars and open house schedules). In several cities, government websites provide e-government services such as online payment of bills and permits and have built links through which citizens and members of the public can access city maps, city services, departmental directories, neighborhood activities, and streaming videos on various issues. Citizens in many parts of the United States and other developed countries can watch city council and board meetings in archived videos and have greater opportunities for both accessing and assessing their leadership.

In a general sense, executives need a feedback process, and evaluation is one way to promote bureaucratic accountability and public satisfaction. Evaluation of ICT projects can be done by contractors or simply be an in-house affair, or both administrators and contractors can be involved at different levels. Whatever the case, evaluation is always done over a specified timeframe and must be designed to measure the project's success or failure against agreed-upon objectives. In all cases, the objectives must be identified before any meaningful evaluation occurs. Objectives must ordinarily be observable and measurable. Therefore, if an e-government project involves constructing a web portal aimed at passing information to a client group, recipients of passport application forms for instance, then the website must have features that allow individuals to download and send these forms. The number of people successfully being processed can be measured to determine the success of outreach efforts. But the evaluator must first determine what the objective to "provide forms" to passport applicants means. In this case, it is relatively easy to design an evaluation. One would most likely measure the frequencies at which the forms are being accessed, the quality of the content on the forms, and especially the ability to serve persons with disabilities and the provision of contacts for follow-up processes.

To illustrate, let us take the example of a hypothetical city government website. We recognize that there are a number of approaches and methods for evaluating a city website. The most frequently stated criteria are drawn from the OMB's Interagency Committee but have been revised here to suit the contrasting objectives of different government agencies. The main criteria are shown in box 9.3. Low-literate or illiterate Americans, whose numbers are in the tens of millions, "continue to struggle with websites that don't address their needs. These are used as guidelines to determine whether or not a specific website is meeting the general standard or benchmark (OMB, 2004).

While these specifications are drawn in relation to city government, the principles are applicable to most other government units. However, we must clarify a few issues with regard to the federal government. For instance, OMB requires that all websites be in compliance with a wide range of legal requirements including the E-government Act of 2002, which has a schedule of acceptable content. Beyond content, there are

Box 9.3. *OMB Evaluation Criteria as Applicable to a City's Website.*

Evaluation Markers	Measurables
Identifiability	The city's website must use government domains, show city sponsorship, and make it clear when citizens are linking to other sites from the city site.
Customer Orientation	The city's website content must be organized to make sense to the public and not just city employees; citizens' satisfaction and usability of the city website must be measured.
Accessibility:	The city's website should use plain and simple language and have consistent navigation and a search engine; document access must be in widely used file formats.
Timeliness	The city's website should be current and should establish a schedule for posting content.
Standardization	The city's website should establish a single point of management to approve common content and links and to coordinate department portals.

Source. Office of Management and Budget, 2004.

concerns for a design that is "senior friendly." The National Institute of Aging (NIA) has in the past made recommendations for agencies developing websites that are usable for older adults. Other interests, including the National Library of Medicine (NLM), have formulated different guidelines. The NIA and NLM collaborated to publish *Making Your website Senior Friendly: A Checklist* (NIA, 2002), which consisted of twenty-five empirically based guidelines for these websites. These evaluation criteria were meant for users aged 60 and above (NIA, 2002). Studies show that the majority of websites comply with the NIA guidelines related to basic navigation and content but not on matters of text size or site map availability (Hart & Chaparro, 2004). Table 9.1 shows guideline adherence rates and the criteria for evaluating websites for elderly users.

Hart and Chaparro's (2004) study reported that designers should recognize that the elderly are a growing segment of consumers of e-government services and should work to address the needs of this special group. Already, software and hardware manufacturers have responded by developing systems that recognize the special attributes of older users.

Much federal law regarding content arises from the need to safeguard against communication that is contrary to constitutional guarantees. For example, content must adhere to rights of privacy and conform to standards of records management as is established in OMB manuals. The one major criterion that is applicable to federal websites and not to local government and city websites is the requirement that websites be integrated or linked to the federal portal FirstGov.gov to avoid wasteful duplication of effort. While integration can be difficult to attain in instances where there are turf wars and budgetary limitations, the chances of a successful outcome can be enhanced wherever there is solid leadership and an ICT champion. Leadership is committed to integration of services and sharing of data among the different departments and related agencies. The agreed upon objective is to establish how well the site meets the goals of the government as prescribed by the city's mission statement, as well as to meet the needs of the public

TABLE 9.1. *Guideline Adherence (Percentage of Sites Adhering to Guideline).*

Guideline Description	%
Phrasing: uses the active voice	100.0
Scrolling: avoids automatically scrolling text and provides scrolling icon	100.0
Mouse: uses single clicks to access information	100.0
Lettering: uses upper and lower case for body text and reserves all capitals for headlines	97.2
Justification: uses left justified text	97.2
Style: uses positive phrasing and presents information in clear manner without need for inferences	97.2
Menus: uses pull down and cascading menus sparingly	97.2
Simplicity: uses simple language for text; glossary provided for technical terms	91.7
Typeface: uses san serif typeface that is not condensed	91.4
Color: avoids using yellow, blue, and green in proximity	90.6
Backgrounds: uses light text on dark backgrounds or vice versa; avoids patterns	88.9
Consistent Layout: uses standard page design and navigation is same on each page	77.8
Organization: uses a standard format; lengthy documents broken into short sections	75.0
Navigation: uses explicit step-by-step navigation procedures; simple and straightforward	72.2
Help & Information: offers a tutorial on website or offers contact information	78.1
Icons & Buttons: uses large buttons; text is incorporated with icon when possible	69.4
Text Alternatives: provides text alternatives for all other media types	67.6
Illustrations & Photos: uses text-relevant images only	63.9
Type Weight: uses medium or bold face type	50.0
Type Size: uses 12 or 14 point for body text	44.4
Site Maps: uses a site map to show how site is organized	38.9
Hyperlinks: uses icons with text as hyperlinks	25.0
Animation, Video & Audio: uses short segments to reduce download time	9.5
Back/Forward Navigation: uses buttons such a “previous” and “next” for reviewing text	5.8
Physical Spacing: uses double spacing in body text	2.8

Source. Hart & Chaparro, 2004.

and general citizenry. The assumption is that most public organization websites are designed to provide specific non-classified information to the public. Such information is not limited to information on taxes, council deliberations, policies, rules and regulations, and other public announcements. Citizens expect that when they click on their government's websites, they will find up-to-date information. Conversely, citizens do not want to click on a government website and find information that is outdated or that compromises their privacy. For example, citizens do not want to find their social security numbers and other demographic information included in a municipal website on residential addresses. Citizens expect the government to be transparent and to provide a forum through which they may be involved in governance on matters affecting their communities.

In addition, the information must be provided in a platform that is secure. Users expect government domains to be secure from malicious software and hackers—a measurable objective. There is always the risk that a website can carry malicious software such as Trojan horses and viruses that can damage the client's CPU, but this risk should be limited as much as possible. There are instances where users of e-government services can be intentionally or unintentionally lured by rogue elements in the cyberenvironment for wrong motives. The risks are numerous. Imagine a client completing an income tax return online and then losing his or her data to an unauthorized third party. Imagine also the detrimental loss resulting from a client disclosing debit card numbers to unauthorized persons. Poor security measures can cause significant distress and inconvenience to users and must be a source for concern. There is also the possibility that clients may receive classified and unauthorized materials. This means that evaluation criteria should incorporate degrees of information and network security as well as risk preparedness. It means that administrators should periodically institute security awareness training for project implementers.

These expectations inform the manner by which governments establish measurable objectives for determining success or failure of e-government projects. Further, the government must have a feedback

Box 9.4. *Collection of Best Practices in E-government Worldwide.*

Institution	website	Brief Description
World Bank	http://www1.worldbank.org/publicsector/egov/	This site focuses on e-government in developing countries.
Institute for Development Policy and Management, University of Manchester, UK.	http://www.egov4dev.org/opic1cases.htm	This website posts 34 cases in the world, dividing them into outcome classification (total failure–total success), reform (e-administration, e-citizens, e-services, e-society), sector, and region (continents).
The Center for Digital Discourse and Culture, Virginia Polytechnic Institute and State University	http://www.cddc.vt.edu/digitalgov/gov-cases.html	The site provides 68 cases with links and a few lines of description on 30 countries.
Inter-American Agency for Cooperation and Development, Application of best practices for development: e-government	http://www.iacd.oas.org/template-ingles/110602_egov.pdf	This paper summarizes 29 cases in the United States, Canada, Australia, Chile, Spain, Brazil, Ireland, Mexico, and the United Kingdom
eGovernment Observatory, IDA (Interchange of Data between Administration), European Commission	http://europa.eu.	Best practices and projects from across Europe
Public Sphere Information Group, The Municipality eGovernment Assessment Project	http://www.psigroup.biz/megap/index.php	Municipal e-government best practices are presented according to four categories (information dissemination, interactive functions, e-commerce, e-democracy) and 29 subcategories.
Texas online: Best Practices in e-government	http://www.state.tx.us/	Governments in Texas
Orange County and Gartner Consulting, Best Practices in County e-government	http://www.cira.state.tx.us/Docs/docs/bestpractices.pdf	Orange County, California asked Gartner Consulting to investigate best practices in county e-government.
Eagleton Institute of Politics, Rutgers University	http://www.rci.rutgers.edu/~eagleton/e-gov/e-ideas.htm	Best practices and ideas are analyzed and divided into 15 areas: e-government administration, budgets/taxes, purchasing, education, environment, human services/health, law, tourism, consumer, data/mapping, politics, elections, legislatures, and judiciary.

mechanism through which it can ascertain whether the e-government project is working and how well it is working. In cases where access is hampered by lack of relevant usage skills, efforts should be made to reverse the situation. In other words, mechanisms should be put in place to ensure that citizens are trained on how to use the Internet resources available through the various e-government infrastructures. The recommended measures include:

- Administrative determination of costs of the project, whether or not budget savings in staff cost for maintaining the site have been realized;
- Increase in public awareness of e-services by measuring usage before and after implementation;
- Ease of accessibility surveys;
- Feedback processes including surveys measuring levels of satisfaction with services provided and involvement in governance;
- Measuring systemic concerns with security, access (broken links), relevance and accuracy of facts.

Conclusions

Governments across the nation have established well-designed websites. websites for e-government purposes cannot be built without comprehensive ICT project feasibility studies and prudent management. Studies show that ICT project failure rates are generally high and can lead to a waste of public funds. In a practical sense, two of the most noted reasons for project termination and hence failure are that the business needs have changed and that the project did not deliver on its promise. Other reasons cited include the project exceeding its initial budget request, no longer having priority, or not supporting the business strategy. These reasons have much to do with the failure to engage in strategic planning, a variable that cuts across all the sectors. It is the responsibility of public administrators and managers to lower the failure rates of ICT projects. They can do so by learning from failed experiences (Crawford, 2011; Ewusi-Mensah & Przasnyski, 1995). Without high rates of project success, there will always be a public outcry and demands for accountability.

These ICT projects are implemented, in part, because of the recognition that the citizenry and public in general have changed and turn to the Internet for information on government work. The Internet has become the primary source for content and services including payment of fees and bills at all levels of government. To meet the growing technological challenges and expectations, governments are adjusting to address the needs of the growing cybercitizenry. Evaluation procedures are important because they allow the administration to understand where problems exist and to take corrective measures. Administrative prudence demands that evaluation be continuous and that agencies establish evaluation plans in consultation with stakeholders and agencies that have institutional expertise, such as the OMB at the federal level. Agencies need to set aside resources for this process to be meaningful. Without a robust evaluation process, ICT project implementation does not amount to much.

KEY CONCEPTS

Accountability
Benchmarks
Best practices
Cost-Benefit Analysis
Evaluation of websites
Feasibility study
ICT project implementation
Ideal e-government
Innovative and visionary leadership
Needs assessment
Partnership
Planning
Process champion
Projects in e-government
Stakeholder interests
Virtualization
websites

Discussion Questions

1. Why should we study implementation of e-government projects? Why is project implementation important for public administrators?
2. What are the main management reasons why e-government projects succeed or fail?
3. Should public administrators outsource experts to conduct needs assessments before e-government projects are implemented? Why or why not?
4. Using recent news items and personal experiences, discuss some cases of successful e-government projects. Do you believe benchmarking was helpful in the cases you identified? Explain your answer.
5. Why should administrators pay attention to evaluation? Discuss the importance of evaluating e-government projects, especially government websites.

Internet Activity

Visit the *Best Practices in E-government Resource List* provided by the E-Governance Institute in box 9.2 (http://andromeda.rutgers.edu/~egovinst/website/bestpracpg.htm).

Then, using information from the resources list, outline the key features of the best e-government sites. Identify those that have received awards from different professional associations and share your list with your colleagues. How do American government websites compare to those from developing countries?

Chapter 10

Comparative e-Government

It has been said you cannot deliver modern government programs without the use of ICTs. This statement is largely true for all countries in the world. There are, however, differences in the manner by which ICTs are applied in different political and cultural settings. Most countries consider ICTs to be integral to the delivery of government information, services, and processes. This chapter focuses on the salient features and trends in the emerging e-government paradigm in global administrative systems.

We begin by noting that hundreds of studies have been written about e-governments from a comparative perspective. These studies look at different jurisdictions or provide different levels of analysis. Comparative studies are evaluative in nature and examine hindrances in implementation, connections to regional networks, and usability of e-government portals in local and state governments, sometimes across a given time frame. For example, studies indicate that different states present a wide variety of web design strategies for promoting computer-based e-governance systems. Evaluative surveys rate governments on how they perform in terms of best practices and interactive features of their web delivery (Withrow, Brinck, & Speredelozzi, 2002). Designs that are user centered are considered superior to those that are not user friendly.

Within a single country, there are also comparisons to be made. In an important comparative study on e-government in New Jersey, Holzer and Melitski (2003) observed that New Jersey is one of the "most technologically advanced states in the country." In 2000 more than 88% of its citizens had access to the Internet. In addition, close to 83% of those surveyed had contact with state government agencies over the Internet. Holzer and Melitski (2003) evaluated different cities' e-government implementation according to the following components: usability, content, services, citizen political participation, security, and privacy. Usability issues concern information dissemination, two-way communication, services, and integration dynamics. The study reports that even websites of the largest cities in New Jersey required improvements, and then provides benchmarks for measuring improvements while recommending formal strategic planning, meaning incorporating e-government planning into overall frameworks for information technologies. They identify successful examples of strategic e-government plans from Long Beach, California; Mesa, Arizona; and Fairfax, Virginia.

These studies are not peculiar to the United States but are becoming an important element of the mosaic of e-government studies. The Information Society Institute (ISI) conducted a survey to benchmark leading e-government applications in Germany, which they then compared to practices in the United States, Germany, Japan, Australia, United Kingdom, France, and Finland. Another study compared e-government practices between two regional authorities and provinces located in different countries, New Brunswick in Canada and Dubai (Choh, Song, & Kim, 2006; Ghafan, 2003; Odgerel, 2009). The latter study shed light on the applicability of the concept and practices of e-government in different cultural settings.

Other comparative studies take an intersectoral perspective to compare e-government practices within a given country's government structure. There are numerous studies that compare e-government in specific policy sectors, such as in the area of social security. Comparative studies have a wide variety of foci. For example, researchers seek to find differences and similarities in how different countries manage their social security systems through computerization and other ICTs (ZDNet UK, 2005). In another example, Dunleavy, Margetts, Bastwo, and Tinkler (2006) provided a "systematic comparison and interpretation of rich qualitative case data" for many countries, comparing their IT programs at the national level (p. 66).

Other comparative analyses also range from specific descriptions of how ICTs are used within single countries to more nuanced cross-country comparisons of performance and utilization of ICTs. Single country case studies are rich in coverage and focus on a variety of topics that include limitations to achieving a mature e-government regime. In Poland, the context of e-administration is the country's institution of a customer-based public service delivery system as well as the need to embrace new technologies. Poland, like other countries in European Union, has an ICT infrastructure that involves several ministries, with the Ministry of Science and Information Technology taking the lead role in policy guidance and formulation. The country has developed its ICT policies along the lines of eEurope and e-Polska (Lisowska & Rutkowska, 2006). Similar to other countries, Poland has witnessed extensive implementation debates in pivotal areas such as level of funding, EU involvement, appropriate legislation, and supply and demand issues of ICTs.

In China, most accounts observe that the country is unique in that there are macro-level impediments to attaining greater success in e-governance. China is said to have a weak managerial or administrative framework characterized by several layers of government management. In addition, its managerial capacity is riddled with far too many redundant processes. There is a feeling that new technologies challenge traditional power structures in the country (Li, 2005, p. 550). Even though China has joined the World Trade Organization and is a major player in the global business community, data show that its e-commerce regime is weak and not as developed as e-commerce programs in the Western countries. Although China enacted an Electronic Signature Law in 2004 to provide guidelines for e-payments and other transactions, the regulatory framework is still weak and cannot provide required linkages to e-government platforms. However, much progress has been made in large metropolitan areas such as Shanghai, which launched a successful municipality-wide e-government program that has provided a model for other enclaves to follow (Chen et al., 2009).

We know that comparisons allow us to go beyond individual country or city analyses. There are useful comparative studies drawn from research funded by multilateral institutions. A majority of cross-national analyses are organized under the auspices of international organizations including the European Union, World Bank, the United Nations, the Commonwealth of Nations, and the OECD. In these organizations, there is considerable discussion of benchmarking and best practices.

European countries have established numerous basic supply-side public services for e-government. The European Union determines which services are best performing and gives examples of income-generating services, registration services, return services, and permits and licenses. These clusters are summarized in box 10.1.

Box 10.1. *Service Clusters.*

Income-Generating	Registration	Returns	Permits and Licenses
Income taxes	Birth & Marriage Certificates	Social security benefits	Personal documents
Corporate taxes	Registration of a new company	Public libraries	Application for building permission
Value-added taxes	Car registration	Public procurement	Enrollment in higher education
Social contribution for employees	Announcement of moving	Job search services	Environment related permits
Customs declaration	Submission of data to statistical offices	Declaration to the police	
		Health related services	

Source. Vogt, 2003.

Countries perform at varying levels in different service clusters (Gasco, 2006; Odgerel, 2006). Because of this, the EU has well-developed parameters for understanding the barriers to e-government that block or constrain progress and attainment of mature e-government systems. The EU regards the comparative approach, especially sharing of experiences and ideas, as an important aspect of improving e-governance. The European Union's portal is not just an opportunity to enhance the delivery of services but an opportunity to improve the relationship between citizens and the state (Norton, 2008). Likewise, the U.N. recognizes that ICTs are a major force for change in the global economy, human understanding, and ideas concerning governance.

E-Participation, E-Readiness, and the Digital Divide Again!

The European Union and the United Nations have commissioned snapshot surveys and detailed studies on ICT utilization in different member countries (UN, 2003; 2003a). These studies are among the growing number of surveys that develop benchmarking and comparative assessments of the willingness and ability of governments to involve the public in e-participation. The former provide an index based on human resources, technological availability, and infrastructures. The latter are based on a comprehensive assessment of e-participation that examines the levels at which different countries have applied ICTs to increase the supply of information useful in the process of consultation and for decision making in the polity.

The United Nations 2003 survey reported that countries were at different levels of e-government readiness and had varying levels of e participation. The survey provides results of inter-regional comparisons and clearly indicates the realities of the global digital divide (UN, 2003a). The digital divide, as we previously described, is the divide between those with access to new technologies such as the Internet, telephones, and computers and those without. It is now one of the world's leading economic and civil rights issues. Overall, the number of people connected to the "information superhighway" has been soaring. Nevertheless, a digital divide still exists, and, in many cases, is actually widening over time. Low-income countries, the less educated, and the poor in rural and urban households are among the groups that lack access to information resources. There are also growing concerns over gender equity in ICT usage (Cullen, 2006). In developing areas more than in the industrialized world, gender equity has become foremost among issues with e-government implementation. Concerns with gendered differentiation of access raise the bar in any discussions on the digital divide and egalitarianism generally.

The problem is not confined to the developing world. It exists in the United States as well. The digital divide has much to do with provision of economic and political opportunities for all genders. The gap in access between women and men has widened because by all indications women are already disadvantaged through structural problems involving both culture and economics. The problem can be exacerbated in communities where women are not offered opportunities to acquire technical education and computers. The longer these inequalities persist the farther women fall behind. According to the U.N. study (2003a), "gender equity issues have risen to the front banner of the e-government implementation strategies." Therefore, any credible and enduring e-government strategy in developing countries must first address the overwhelming digital divide concerning women. Without women being able to e-participate in local governance, a large percentage of the population does not access the services e-government seeks to provide. There can be no real transparency without first closing these digital divides. Although the United Nations may have good intentions to create awareness of the problem, it does not have the resources to narrow the global digital divide. The U.N. system is a G2G system that has taken steps to bring this issue to the attention of world governments but cannot solve the problem unilaterally. In 2001, the U.N. General Assembly endorsed the idea of holding a summit on the problem of the digital divide. The summit was actualized in 2003.

The UN General Assembly 2003 issued a declaration of principles, in which delegates declared the international community's "common desire and commitment to build a people-centered, inclusive and development-oriented Information Society" and a plan of action laying out what everyone involved would accomplish before the second meeting (Hesseldahl, 2005).

The next meeting, dubbed the United Nations World Summit on the Information Society, was held in Geneva in 2005. The meeting laid out a "plan of action" that declared the goal of connecting villages, schools, universities, public libraries, health centers, and local governments to ICTs by 2015 (Hesseldahl, 2005). While these objectives are good intentions, the practicalities of the international global economy do not indicate the possibility of ending the divide.

All in all, the U.N. Global Readiness Report in 2005 (2005a) indicated that disparities between countries in information technology broadly mirror disparities in income and other socioeconomic factors. In all areas, advanced countries are ranked as better prepared for absorption of ICTs in public service delivery than the poor developing countries. The U.N. survey (2003a) goes beyond placing countries on different continuums of progress in ICT utilization. It also discusses the challenges involved in building ICT infrastructures. E-government readiness strategies and programs are about having a population that is functionally literate and has access to technologies, especially the Internet, and at the very minimum, e-connectivity and the financial and human resources to manage the infrastructure. Richer countries have a greater ability to manage the ICTs at the core of e-government services. The United Kingdom, a leading global power, has an e-government unit that formulates information and technology strategy and policy and represents the largest unit in the cabinet office. The U.N. report (2003a) noted,

Considerable financial resources are required to establish, expand and constantly update e-networks. Effective integration of e-strategy delivery into development strategies requires programming and planning; research and development; and creating, monitoring and feedback systems, all of which require outlays of government expenditure. (p. 4)

E-READINESS

As the two U.N. reports showed, e-readiness is a function of a country's resources or relative wealth. With 24 percent of the world's population living below the poverty line, and only 9.5 percent of the world's population having Internet access in 2003, the gap between the advanced countries and countries of the developing world is substantial. In general, African and South Asian countries are falling behind while OECD and Southeast Asian countries have gotten ahead (OECD, 2005; U.N., 2003b; West, 2003b). The U.N. system is aware of this anomaly and provides assistance to member states to avail themselves of the opportunity to move ahead in this development stage. For example, in Sri Lanka, United Nations Educational, Scientific, and Cultural Organization (UNESCO) initiated programs that expanded e-government in rural areas. The Kothmale Community Radio Internet Project utilizes an interface with radio systems to provide e-government services closer to the rural masses. The World Health Organization provides support to hospitals to mount e-health websites for communicating health-related issues across the globe.

E-readiness reports also seek to illuminate the obvious connections between e-government and prospects for expanding global trade. More than 100 countries provide data for the annual *Global Information Technology Report*, which provides an assessment of the impact of ICTs on a nation's readiness to use e-government technologies in support of business interests. The report, published under the auspices of the World Economic Forum and Institut Européen d'Administration des Affaires (INSEAD), based in France, features a network readiness index (NRI) that ranks countries according to policies adopted in the service of economic growth and development. Recent reports show that the United States has fallen from first place to seventh place in the NRI

(Dutta & Mia, 2008). According to these rankings, the United States has fallen due to change in the following areas:

- Networks and changes in everyday life, Generation networks in telecommunications, Cities' e-government and global competition, and Filtered Internet and the moral dilemmas for multinational corporations.

Several factors account for the aforementioned criteria. There are concerns that the regulatory environment in the United States is contributing to the decline in ICT investments. In the 1990s, the United States forged ahead by investing in miles and miles of fiber-optic cables, providing fast Internet access, but usage by ICT stakeholders has not grown to the extent it has in other industrialized countries such as Denmark, the emerging new leader in ICT readiness. Several poor African countries are currently investing huge percentages of their GDP in ICT infrastructures, thereby changing the nature of global e-readiness forever.

The World Bank and other Multilateral International Agencies

The World Bank has initiated several programs within its poverty reduction strategies to promote e-government strategies. These programs are linked to several development efforts, especially those in the realm of governance and promotion of transparency. Though public figures have touted e-governance to be an important force in enhancing accountability, empirical data provide less than conclusive evidence. Wong and Welch (2004) found that in some cases accountability rose but in others web-based services merely reinforced existing practices. In their study, accountability gaps between various bureaucracies remained intact. Countries considered prone to endemic corruption by the World Bank and Transparency International did not necessarily improve on their corruption index if they incorporated ICTs in service delivery. International agencies such as the

World Bank have consistently identified accountability and transparency as key points of entry into correcting bureaupathologies at the core of international public administration.

Among other entry points posited by the World Bank are improved public finances, greater private sector development and competitiveness, and improved service delivery. The World Bank considers the role of e-government to be an integral part of a country's overall development agenda. World Bank country reports indicate a desire on the part of most poor nations to acquire information and communication technologies. Most countries have established units through ministries of science and technology and national knowledge commissions to manage changes. Increasingly often, the World Bank has organized forums through which countries exchange ideas on e-transformations and best practices and lessons. E-government is already big business for the World Bank, which provides financial and technical support for ICT development in countries across the world. The World Bank has an established track record in managing macro and micro projects in many developing areas. It has a reservoir of data on development and growth of vital sectors in these countries. Certainly, it has connections to the business sector and has an agenda to promote the development of private sector activities in developing countries. These and other factors make it an important player in promoting global e-government.

According to World Bank initiatives, successful e-government strategies require technological innovations, transparent client-oriented governments, and efficient and effective empowerment. The World Bank has advocated integrative systems of information management and considers the area of ICTs to be a cutting edge frontier in the development agenda. A summary of the U.N. 2003 survey (2003a) follows:

- Governments worldwide embraced ICTs; North America and Europe lead in ICT usage; South and Central America have the highest aggregate state of e-government readiness, followed by South and Eastern Asia, Western Asia, the Caribbean, Oceania, South Central Asia, and last, Africa.

- The leading countries are the United States, Sweden, Australia, Denmark, the United Kingdom, Canada, and Norway; other important leaders are Singapore, South Korea, Estonia, and Chile.
- English is the dominant e-government language (125 out of 173 countries surveyed used English on their websites); 88 percent of South American and Caribbean countries used either Spanish or French.
- There is no one model of e-government development and no evolutionary stages in e-government.
- National one-stop portals are increasing in deployment and functionality.

The U.N. survey results follow in box 10.2.

Vogt (2003) examined specifically how European e-government initiatives compared with each other. Vogt reported that EU member states, EU candidate countries, and European Free Trade Association countries have periodically examined how each performs in terms of ICT usage.

Box 10.2. *2004 U.N. Survey Results.*

E-government Readiness Index Top Ten Countries		E-Participation Index Top Ten Countries	
United States	0.9132	United Kingdom	1.0000
Denmark	0.9047	United States	0.9344
United Kingdom	0.8852	Canada	0.9016
Sweden	0.8741	Singapore	0.80361
Republic of Korea	0.8575	Netherlands	0.8033
Australia	0.8377	Mexico	0.7705
Canada	0.8369	New Zealand	0.7705
Singapore	0.8340	Republic of Korea	0.7705
Finland	0.8239	Denmark	0.7377
Norway	0.8178	Australia	0.6721

Source. United Nations, 2004.

European countries have adopted a pan-European approach to managing the e-government infrastructure. This approach emerged out of the March 2000 EU meeting in Lisbon, where the European Council set an ambitious goal for Europe to become the most "competitive and dynamic knowledge based economy in the world"(Vogt, 2003). The project was sold as eEurope even though numerous country-level discussions preferred to internalize the concept as e-administration.

According to Vogt (2003), e-government includes all ICTs in the public sector. The term narrowly refers to the use of electronic means by government to deliver information and services to individuals, NGOs, and businesses. This conceptualization is not any different from the U.S. variant. There is also consensus among some European researchers and administrators that e-government is not a goal in itself.

Why Do Countries Move Toward e-Government?

The instrumental reasons for e-government include its proven ability to deliver public services more efficiently and at lower costs. The banners for these initiatives are loud and speak to the possibility of a flourishing reform movement. In the United States the drive to e-government was originally touted as a project to re-engineer government through information technologies. In Britain the phrase was to develop "Direct Government."

As Hernon (2006) contended, the central government in the United Kingdom considers e-government as a means to

> exploit information and communication technologies for the benefit of society, the economy, and public services; modernize public services; and make those services electronic and more responsive to a knowledge economy in which higher education, businesses, and other segments of the UK society are able to compete more successfully in a global electronic economy. (p. 55)

The terminology in Canada is similarly couched in reformist language as the "Blueprint for Renewing Government Services Using IT."

The Canadian model regards the e-commerce model as an example for governments to embrace. The blueprint set the goal "of making e-commerce the 'preferred way of doing government business by 1998" (Nilsen, 2006, p. 67). In Australia, three goals were identified: first, to employ ICTs in the efficient, timely, fast delivery of services electronically for the business and community in general; second, to provide opportunities for citizen interaction with government; and third, to enhance e-democracy across all government jurisdictions (Burgess & Houghton, 2006). In brief, governments all over the world no longer consider e-government a fad or fashion. It is not an option but rather has become a necessity.

Moreover, some evidence suggests e-government can mean higher levels of productivity. E-government creates greater transparency in government, and through links to frequently asked questions, citizens may be directed to important public services. New Zealand, Japan, and Taiwan offer excellent examples of such usage. E-government also creates opportunities for citizens to follow what their governments are doing. Another important reason for e-government, mostly reported by developing areas such as Nigeria and Sri Lanka, is that embracing e-governments serves a symbolic purpose. It is a status symbol for modernization of public service delivery systems. In middle-range transitioning countries such as Poland, e-administration is embraced for purposes of building an information society (Lisowska & Rutkowska, 2006). This is not to say these countries ignore the reform nature of e-governance. Governments consider ICTs as an aspect of reform in overall public administration systems that provide important services such as social insurance, pension reform, and health insurance, all of which are heavy consumers of digital data storage and retrieval systems.

There is also general consensus that adopting e-administration is a means to achieving a paperless office. However, we must recognize that implementation strategies, plans, and focus vary from country to country (Weerakkody, Jones, & Olsen, 2007). Countries focus on different components of e-government. There are those that are more interested in modernization, automation, and rationalization of processes, whereas others pay more attention to issues of access.

In India's state of Tamil Nadu, the government purposefully frames its e-administration strategy as a means of realizing its goal of a paperless administration or, at the minimum, *less paper* administrative systems. The system in Tamil Nadu involves installation of software that tracks workflow in government offices. The status of every file can now be known at the click of a mouse. The state defined e-administration as a web-enabled, browser independent, paperless office tool. Much like other government entities, e-administration involves creating new institutions, responsibilities, relations, and roles for public servants. E-administration is considered meritorious because it enhances efficiency in workflow between and among sections of the workforce. Indian authorities also regard e-administration as a means toward greater transparency in provision of public services.

While it is not possible to have a full discussion of all countries embracing e-government, some common threads are clearly visible. There are indicators that we can employ when we compare and contrast the context of each country's e-government strategy. A simplistic approach is to see the differences and similarities in terms of the varying political and economic conditions in each country under consideration. The descriptive key indicators for countrywide comparisons are summarized in box 10.3.

However, the comparison of context goes beyond the specific indicators, because countries are somewhat interconnected. In Friedman's *The World Is Flat* (2005), he argued that the flattening of the world has already taken place. The dawn of the 21st century witnessed the proliferation of events that support the thesis of globalization. So strong are the forces of globalization that countries, corporations, communities, societies, governments, and individuals must adapt. Friedman suggested the world is flat, or connected, in part, because of the weakening of trade and political barriers and the rapid growth and diffusion of ICTs. Through the digital revolution, people instantaneously do business or socialize with others thousands of miles away.

Friedman asserted that contemporary "Globalization 3.0" was driven by individuals and not by multinational corporations, as were past phases

Box 10.3. *Context of Country Comparisons Indicators.*

Categories	Indicators
Economic	Investment in ICTs as % of GDP % of business using e-commerce Availability of Digital Subscriber Lines/Wireless LAN Availability of new technologies (Web 2.0 apps)
Political	Leadership and bureaucratic accountability Levels of budgetary provisions Legislative support and constrained regulatory framework Ability of e-government lead organization to drive change
Societal	Citizen access to broadband (subscriptions) Households with internet access or hand-held internet capable devices Trust and openness in society and level of e-democracy Training of tele-workers and ICT specialists

of globalization. Individuals can now start businesses online from any part of the world. Much high-end research and design work now originates from far off places such as in India and China. Friedman, like other future- and present-minded observers, suggests that the world has gotten too small too fast, which has forced governments to rethink their governance structures.

The downside is that the emerging globalization has its ugly side in the form of Al-Qaeda and other non-state actors capable of destabilizing countries. And, there is the unparalleled proliferation of cybercrime, which transcends the purview of a single state (Glenny, 2008). Glenny's (2008) work is perhaps the dark side of Friedman's more optimistic view of the world. Glenny (2008) showed that the connected globe is more dangerous than is generally acknowledged. Cybercrimes including identity theft, hacking, and phishing cost over $52.6 billion in 2005 alone. Some countries such as Brazil now have Internet police to combat the growing problem.

Glenny (2008) reported that trickle-down criminal activity, much of which has involved the Internet, amounts to 20 percent of global GDP. The underworld, he argued, is also connected to the global village.

The Internet in particular has opened the gates for criminal networks that deal in narcotic drugs, sex, contraband goods, nuclear materials, and so on. Glenny (2008) traced part of the growth of organized crime to the fall of the communist states in Eastern Europe and demand for easy money in the west.

Arguably, e-government opens up more opportunities for global interconnectedness because services can be accessed 24 hours seven days a week from any part of the world. An important observation in the U.N. report (2003b) is that globalism and globalization have made it possible for countries to network and seek new ways of providing government services. This is hardly surprising, and is evident in comparative public administration literature (Jreisat, 2002).

A careful examination of academic literature and work by consultants reveals a rich array of work in this area of comparative studies. The point about these comparative studies is that they provide important perspectives for the emerging subfield of comparative e-government. To explain further, there is the possibility of teasing out the pros and cons of these complex studies. We chart out at least five merits and two distinct areas that one might consider demerits of these comparative approaches.

MERITS OF COMPARATIVE e-GOVERNMENT

First, comparative e-government has brought forth an important vocabulary that enriches public administration's practice. Public administration scholars have added to their vocabulary new neologisms such as e-notify, e-democracy, online democracy, cyberdemocracy, e-rulemaking, e-manager, portals, e-procurement, e-administration, and websites. One might add that without e-government, levels of computer literacy might be lower than they are at present. These technologies inform daily discourses on how governance is conducted all over the world.

Second, comparative e-government has developed a framework for studying e-government models. The typical model includes establishment of core organizations and networks through which ICTs are integrated or from which they radiate. For example, the CIO Council is an important locus for ICT discourses in the United States. Comparative e-government vividly describes practices of transparency and accountability in governments. It establishes patterns for studying various aspects of policy implementation within an increasingly networked world. From a technical standpoint, comparisons enable CIOs and other executives within states to determine levels of cooperation, especially where there is need for data collaborations. It is widely expected that many in the enterprise architecture community regard the creation of one-stop portals or data catalogues as vital to enhancing the level of citizen engagement and governance. Without comparative evaluation it is not possible to determine how different state and local governments are moving toward transparency and the use of metadata models, which are proving to be helpful in federal governance.

Third, comparative e-government provides comparative public administration with discussions about levels and phases of e-government that build on the extensive literature generated by development studies. The proliferation of e-government adds to our understanding of developments in the new ICT environment, especially interconnectivity and wired or wireless networks. The existence of the digital divide is exacerbated by the awareness of e-government processes across different regions. This fresh approach enriches not only the literature on organizational development, but that on societal growth and quality of life indices as well.

Fourth, comparative e-government has made significant contributions to our understanding of globalism, comparative government, and the diminishing role of states. E-government has made scholars pose more forcefully the question: what services should the government be making more public? For example, access to blog activity might be confined or structured by governments wishing to suppress public speech. The ability of the Internet to break boundaries reinforces its importance as a tool for public engagement. This also applies to its roles in rule making delivery of public information, and the implementation of education and training programs. These applications afford scholars opportunities to study different levels of political development.

Fifth, comparative e-government has the potential to rejuvenate the field of comparative public administration. Cross-national studies benefit the discipline in a variety of ways, including establishing principles for best practices and strategies in e-government. Formulating general principles concerning application of ICTs in government sectors is a difficult enterprise, but this is now made possible through the global outreach of computer-based communication systems such as the Internet. This is regardless of the possibility of distortion brought about by the digital divide. As Heady (2001) observed, "The increasing interdependence of nations and regions of the world makes comprehension of the conduct of administration of much more importance than in the past" (p. 7).

Disadvantages of Comparative Approaches to e-Government

It is difficult to compare countries with drastically different levels of technology and e-government readiness. Countries have different resource levels and political and cultural norms. The digital divide exists at varying levels worldwide, making it difficult to establish a true benchmark. The most widely cited comparisons were done by a private firm, Accenture, which analyzed several countries and ranked them in four groups depending on the maturity of their e-government systems (Accenture, 2001). The broad categories are (1) innovative leaders, (2) visionary followers, (3) steady achievers, and (4) platform builders. The 2001 Accenture study ranks Canada as the global leader in e-government, with the highest efficiency levels, measured in terms of rate and ease of access and unit cost of service delivered online, at 72%. Canada, Singapore, and the United States are considered innovative leaders (Accenture, 2001). In the visionary followers group are countries such as Norway, Australia, Finland, the Netherlands, and the United Kingdom. The study distinguishes the two categories by the level at which the integrated delivery portals had developed across the different national agencies (Accenture, 2001).

The problem with such a comparative ranking system is that the method of ranking is not immediately verifiable. This means that this popular approach in comparative studies cannot, therefore, be the basis for universally agreed-upon benchmarking. As O'Donnell, Boyle, and Timonen (2003) pointed out with reference to their case study of Ireland, benchmarking surveys "do not delve behind the headline figures to look at the consequent degrees of impact of information and communication technologies on organizational change or development" (p. 22). Their study examined the comparative impact of and synergies between ICT development and organizational change, noting that though Ireland performs relatively well in a number of government benchmarks, the story changes when one turns attention to assessing productivity changes. Ireland was ranked second to Sweden in terms of sophistication of services online, but there are sizeable differences when it comes to comparing organizational capabilities (O'Donnell, Boyle, & Timonen, 2003). There are nuanced differences in technological capabilities for digitizing information as well as in the legal frameworks through which e-government operates. In a nutshell, benchmarking has limitations, especially when studies examine organizational changes in different countries. Where there is a marked lack of an informatics system, there is also a strong likelihood that the government does not have a robust enough legal environment for e-governance. An example of this is China (Li, 2005). This complicates the process of making comparisons. If only a few citizens can access government information, it is hardly useful to engage in comparative debates.

In addition, there is some possibility that comparisons would lead to models that may oversimplify the challenges that government units confront in developing their e-government capabilities. One could argue that comparisons across differing levels of governments in different locations do not account for disparities that may be due to other sources than government failures. These other areas may include language and cultural issues.

Other International Organizations Involved in e-Governance

The Commonwealth Center for e-Governance (CCEG) is a think tank based in London. CCEG has been at the forefront in conducting studies that compare e-governance in Canada and the United Kingdom. The center provides insight and knowledge on the changing nature of governments in ICT infrastructures. The CCEG develops best practices on how ICTs can be used to provide public services to members of the commonwealth, including most of the developing countries. Many of its study reports are posted online for worldwide circulation. CCEG distributes published documents on e-democracy, e-governance, and e-government and provides tracking services, in chart form, on the progress of countries in government online initiatives.

For its part, the OECD conducts periodic public administration analyses on management of cross-national or country data (OECD, 2006). OECD issues reports on progress made and experiences had by different member countries with public management reforms. A common theme is to determine best practices and to develop broad measures for assessing governance data. The robust data collected by OECD are incorporated into administrative practices in areas such as human resource management, regulation, and budgeting. Data cover all the key sectors, including health, education, labor, and national accounts.

The World Bank considers e-leadership to be a critical factor in achieving success in ICT-enabled reform and development. The World Bank recognized the important roles played by empowered CIOs and stated that leadership needs to be properly institutionalized according to local needs and conditions with appropriate incentives and agencies created (World Bank, 2006). Among the institutions that must be created are monitoring and evaluation entities as well as public-private partnerships.

e-Government Global Agenda

After this review, it is now possible to arrive at some thoughts on what constitutes a global e-government agenda for the international community.

If one extrapolates information from the various interests, including the World Bank and other international agencies, a possible global e-government agenda would be concerned with at least four big ideas. First is the goal of reducing the digital divide, which can be addressed through various approaches involving partnerships between some private corporations, such as Dell, Microsoft, and IBM, and developed countries, foundations, and donor agencies. For example, the One Laptop Per Child Foundation (OLPC) has helped provide inexpensive laptop computers to schools in developing countries. Formed in 2005, the not-for-profit organization provides low-cost laptops to children around the world. Its founder Nicholas P. Negroponte's philanthropic mission took root while he worked at MIT in the late 1960s. Influenced by MIT mathematician Seymour A. Papert, an expert in artificial intelligence, Negroponte envisioned the concept of cheap laptops to serve children in low-income communities. Initially, the idea failed to gain much traction and support from commercial interests. Later, the idea began to grow and attracted the interest of business giants Intel and Microsoft. As well as promising market completion, the idea of inexpensive laptops to children morphed into a cause for social inclusion and global justice. The United Nations saw this as an opportunity and joined hands with other organizations to promote the idea. As of 2011, OLPC has provided low-cost laptops to at least 2.5 million children in 40 countries.

But more needs to be done in expanding broadband technologies, especially in lowering infrastructure development costs. Already much is being achieved globally. In Africa, the expansion of broadband capabilities received a boost in 2009 when European-based companies collaborated with African partners to install fiber-optic cables through the ocean, just in time for the summer 2010 World Cup soccer bonanza held in South Africa. The East African region, in particular, benefitted from two undersea fiber-optic cables running under the Indian Ocean from the Middle East to South Africa. Seacom and the East African Marine System manage the undersea cables cooperatively. Another system, code-named ESSAY for East African Submarine System, commenced in 2010. The West African coast is covered by another undersea cable managed by South Atlantic cable that runs from Portugal through West Africa to South Africa. This broadband infrastructure, along with satellite service presented by corporations such as Sky Vision Networks, has led to increased computing power and a rapid growth of mobile telephony devices that permit Internet access to millions of people. Africa as a whole has well-developed mobile phone networks, which have led to a major shift in the region's access to ICT based applications. These permit not only social networking opportunities but are creating prospects for greater e-government services.

In terms of policy, most developing countries are reforming their policy environments to allow for greater liberalization of ICT markets. Several countries regard ICT industries as the driving force in their new economies. ICTs present an opportunity not only to engage the world but for economic development. Developing countries have embraced the World Bank's millennium development goals, which focus on reducing poverty. In response to these goals, these countries, Bangladesh and India among them, are positioning themselves as centers for business process off shoring (or outsourcing), which involves providing business services via the Internet to corporations.

Within the United States, minority communities such as the Navajo in the Southwest are regularly represented in international summits that address issues of the digital divide. The Navajo Nation's leadership has been regularly featured in the U.N. World Summit on the Information Society. At the global level, there is consensus that indigenous communities must be a part of the digital revolution. For instance, this realization informs the decision by the Navajo leadership to sign a memorandum of understanding with the ITU and UNESCO's Observatory for Cultural and Audiovisual Communication (OCCAM) that established a regional office in Window Rock, Arizona (International Indigenous Portal, 2007). Together with other initiatives, such as the Navajo Nation Department of Information Technology's plan "Internet to the Hogan: Entering the Information Age," this presents a real drive to shrink the digital divide (Pyrillis, 2007). A great boost came from President Barack Obama's administration, which has supported additional broadband mapping and upgrades in Native American country. Through the American Recovery and Reinvestment Act of 2009, the administration granted federal stimulus funds to support further broadband capabilities in the reservation.

The second item on a possible global e-government agenda is to continue cooperation in matters of ensuring Internet security and the enforcement of laws governing issues such as privacy, data mining, regulations, identity theft, patents and copyrights, and intellectual property rights. There are concerns with the enforceability of some laws across jurisdictions. An additional area of concern is e-commerce practices, especially fraudulent practices that must be managed and resolved. Governments must enforce the law and eliminate counterfeiting and copying original products with the intent to deceive, especially in the e-commerce framework. E-commerce or e-business is important because partnerships between government and the private sector are crucial in the provision of certain services.

The third area of concern is the delivery of services that must conform to agreed-upon safety standards. Policies and regulations about cyberterrorism are of concern to all countries and are an area that requires international focus and attention. Although difficult to define and often referred to as electronic terrorism or information war, cyberterrorism can, for our purpose, be operationalized as follows:

> Cyber terrorism is the convergence of terrorism and cyberspace. It is generally understood to mean unlawful attacks and threats of attack against computers, networks, and the information stored therein when done to intimidate or coerce a government or its people in furtherance of political or social objectives. Further, to qualify as cyber terrorism, an attack should result in violence against persons or property, or at least cause enough harm to generate fear. Attacks that lead to death or bodily injury, explosions, plane crashes, water contamination, or severe economic loss would be examples. Serious attacks against critical infrastructures could be acts of cyber terrorism, depending on their impact. Attacks that disrupt nonessential services or that are mainly a costly nuisance would not. (Denning, 2000)

As Denning (2000) observed, the next generation of terrorists will grow up in a digital world with ever more powerful and easy-to-use hacking tools at their disposal. According to the U.S. Commission on Critical Infrastructure Protection, possible cyberterrorist targets include the banking industry, military installations, power plants, air traffic control centers, and water systems. Combating cyberterrorism requires international cooperation and is an emerging agenda for administrative units all over the world.

No one is safe from expert hackers. Beyond the WikiLeaks international megascandal described in chapter 7 of this volume, incidents of hacking continue to be reported by media outlets across the globe. The list of political leaders whose e-mails have been hacked is growing and includes Republican vice presidential candidate for the 2008 election Sarah Palin, then governor of Alaska. Palin's Yahoo e-mail account (gov.palin@yahoo.com) was hacked in 2008. WikiLeaks published the hacked data.

Perhaps the most interesting case is the hacking of Spain's prime minister's website. In January 2010, the government in Spain acknowledged that Prime Minister José Luis Rodríguez Zapatero's official European Union website had been hacked. In a bizarre incident, Zapatero's image was replaced with the caricature of comedian Rowan Atkinson in character as Mr. Bean. Zapatero was seeking election as EU president. The *Guardian* captured the moment in these words: "Where Zapatero's warm, smiling image should have been reassuring millions of Europeans that they were in his capable hands, the hacked website featured the radiant, if dangerously incompetent, Mr. Bean. 'Hi there!' was the suitably Beanish greeting to Spain's European presidency" (Tremlett, 2010).

Mahmoud Ahmadinejad's website was also hacked in January 2010 to display a message that called on God to take the Iranian leader's life. More recently, in March 2011, Australian Prime Minister Julia Gillard's parliamentary computer was hacked. Other senior administration officials, including Foreign Minister Kevin Rudd and Defense Minster Stephen Smith, also suffered a similar fate. These individually executed hacking crimes affecting the most powerful men and women in society show how vulnerable e-government systems are and the depth to which hackers can go to discredit the potential for the new technologies.

A similar issue has arisen between countries suspecting each other of recently developing and deploying cyberwarfare capabilities. Although there is no clear definition of what cyber warfare means, the number of high-profile international incidents has increased. Among these were the blackouts in Brazil in 1998 and the Stuxnet virus that damaged Iran's nuclear power facilities. The Soviet Union's July 2008 attack on Georgia's Internet system and China's gag on Google constitute events that show the vulnerability of ICTs.

The *New York Times* reported that in the cases of countries that don't have much of an Internet infrastructure, the likelihood of a cyberattack having much of an impact is limited. While describing the events in Georgia, the *New York Times* reported that Georgia ranks 74th out of 234 nations in terms of the number of hosted Internet sites, behind Nigeria, Bangladesh, Bolivia, and El Salvador, according to Renesys, a Manchester, New Hampshire, firm that provides performance data on the state of Internet. Cyberattacks have far less impact on such a country than they might on a more Internet-dependent nation, like Israel, Estonia, or the United States, where vital services like transportation, power, and banking are tied to the Internet (Markoff, 2008).

In the case of Stuxnet, though the true source of the attack has not been fully disclosed, research shows that "it is the first-known virus specifically designed to target real-world infrastructure, such as power stations" (Fildes, 2010). The worm repeatedly targeted Iran's industrial facilities and reportedly slowed down the country's ambitions to build a nuclear bomb. There were fears from Russian agents that similar attacks "could lead to a new Chernobyl" (Fildes, 2010) type of nuclear meltdown.

Attacks on infrastructure are not imagined or confined to other cultures. In 2009, U.S. Secretary for Homeland Security Janet Napolitano admitted that the nation's power grid was vulnerable to cyberattacks. There had been media leaks that Chinese and Russian agents had breached the system (Shiels, 2009). However, the North American Electric Reliability Corporation, which oversees the system, denied significant cyberattacks had occurred. On the other hand, U.S. authorities blamed the security breach on dated software and called for a review of the systems.

A *Wall Street Journal* article dramatized the prevalence of cyberattacks by reporting that specialists at the U.S. Cyber Consequences Unit, a nonprofit research institute, said attack programs search for openings in a network, much as a thief tests locks on doors. Once inside, these programs and their human controllers can acquire the same access and powers as a systems administrator. (Gorman, 2009)

The well-researched article pointed out that though hackers attack all segments of society, individuals, government, and commerce, the problem has international dimension. Although China and Russia are considered to be the most likely candidates to spy on American ICT installations, the motivations for hacking remain unclear except for wartime tactical logistics. Government intelligence officials acknowledge, "a cyber-attack had taken out power equipment in multiple regions outside the United States and that the outage was followed with extortion demands" (Gorman, 2009). Attacks are not only limited to the power grid and could be extended to sewerage and water systems as well. A brief overview of this most interesting story is captured in Marshall Abrams and Joe Weiss's excellent technical and scientific work, as follows:

> Vitek Boden, a man in his late 40s, worked for Hunter Watertech, an Australian firm that installed SCADA (Supervisory Control And Data Acquisition) radio-controlled sewage equipment for the Maroochy Shire Council in Queensland, Australia. Boden applied for a job with the Maroochy Shire Council, apparently after he walked away from a "strained relationship" with Hunter Watertech. The Council decided not to hire him. Consequently, Boden decided to get even with both the Council and his former employer. He packed his car with stolen radio equipment attached to a (possibly stolen) computer. He drove around the area on at least 46 occasions from February 28 to April 23, 2000, issuing radio commands to the sewage equipment he (probably) helped install. Boden caused 800,000 liters of raw sewage to spill out

> into local parks, rivers and even the grounds of a Hyatt Regency hotel. (Abrams & Weiss, 2008, p. 1)

Even before the story of the nation's power grid vulnerabilities had appeared in the *Wall Street Journal* and in online media outlets, the Obama administration had already made the issue of cybersecurity an area of priority concern. While campaigning for president, Obama had likened cyberattacks to nuclear or biological threats. Speaking at the Summit on Confronting New Threats at Purdue University on July 16, 2008, candidate Obama stated, "As president, I'll make cybersecurity the top priority that it should be in the 21st century" (Moscaritolo, 2009).

Just before George W. Bush's term as president expired, the U.S. GAO had warned of an impending crisis if the DHS failed to deal with cybersecurity threats. A congressional panel issued similar warnings in December 2008 and specified that Chinese agents were hacking or stealing vast arrays of sensitive material from U.S. computer networks. At the same time, the Commission on Cybersecurity reiterated the charge that cybersecurity was a major national security issue. And it must be noted that in January 2008, new Federal Energy Regulatory Commission protection measures that "required improvements in the security of computer servers and better plans for handling attacks" were initiated (Gorman, 2009).

After he took office, President Obama ordered a cybersecurity review. In December 2009, the administration appointed Howard Schmidt as White House cybersecurity coordinator. Schmidt had previously served the George W. Bush administration, where he helped formulate the U.S. National Strategy to Secure Cyberspace. The post, dubbed "cyberczar," was a response to increased focus by the Pentagon on computer systems. Organizationally, the cybersecurity coordinator reports to the White House through the National Security Council and the national security adviser for homeland security and terrorism. President Obama, while making the organizational changes at the White House, described the task ahead as an effort to "deter, prevent, detect, and defend" against cyberattacks (Sanger & Markoff, 2009). The post had a twofold charge: to examine and manage domestic and foreign-based cybersecurity threats. The cyberczar's job description included the coordination of cybersecurity policy across the federal government and from military to civilian agencies. The Pentagon also established a "cyber command." However, the administration declined to actively endorse proposals to ban the offensive use of cyber weapons. There are ongoing discussions on this subject among world powers.

The fourth area is the incorporation of the greener ICT agenda in both e-business and e-government. This means that government CIOs will work toward using energy efficient infrastructures, including increasing use of solar-powered equipment as well as working in energy efficient buildings that embrace the concept of green government. CIOs recognize the importance of savings accrued from prudent use of energy resources in data centers. It makes sense from an investment point of view. Being sensitive to green government entails greater decentralization and usage of telecommuting. Eco-minded administrators are likely to develop systems that encourage ICT resource sharing as well as rewarding individuals and units that have the best eco-friendly practices. Governments all over the world are aware of the challenges of global warming and the need to embrace eco-friendly ICT systems. The most prosperous group of countries, the G-20, has in many agreements reinforced the move toward greener, more sustainable growth. This is an agenda that the discipline of e-government will focus attention on.

CONCLUSIONS

In recent years, e-government has spread across the world. The spread can be considered an epochal shift in the way governments deliver public services. It is part of the reform tradition of public administration. While comparative studies of these changes have proliferated, the discourse has embraced the perennial concern for reducing the global digital divide. International organizations as well as regional groups recognize this problem and seek to provide benchmarks on best practices in addition to a wealth of information on different approaches to e-government. The data generated from various reports, as well as individual country reports generated internally, are useful for understanding e-government from a comparative viewpoint. Similar to other comparative studies, much benefit can be derived from a policy point of view. Comparisons help public administrators and policymakers understand better what works and what does not work. Public administrators need to know common features of barriers to achieving egalitarianism and specific policy mechanisms to address hindrances to achieving an efficient new economy. Comparisons are also a means of sharing important skills occasioned by advances in the global information society.

Key Concepts

Accountability
Benchmarking
Comparative Administration
Cybersecurity
Cyberterrorism
Digital divide
E-administration
E-commerce
E-connectivity
eEurope
E-health
E-participation
E-readiness
European Union (EU)
Greener ICT agenda
International e-government
Metagovernance
Paperless office
Portals
Public Private Partnerships
United Nations
World Bank

Discussion Questions

1. Define comparative e-government. Identify the levels at which comparisons may be made. In general, why are comparative studies useful?
2. What are the advantages and disadvantages of making comparisons in e-government strategies across different units of government?

3. Does either the World Bank or United Nations have a comparative advantage in providing leadership in formulation of an e-government agenda? Why?
4. Why does the United States lead other nations in developing e-government strategies? Why has it declined in the e-readiness index?
5. Attempt to provide an itemized list of what qualifies to be on the global e-government agenda. Provide justifications for what is on the list. With reference to the concept of benchmarking, how would you go about developing an e-government program? What factors would you consider before launching an e-health program in a developing country?

INTERNET ACTIVITIES

1. Use search engines to examine and compare the roles of think tanks and international multilateral agencies in promoting e-government strategies. What are the common themes in their approaches to supporting e-government initiatives?
2. Use search engines to determine the latest ranking of nations in usage of e-government strategies.

Chapter 11

The Future of e-Government

At the conclusion of this book, we consider the future of e-government. We note that the emerging field of e-government has distinct features. With the growth of numerous e-government centers across the world, we now know that a coherent body of literature describing how different governments utilize ICTs for delivery of public services exists and is expanding. The introduction and first two chapters of this volume charted some of the paths and directions taken in understanding the field. To be sure, sometimes, much of this emerging field of interest relies on untested theoretical assumptions regarding technological capacities of the enabling public administrative institutions. Therefore, more frequently than not, the preferred way to comprehend the future of e-government is to look at trends that have developed since the early 1990s. This concluding chapter also considers trajectories for future growth of e-government.

As Toffler (1981) observed, three major changes took place in the 20th century. According to Toffler (1981), the most basic raw material of all, which can never be exhausted, is information. The 21st century has experienced exponential growths in information technologies. Indeed, these mark the defining moments of the information or knowledge society. Perhaps, one might add, we are already living in a new global economy heavily enabled by ICTs. Already a good number of people believe the invention of mobile telephones and other ICTs redefines human connectedness to beyond previous levels. A CNN program aired in 2005 acknowledged ICTs to be among the greatest inventions of all time.

Kurzweil (2005) explored the idea of singularity, in which human intelligence is increasingly non-biological. Emerging from the expansion in knowledge is the singularity of humans and machines, which is recognizable because we no longer have a clear distinction between actual reality and virtual reality, or between humans and machines. He builds on ideas established in futurist discourses that acknowledge the exponential growth and speed in knowledge creating and sharing afforded through new technologies. In his own previous work, Kurzweil (2000) made the case that computers could now rival human intelligence in a wide range of activities.

Perhaps he was right! For those who watch the popular TV quiz show *Jeopardy*, it became quite clear that we are living in the future. In an episode taped in January 2011 and aired early February, an IBM computer named Watson after IBM's founder Thomas J. Watson competed against Ken Jennings, who had a previous winning streak of 74 games. Also competing was another ace human player, Brad Rutter. After three days of competition and tallying, Watson emerged the winner. Computer experts saw Watson's victory as vindication of the field of artificial intelligence, a field that emerged in the 1960s with a vision to create thinking machines. A *New York Times* technology writer noted, "for IBM, the showdown was not merely a well-publicized stunt and a $1 million prize, but proof that the company has taken a big step toward a world in which intelligent machines will understand and respond to humans, and perhaps inevitably, replace some of them" (Markoff, 2011). In the end, Jennings acknowledged that Watson's stellar performance was "not about the results" but "about being part of the future" (Markoff, 2011). IBM announced that it was developing "Watson-like tools" to assist medical professionals (Markoff, 2011). Similar interactive devices to be used in technical support and customer relations are also in the works in partnerships between IBM and other electronics companies.

In *The Singularity* (2005), Kurzweil added that ICTs have made it possible for humans to transcend our biological limitations more than ever before. Kurzweil (2005) observed that humans now have a union with machines and that technology will supplement human brainpower to vastly increase our abilities and transcend human limitations. In this new civilization, thanks to nanotechnology, he predicts the possible end of disease, poverty, and possibly death. The future for him will be about humans taking advantage of inexpensive information processes to create any physical products we desire or want. Kurzweil's (2005) predictions are echoed in new editions of *The Futurist* magazine, published by the World Future Society. With the development of nanodevices and especially nanoimplants, it will be possible for humans to experience seamless communication and surveillance among all people everywhere. The thought of humans having unique IP addresses seems to fit into Kurzweil's conceptualization of the singularity.

Inventions like nanotechnologies are hardly surprising. The history of humankind's curiosity and attendant inventions is as long as human life. New forms of technologies will, therefore, continue to be discovered, changing the way we live. In general terms, Gates (1995) put it well when he described government disdain for encryption capacities. He added, "unfortunately for them, the technology can't be stopped" (p. 270). He was right. Already stories of wireless cities and mobile technologies tied into computer-mediated devices demonstrate the frontier has not been fully realized (Moon, 2005). These wireless fields of presence will continue to have important implications for the way public administrators design and plan cities and provide public services (Mitchell, 1996). Of particular relevance are issues of designing recreational facilities, homes and residential quarters, workplaces, and of course access services. Yet access will continue to be a subjective matter, confined by the digital divide. ICTs have not proven to be fair systems for open democratic deliberations; we briefly touched on this issue in the discussion on e-democracy.

Yet for what it is worth, entrepreneurial leadership, beginning in the U.S. private sector, opened the doors after 1991 for great possibilities in e-commerce. Early pioneers including Amazon.com and others demonstrated great potential for business applications of the new developments. Electronic mail and the World Wide Web became the most powerful Internet applications worldwide, even for noncommercial purposes (Gleick, 2000; 2003). By 2000 there were more than 435 million active e-mail accounts in the world and least 2.2 million websites. These represented great opportunities for both commerce and provision of public services. The vision of e-government pioneers was to deliver government services electronically. For its part, the federal government embraced the virtual state and aggressively exploited the possibilities of digital technology. For the most part, the new appeared more promising that the old. Box 11.1 outlines the key differences between new and old government operation systems. The federal government's real challenge was not to achieve the technical capability of creating a government on the web but to adapt the organizational and political environments in which public policy is made and executed (Fountain, 2001).

Different countries establish their own comfort zones in which e-government is permissible or affordable. For the most part, not all services can be delivered electronically. The United Kingdom, for example, had previously targeted only 25% of its services for delivery through online outlets. This figure could be higher if e-government is defined more broadly to include non–Internet-based electronic service delivery. The point is that e-government is now an integral part of our civilization. It must be studied and understood in its entirety. Therefore, comparing ICT usage in different settings, as observed in chapter 10, enriches the depth of the emerging field of study.

There are common threads in all these studies. For instance, all modern day governments will continue to develop e-government and administrative systems. Without policy frameworks, committed leadership, and managerial competence, progress will be slower than is needed or intended. Moreover, new technologies will continue to be developed, forcing public bureaus to reorganize their structures and at the same time

Box 11.1. *Comparing Non e-Government (Old) and e-Government (New) Operations.*

Criteria	Non E-government (old)	E-governments (new)
Public Services	Service hours are available during "office hours"	Services available 24/7
	More paperwork systems	Less paperwork
	Responses to phone calls and letters take longer	Response to e-mail is instant
Information Systems Management	Practical logistics and organization much more difficult to manage, often labor intensive	Data and information management based on "artificial intelligence" techniques and electronic forms
Client and Customer Relations	Public takes time finding out whom to contact for services	Public accesses contacts via one-stop web portals
	Information difficult to find	Information relatively easy to find
	Less automation implies relatively lower productivity	Automation contributes directly to greater productivity, if used appropriately
	Clients and customers cannot easily track status of government services applied for or needed	Clients and customers can track work flow instantaneously
Physical Locations	Complex organizations with regional and local subsidiaries	Virtual office, accessible from multiple locations
Privacy and Security	Agency vulnerability varies with organizational type	Governments standardized PKI and other security and privacy protocols

Source. Kendrick, J. 2003. Federal Sector Report, P2C2 Group, Inc. (January), Retrieved from: http://www.p2c2group.com/jan03nws.html

institute massive training programs. Learning, therefore, will continue to be an important mission in projection of governance models. It will be two-way: the public will have to acquire skills to function in a highly ICT-based environment, just as service providers will need skills to manage the fast-changing world.

CYBERSCHOOLS AND THE FUTURE

We must pause here and address the issue of cyberschools one more time. While the future is unknown, based on current trends in ICT absorption, we offer some insights into the emerging e-government structures, starting with the industry we are most familiar with—education. Education remains the key variable in addressing many global challenges and needs. It is a major influence on political and cultural socialization. Within the realm of education policy, the most visible debate is that of quality and relevance of education. Many times, political and education leaders all over the world debate what are the best solutions for managing what is frequently termed a crisis in education systems.

Outstanding scholarship on this topic is multidisciplinary and growing. Among the most recent works that raise important and pertinent questions about our use of ICTs in education that merit our focused attention is Moe and Chubb's compelling and controversial book *Liberating Learning* (2009). Moe and Chubb (2009) addressed the issue of education in light of the exponential growth of an information society and advances in computing. More precisely, they spoke to the issue of cyberschooling and virtual or e-learning. Their work is controversial for at least one reason; it offers an optimistic appraisal of the future role of ICTs in education and learning. Moe and Chubb (2009) were not the first to do so. Microsoft founder Bill Gates (1995) saw this unfolding scenario as inevitable when he noted that citizens of the information society will "enjoy new opportunities for productivity, learning, and entertainment" (p. 150). But he added, "Just because I'm optimistic doesn't mean I don't have concerns about what is going to happen to all of us. As with all major changes, the benefits of the information society will carry costs" (p. 151).

Moe and Chubb (2009) made the point that technology offers far more benefits for school children than are necessarily appreciated. New technologies, especially cyberschooling devices, have profound implications for how children learn and will continue to learn. They argued that among the many benefits of cyberschooling is that it is customized to individual students. In traditional schools, students are frustrated and bored by not being allowed to take courses that are available in other parts of the world and country. Cyberschools can allow students to take classes anywhere, anytime, and from the best teachers. In other words, cyberschools offer more choices than traditional schools.

Moe and Chubb (2009) also explain that cyberschools have the advantage of enhancing student abilities. Students in cyberschools learn at their own pace and are not distracted by restrictions placed in traditional curriculums offered in brick and mortar schools.

In their estimation, cyberschools may cost less to society for a variety of reasons. First is that for the first time in human history labor in the education sector can be eliminated through increased use of ICTs. This is where the costs can be cut and is also the controversial part of the discourse. Moe and Chubb (2009) saw labor unions as obstructing the cyberschool movement. Here is how: unions naturally oppose the idea that teachers should be laid off and replaced by computers. In cyberlearning, the substitution occurs because schools hire fewer teachers to manage courses delivered online. As the book argues, technology is transformative but threatening to some groups. Teachers' unions in particular are threatened because their membership numbers will go down farther, which will also weaken them politically. With fewer students in classes, school districts will hire fewer teachers and hence there will be less union dues. In terms of organizing, unions will be disadvantaged by the decentralized nature of cyberschools. Moe and Chubb (2009) argued that centralization of school districts has in the past boosted union ability to mobilize for political action. This is no longer going to work in an environment saturated with decentralized and dispersed cyberschools.

According to Moe and Chubb (2009), unions have traditionally blocked major efforts to institute reforms in the education sector. For them, unions opposed efforts to increase accountability and pay for performance policies. However, the authors argued that new ICTs and other technologies do not necessarily imply reform and instead should be considered a massive social force that human societies all over the world must interact with and leverage to their advantage. In the end, their point is that the liberation of learning means that groups such as powerful unions will not in the future have the same level of success at blocking reforms in education and that students will be offered more choice in what they learn, thanks to the advances in ICTs.

Moe and Chubb (2009) argued that in the near future there are going to be more hybrid programs whereby students will go to traditional schools but also take other classes online. Blended models of learning are already taking place and will probably grow in stature and prominence.

As with schools, the transformation in scope of information storage and retrieval has greatly affected libraries. Expert commentators observe that the new libraries are frequently referred to as "information centers." The emerging trend is for information to be available at users' fingertips. This has changed the traditional view of libraries as places with limited access, open for only 12 hours a day. Today's virtual library is open 24/7 (Makulowich, 2000). With the proliferation of computer-based devices and terminals, gone are the days of huge buildings. Today, books take far less space, thanks to audio recordings, videotapes, DVDs, CD-ROMS, databases, and limitless "networks linking remote resources via the Internet" (Makulowich, 2000).

Northern Arizona University library announced in 2011 that it would replace its paper-based periodical selection with a digitized online collection. It is not alone, because hundreds of other institutions of higher education have already done so. A few examples illustrate this point. The online-based University of Phoenix, whose motto is "thinking ahead," replaced the majority of traditional textbooks and course materials with an e-source and e-book program that allows students to use an online library. The online library has more than 20,000 periodicals. Schoofs (2007) reported that Grand Valley State University, an institution with around 20,000 students located in western Michigan, abolished its periodicals department in response to the opportunities afforded by the Internet and ICTs. The new reality required reorganization of the library system and established a new position called the electronic resources administrator. The job involved setup and maintenance of electronic resources of various kinds, including electronic journals (Schoofs, 2007). These organizational changes have implications for library acquisition units that will also be reorganized as more libraries adapt to new changes.

This brief illustration of the implication of ICTs for comparative analysis and reflection is merely indicative. As libraries reinvent themselves, the focus toward online access and use will be a part of the conversation for a long time to come. The question for consideration will be whether or not libraries embrace technological changes in the quest to seem relevant or as a matter of rationality (Bivens-Tatum, 2006).

Role of Government

Will the role of government change in the wake of increased proliferation of technology? The direction of change will, of course, be in the manner in which services are delivered, but as West hinted, the much-touted promise of e-government will not redefine the core functions of government (West, 2005). More specifically, he argued that e-government has not dramatically improved interactivity and responsiveness of governments across the globe. Economists might suggest government should do what it does best—mostly correct market failures while the market does its part to reallocate resources. Although Galambos and Pratt (1988) argued that government regulation is "a distinctively American approach to balancing public and private interests." The practice is also well developed in other cultures (p. 56). It is precisely because governments across the globe have deregulated ICT sectors that e-government is now possible.

Perhaps it is fitting to explore this idea further through revisiting the fate of one of public administration's oldest institutions, the postal service. During the paper age, postal services were government monopolies and, in many parts of the world, emerged as the quintessential public service. Market forces have changed this old reality, and in the new ICT-driven age, postal services are on the decline. We may pose the question of what the spread of e-government will do to the U.S. Postal Service (USPS). There are several ways to think about the impact of ICTs on organizational and business changes at the USPS.

First, the 1990s were a period of tremendous growth in the mail and courier industry. The use of e-mail drastically reduced the role of handwritten correspondence across the board. And with the new Web 2.0 proliferation, for the first time in USPS's more than two centuries of history, it must rethink its business and managerial strategies. The USPS has never lost the vision to continue playing a vital role in enabling businesses, government, and citizens to receive secure and fast mail services. As a response to new technologies, USPS introduced in 2001 "an Internet-based service designed to enable government agencies to secure and authenticate electronic correspondence" (USPS, 2001). According to Deputy Postmaster General John Nolan, the service NetPost. Certified "was specifically designed to support e-government initiatives by expediting the movement of documents online and ensuring users so that those documents sent electronically would be secure and private at all times while in transit" (USPS, 2001).

Among the first beneficiaries of this service was the Social Security Administration, whose long-range plan had been to create an electronic infrastructure that would enable customers to securely send electronic packages of information in the new media. Official replies would also be transmitted through the electronic infrastructure.

USPS demonstrated its commitment to e-government and efficient service delivery by complying with the E-Government Act of 2002. The law, as we described in chapter 3, "requires government agencies to conduct a Privacy Impact Assessment when buying or developing an information technology system that contains personal information about members of the public" (USPS, 2011). USPS's website functions as a service to customers wishing to track registered mail and packages in transit. The site complies with all government privacy policies and is designed to meet the highest standards such as using user-friendly and machine-readable P3P form features.

Although the USPS and its British counterpart, the Royal Mail, have attempted to meet the new market on its own terms, adaptation to new technologies is not enough to catapult these corporations to the desired financially sustainable level. Postal business models will continue to confront changes in preferences on both the senders' and receivers' sides.

Current innovations involve greater use of automation in sorting based on Optical Character Recognition, among other well-established systems. As was pointed out, customers can now track packages posted through USPS. Tracking is a function of advances in bar coding and the use of RFID tags. New approaches to shortening delivery times through providing tailor-made last mile delivery services are all meant to satisfy the increasingly complex customer. Overall, customers now have a wide range of receiving and sending approaches to use. We may speculate that the era of large size postal establishments in developing countries is also over. ICTs will continue to provide an opportunity structure for postal services to innovate, streamline processes, and develop new services or suffer organizational decline and extinction.

Granted that classical thinking favors market solutions to resource allocation, e-government should support the development of new markets while at the same time reifying good governance processes. How is this going to be realized? The answer lies in appreciating ongoing e-government innovations that have already made an impact on governance. More profoundly, e-government's ability to offer greater interaction between governments and the people is widely acknowledged to be a feature of 21st century political development. If investments in ICTs are profitable, as they are, then e-government serving both business and society is a part of the new world order.

Under this belief, the relationship between governments and the market is both closer and more scrutinized. Few, however, will expect their governments to use ICTs in intrusive ways. Active government intervention to promote diverse speech through ICTs will generally be favored but not by all political doctrines. Besides, there is a real danger that large corporations controlling knowledge-based industries might become all too powerful (Postman, 1993).

Having observed technology, Simon (2007) pointed out that it "plays a significant role" in shaping public policies (p. 394). More specifically, ICTs will in the future play a crucial role in policy formation, implementation, and evaluation. ICTs are the avenues through which ideas are discussed and actualized into plans of action. It is through ICTs that citizen concerns will continue to reach the doorsteps of policy makers. Moreover, politicians will have to pay attention to the make-or-break capabilities of the vast array of ICTs in the modern political environment, including any opponents who mobilize for action through those tools. ICTs, more than other technologies, will be the force through which both government and citizen power is contested. Importantly, the post–baby boomer generations, Generations X and Y, have all been born experiencing the full benefits of a myriad of computer-mediated systems. For them, life without these gadgets is inconceivable or boring to say the least. Therefore, the cultural internalization of e-government will continue to reinforce its sustainability.

For these generations, seeking information online and through a variety of computer-mediated devices are core values. They will seek health, entertainment, educational, and other varieties of information from these gadgets, often on handheld devices. What is important for the future is the continuation of the advanced information age in which access and accessibility are core practical issues for both policy and politics.

What do we mean by access and accessibility issues? Members of the public, especially in developed countries, have access to ICTs and will therefore continue to receive a variety of public services. Having access means being able to search for specific government information as needed. Yet the design of these ICT systems is crucial and is what accessibility refers to. Ironically, enhancing accessibility online and through other ICTs can best be achieved through the systems which must also be designed appropriately. Key to design issues is the perennial goal of ensuring the correct balance between data privacy, security, and integrity.

In the discussion about the design and policy foundations of e-government, we touched on some of the core issues that will continue to present challenges for administrators all over the world. Our discussions on different e-government practices allow us to recognize the essentiality for benchmarking and sharing of information on best practices. Indeed, the countries that lag behind can only be expected to see their futures through the lens of those ahead in the development and use of ICTs as manifest in e-government or governance structures. The future, therefore, lies in developing systems that progressively engage publics with their networked governments. This entails building on experiences gained from past endeavors and incorporating statutory provisions that favor inclusiveness.

Much as in the past, technical design will continue to be collaborative work between consumers and developers of software and hardware. Designs of e-government web portals will continue to coalesce around acceptable standards for interoperability emanating from the growing networking among different governments within the avenues provided by ICTs.

Specifically, the emergence of virtual communities, especially the ever improving Web 2.0 initiatives and forces of globalism, have necessitated government support for publics who now increasingly interact with friends and relatives overseas. The move to greater use of advanced computer-based appliances and web services has expanded human experiences in the information space. New communities are emerging from technological advances that place greater premium on data portability. Mobile phones, Blackberry devices, and even video game consoles operate on software that is portable. In other words, files and data are operable or exportable in more than one application. As Zittrain (2008) wrote, "the pull of interoperability compelled most software developers to allow data to be exportable in common formats" (p. 176). This reality has helped developing countries migrate aspects of online computing to mobile phone devices, thereby significantly shrinking access issues and expanding the potential for expanding e-government and virtual communities. Portability also implies that the wave of Internet-centered products and other tethered appliances, like iPods, Xboxes, TiVos, and iPhones, are woven into the already robust social networks that include Facebook, Google and other new Web 2.0 platforms. The emerging communities will continue to engage the political leadership in all countries.

Governments, both rich and poor, support these communities for political and social reasons. Beyond having to participate in civic duties through computer-mediated communication systems, they also participate in knowledge production and dissemination. Thus, governments will not ignore ICTs for the simple reason that they create new opportunities for individuals and organizations. Besides, they have shortened distances and permitted wider interactions, therefore enhancing opportunities for greater participation in governance, including in rule-making administrative endeavors.

Yet it is absolutely limiting to construe ICTs to be the primary movers of how governments will perform in the future. While ICTs have created tremendous opportunities for establishment of e-governments, especially in the developed areas of the world, human history shows change to be a constant phenomenon. Thus, ICTs might after all be only a piece of the change dynamic, in which case e-government will be seen as a tool rather than an enabling vision or way of life. The choices to be made will, of course, be political. This point might not be obvious to all, but we need to be reminded that only political institutions can promote and protect the integrity of such a massive and expensive human endeavor as the Internet, on which much of e-government is premised.

Politics, therefore, remains at the core of e-government much as it has for traditional public administration. Politics is what will determine the choices to be made. Politics determines whether or not to outsource e-government technologies and management. As was shown at the beginning of this book, much of e-government was initially embedded in the refounding paradigm of public administration. This school, more than its predecessors, touted privatization as key to successful government. Again, no direct correlation exists between e-government performance and privatization. But it is embedded in the "reinvention of government" discourses that seek to change government operations and embrace private sector practices (Fountain, 1992; Heeks, 2001).

However, if privatization saves money, as has been claimed by scholars in the New Public Management frameworks of analysis, it is not a panacea to all administrative problems. No empirical studies show it enhances the quality of e-government services. What has been demonstrated is a strong movement toward partnerships in building viable e-government structures.

The bottom line is that the revenues to be raised and monies spent for e-government endeavors must be a political choice. Even when money is available, rates at which different governments absorb e-government practices will continue to vary. Governments will seek partnerships with the private sector and citizen groups to make e-government work. The future will not be about privatizing e-government services to save money or achieve a higher level of performance alone; there is more to it than that.

Politics also implies managing the legal environment in which e-government operates. This implies providing a framework "through which we live our civic instincts online, trusting that the expression of our collective character will be one at least as good as that imposed by outside sovereigns" (Zittrain, 2008, p. 195). The extrapolation here is that net citizens meeting in cyberspace must follow the law and use available applications responsibly. Matters of security and privacy will not diminish in importance but instead are expected to occupy government administrators across the globe. As Zittrain (2008) posited, there is already a generational divide in terms of those willingly sharing their personal information over the Internet and those not ready to have their information easily displayed through Internet search engines. There is no privacy commons license to police how individual information available in searchable data banks will be used in different situations. The (international) law is behind on these matters of privacy and other unintended issues emerging from the ICT revolution. This and other aspects of the Internet will affect policy toward e-government. Democratic countries are likely to continue to review all legal issues that affect e-government. Much is happening in this regard. Privacy concerns have now forced ICT providers to reconfigure appliances such as

GPS devices to establish standards that respect individual rights. But illicit eavesdropping through these devices remains a challenge even in advanced industrial countries. For the developing world, much uncertainty exists, and it will take political will to provide legal protection against violation of rights in non-democratic states.

Before closing, we need to return to the issues we raised at the beginning of this book—namely, the context of e-government. We had discussed in detail the environmental factors in which e-government functions. Now we must close by stating that these factors are time sensitive. The future will present new technologies. Time will dictate the pace at which public bureaus will be transformed. If the current zeitgeist, marked by scarcity of global resources, impedes certain changes in human abilities to create ICTs, then e-government models will be reshaped accordingly to reflect scarcity. Much as in the past, when cutback management becomes the norm, most likely e-governance will follow similar rational courses of action. Cyberorganizations that have arisen will no doubt shrink and expand in tune with overall environmental opportunity structures.

Finally, one feature of e-government that led to the writing of this book was the sense that e-government must be understood in its most simple terms. The problem was not the shortage of books on the subject or the lack of an administrative treatise on reforming public administration. The problem was the very nature of the discourse and, most importantly, its lack of connection to basic administrative thinking. Hopefully, this introductory book provides a framework through which e-government can be disentangled. This volume suggests, therefore, that rather than disentangling e-government studies from mainstream administrative studies, attempts ought to continue to situate emerging developments in the larger themes of administrative development.

References

Abrams, M., & Weiss, J. (2008). *Malicious control system cyber security attack case study-Maroochy Water Services, Australia*. Retrieved from National Institute of Standards and Technology, Computer Security Resource Center website: http://csrc.nist.gov/groups/SMA/fisma/ics/documents/Maroochy-Water-Services-Case-Study_report.pdf.

Accenture. (2001). *E-government leadership: Rhetoric vs. reality—closing the gap*. Retrieved from http://www.ucis.pitt.edu/euce/events/policyconf/01/Davies-eGovernmentLeadership.pdf.

Affiliated Computer Services (ACS). (2008). *Modernizing health and human services (HHS) programs: Empowering the caseworker: Enabling success*. ACS@Advantage Solution. Retrieved from http://www.acs-inc.com/ov_vantage_brochure.aspx.

Allett, J. (1996). Crowd psychology and the theory of democratic elitism: The contribution of William McDougall. *Political Psychology*, *17*(2), 213–227.

Allison, G. I. (1994). Public and private management: Are they fundamentally alike in all unimportant respects? In F. L. Land (Ed.), *Current issues in public administration* (pp. 16–32). New York: St. Martin's Press.

American Computer Science Association (ACSA). (2004). EINAC was not the 1st Programmable Electronic Computer. Colossus was! And it may have saved the free world. Retrieved from http://www.acsa2000.net.

Andersen, D. F., Belardo, S., & Dawes, S. S. (1994). Strategic information management: Conceptual frameworks for the public sector. *Public Productivity and Management Review*, *17*(4), 335–353.

Andersen, K. V., & Henriksen, H. Z. (2005). The first leg of e-government research: Domains and application areas 1998–2003. *International Journal of Electronic Government Research*, *1*(4), 26–44.

Anderson, R. (2003). Ethics and digital government. In A. Pavlichev (Ed.), *Digital government: Principles and best practices* (pp. 218–234). Hershey, PA: Idea Group.

ArticSoft Technologies Ltd. (n.d). An introduction to PKI (Public Key Infrastructure). Retrieved from http://www.articsoft.com/wp_pki_intro.htm.

Asia Oceanic Electronic Marketplace Association (AOEMA). (2007). *E-government from a user's perspective, stages of e-government.* Retrieved from http://www.aoema.org/E-government/Stages-Phases.

Associated Press. (2004, May 3). California official seeks criminal probe of e-voting: Machines banned in four counties; 10 more must meet condition. Retrieved from MSNBC website: http://www.msnbc.msn.com/id/4874190/ns/politics-voting_problems/.

Associated Press. (2006, March 9). Dubai to give up control of U.S. ports: Deal ran into tough opposition in Senate over security. Retrieved from MSNBC website: http://www.msnbc.com/id/11741617.

Associated Press. (2006, September 13). Princeton prof hacks e-vote machine: Students uploaded viruses able to spread to other machines. Retrieved from MSNBC website: http://www.msnbc.msn.com/id/14825465/.

Atkinson, R D. (20040). Unsatisfactory progress: The Bush administration's performance on e-government initiatives. Progressive Policy Institute Briefing. Retrieved from http://www.ppion-line.org/ndol/print.cfm?contentid=252960.

Bachrach, P. (1967). *The theory of democratic elitism: A critique*. Boston: Little, Brown, & Co.

Bagdikian, B. H. (1997). *The media monopoly*. Boston: Beacon Press.

Bailey, P. J. H. (2008). *Procurement principles and management*. Harlow, UK: Prentice Hall.

Bangladesh Observer. (2005, March 10). Cyber schools ILC program launched at UCEP. Retrieved from http://www.bangladeshobserveron-line.com/new/2005/03/10/it.htm.

Banks, A. J. (2006). *Race, rhetoric, and technology: Searching for higher ground*. Mahwah, NJ: Lawrence Erlbaum.

Barbaro, M. (2006, March 7). Wal-Mart enlists bloggers in P.R. campaign. *New York Times*. Retrieved from http://www.nytimes.com/2006/03/07/technology/07blog.html.

Bardach, E. (1977). *The implementation game*. Cambridge, MA: MIT Press.

Barnard, C. (1938). *Functions of the executives*. Cambridge, MA: Harvard University Press.

Barr, E. (2007). Fixing federal e-voting standards. *Communications of the ACM, 50*(3), 19–24.

Barrett, K., & Greene, R. (2001). *Powering up: How public managers can take control of information technology*. Washington, DC: Congressional Quarterly Press.

Bartis, E., & Mitev, N. (2008). A multiple narrative approach to information systems failure: A successful system that failed. *European Journal of Information Systems, 17*, 112–124. DOI:10.1057/ejis.2008.3.

Barzilai-Nahon, K. (2006, October 16). Measuring the digital divide: Access or competency? *The Information Society*. Retrieved from http://www.zdnet.com/blog/education/measuring-the-digital-divide-access-or-competency/585.

Bellamy, C., & Taylor, J. (1998). *Governing in the information age*. Buckingham: Open University Press.

Bekkers, V. J. J. M., & Korteland, E. H. (2006). Governance, ICT and the innovation agenda of public administration: A comparison of some European policy initiatives. In V. J. J. M. Bekkers, H. van Duivenboden, & Thaens, M. (Eds.), *Information and communication technology and public innovation: Assessing the ICT-driven modernization of public administration* [Monograph]. *Innovation and the Public Sector, 12* (pp. 22–52). Amsterdam: IOS Press.

Bellis, M. (2011). History of email & Ray Tomlinson. Retrieved from About.com website: http://inventors.about.com/od/estartinventions/a/email.htm.

Bennis, W. (1999). The end of leadership: Exemplary leadership is impossible without the full inclusion, initiatives, and cooperation of followers. *Organizational Dynamics*, *28*, 71–80.

Berkley, G., & Rouse, J. (2004). *The craft of public administration*. New York: McGraw Hill.

Bertot, J. C., Jaeger, P. T., & Grimes, J. M. (2010). Using ICTs to create a culture of transparency: E-government and social media as openness and anti-corruption tools for societies. *Government Information Quarterly*, *27*(3), 264–271.

Bertot, J. C., Jaeger, P. T., Langa, L. A., & McClure, C. R. (2006, August 15). Drafted: I Want You to Deliver E-Government: Public access computing grows, but libraries need more funding to serve as the first refuge and last resort for e-government support, public computing, and internet access. *Library Journal*. Retrieved from http://www.libraryjournal.com/article/CA6359866.html?q=drafted+public+computing.

Better Government Association. (2011). About the watchdog center. Retrieved from http://www.bettergov.org/watchdog/about.aspx.

Bhatnagar, S. C. (2004). *E-government: From vision to implementation—A practical guide with case studies*. London: Sage Publications.

Bimber, B. (1998). The internet and political transformation: Populism, community, and accelerated pluralism. *Polity*, *31*(1), 133–160.

Bishop, M., & Wagner, D. (2007). Risks of e-voting. *Communications of the ACM*, *50*(11), 120–121.

Bissell, T. (2004). The digital divide dilemma: Preserving Native American culture while increasing access to information technology on reservations. *Journal of Law, Technology & Policy*, *1*, 129–150. Retrieved from http://www.jltp.uiuc.edu/archives/bissell.pdf.

Bivens-Tatum, W. (2006). Technological change, universal access, and the end of the library. *Library Philosophy and Practice*, *9*(1). Retrieved from http://www.webpages.uidaho.edu/~mbolin/bivens-tatum.pdf.

Blackstone, E., Bognanno, M. L., & Hakim, S. (2005). *Innovations in e-government: The thoughts of governors and mayors*. Lanham, MD: Rowman & Littlefield Publishers.

Bonneville Power Administration (BPA). (2011). About BPA. Retrieved from http://www.bpa.gov/corporate/About_BPA/Tribes/Trblpolicy.pdf.

Bovens, M., & Zouridis, S. (2002). From street-level to system level bureaucracies: How information and communication technology is transforming administrative discretion and constitutional control. *Public Administration Review, 62*(2), 174–184.

Boyer, W. W. (1990). Political science and the 21st century: From government to governance. *Political Science and Politics, 23*(1), 50–54.

Bratton, W., & Knobler, P. (1998). *Turnaround: How America's top cop reversed the crime epidemic*. New York: Random House.

Brock, D., & Waldman, P. (2008). Al Gore on technology. Retrieved from http://www.ontheissues.org/Archive/Free_Ride_Technology.htm.

Brown, D., & Lee, J. (2002). DORBOS. Paper presented at Federation of Tax Administrators 18th Annual Technology Conference. Retrieved from http://www.taxadmin.org/Fta/meet/tech_sum02/brown.pdf.

Brown, M. (2000). Mitigating the risk of information technology initiatives: Best practices and points of failure for the public sector. In G. D. Garson (Ed.), *Handbook of public information systems* (pp. 153–164). New York: Marcel Dekker.

Burgess, S., & Houghton, J. (2006). E-government in Australia. In P. Hernon, R. Cullen, & H. Relyea (Eds.), *Comparative perspectives on e-government: Serving today and building for tomorrow* (pp. 84–101). New York: Rowman and Littlefield.

Burkert, H. (1985). Representative democracy and information and communication technology: The malady, the cure and its effect. In L. Yngstrom, R. Sizer, J. Berleur, & R. Laufer (Eds.), *Can information technology result in benevolent bureaucracies?* (pp. 113–123). Amsterdam: Elsevier.

Burks, A. R., & Burks A. W. (1988). *The first electronic computer: The Atanasoff story*. Ann Arbor: University of Michigan Press.

Burns, T., & Stalker, G. M. (1961). *The management of innovation*. London: Tavistock Publications.

Bush, G. (2006). President Bush's State of the Union Address, Transcript, Retrieved from the (January 31). Washington Post. http://www.washingtonpost.com/wp-dyn/content/article/2006/01/31/AR2006013101468.html.

Cable News Network (CNN). (March 9, 1999). Wolf Blitzer late night edition. Retrieved from http://www.youtube.com/watch?v=BnFJ8cHAlco.

Cable News Network (CNN). (2004). Survey: Cell phone most hated, needed invention (January 21, 2004). Retrieved from http://www.cnn.com/2004/TECH/ptech/01/21/tech.survey.ap/index.html.

Cable News Network (CNN). (2005, November 4). "Can I quit now?" FEMA chief wrote as Katrina raged: E-mails give insight into Brown's leadership, attitude. Retrieved from http://www.cnn.com/2005/US/11/03/brown.fema.emails/.

Cabrera, A. (2009). No end in sight for globalization: The first global crisis will make the world more global. Presentation at Thunderbird School of Global Management, Phoenix, AZ, September.

Caiden, G. (1991). What really is public maladministration? *Public Administration Review*, *51*(6), 486–493.

Caiden, N. (1981). Public budgeting amidst uncertainty and instability. In J. M. Shafritz, A. C. Hyde, & S. J. Parkes (Eds.), *Classics of public administration* (pp. 423–433). Belmont, CA: Wadsworth.

Carter, L., & Belanger, F. (2004). The influence of perceived characteristics of innovating on e-government adoption. *Electronic Journal of e-Government*, *2*(1), 11–20.

Castells, M. (1997). *The power of identity, the information age: Economy, society and culture* (Vol. 1). Oxford, UK: Blackwell Publishers.

Castells, M. (2000). *The rise of the network society*. Oxford, UK: Blackwell Publishers.

Center for Democracy and Technology. (2009). Retrieved from http://www.infodev.org/en/Document.16.pdf.

Chadwick, A., & Macy, C. (2003). Interaction between states and citizens in the age of the Internet: "e-government" in the United States, Britain and the European Union. *Governance: An International*

Journal of Policy, Administration, and Institutions, *16*(2), 271–300. DOI: 10.1111/1468-0491.00216.

Chakraborty, J., & Bosman, M. M. (2005). Measuring the digital divide in the United States: Race, income, and personal computer ownership. *The Professional Geographer*, *57*(3), 395–410.

Chan, C. M. L., & Pan, S. L. (2008). User engagement in e-government systems implementation: A comparative case study of two Singaporean e-government initiatives. *Journal of Strategic Information Systems*, *17*(2), 124–139.

Chen, A., Pan, S. L., Zhang, J., Huang, W. W., & Zhu, S. (2009). Managing e-government implementation in China: A process perspective. *Information and Management*, *46*(4), 203–212.

Chen, M. (2004, December 29). Wireless politics may determine future of digital democracy, Part 1 and 2. *The New Standard*. Retrieved from http://dissidentvoice.org/Jan05/Chen0102.htm.

Chen, Y. N., Chen, H. M., Huang, W., & Ching, R. K. H. (2006). E-government strategies in developed and developing countries: An implementation framework and case study. *Journal of Global Information Management*, *14*(1), 23–24.

Chester, J. (2007). *Digital destiny: New media and the future of democracy*. New York: New Press.

Chief Information Officers Council. (1999, September). *Federal enterprise architecture framework, Version 1.1*. Retrieved from http://www.cio.gov/documents/fedarch1.pdf.

Chief Information Officers Council. (2002). One Hundred Seventh Congress of the United States of America: At the second session. Retrieved from http://www.cio.gov/documents/e_gov_act_2002.pdf.

Chief Information Officers Council. (n.d.). About the Chief Information Officers Council. Retrieved from http://www.cio.gov/index.cfm?function=aboutthecouncil.

Chiger, S. (2009). Has terrorism curtailed e-government?: You'll find fewer government resources online in the post-9/11 security crunch. Retrieved from PCWorld.com website: http://www.pcworld.com/article/104796/has_terrorism_curtailed_egovernment.html.

Choh, K., S. H. Song, & Y. Kim. (2006, April 2). An International Comparative Study on E-government Policy of World Cities: How Can We Foster Citizen Participation. Retrieved from http://www.aspanet.org/scriptcontent/custom/staticontent/2006PDworkshops/egov.cfm (Accessed September 15, 2008).

Chook, V. (2007). *World broadband statistics: Q4 2006*. London: Point Topic Ltd.

City of Chandler. (2007). State of city highlights. Retrieved from http://www.chandleraz.gov/Content/Highlights_2007.pdf.

City of Fairfax, VA. (2004). Homepage. Retrieved from http://www.co.fairfax.va.us.us/gov/dit/itplan.htm.

Clift, S. (2004). E-government and democracy: Representation and citizen engagement in the information age. Retrieved from http://www.publicus.net/articles/cliftegovdemocracy.pdf.

CodeAmber.org. (2007, March 2). The web's Amber alert system. Retrieved from http://www.codeamber.org/.

Cohen, S., & Eimicke, W. (2002). *The effective public manager achieving success in a government*. San Francisco: Jossey-Bass.

Coll, S. (2011, January 31). Democratic movements. *The New Yorker*. Retrieved from http://www.newyorker.com/talk/comment/2011/01/31/110131taco_talk_coll.

Commonwealth Center for Electronic Governance. (2002). E-government 2002: Part II: Applications of e-government in five countries and a review of electronic democracy. Retrieved from http://www.electronicgov.net/about/introletter.shtml.

Compaine, B. N. (2001). *The digital divide facing a crisis or creating a myth*? Cambridge, MA: MIT Press.

Computer Science and Telecommunications, National Research Council Staff. (2002). *Information technology research, innovation, and e-government*. Washington, DC: National Academy Press.

Congressional Research Services (CRS). (2009). Homepage. Retrieved from http://www.loc.gov/crsinfo/.

Cooper, J., & Weaver, K. D. (2003). *Gender and computers: Understanding the digital divide*. Mahwah, NJ: Lawrence Erlbaum.

Cooper, M. (2002). Does the digital divide still exist? Bush Administration shrugs, but evidence says "Yes." *Civil rights forum on communications policy*, Report (May 30). Washington, DC: Consumer Federation of America.

Cooper, P. J. (2000). *Public law and public administration*. Itasca, IL: F. E. Peacock Publishers.

Cooper, P. J. (2003). *Governing by contract challenges and opportunities for public managers*. Washington, DC: Congressional Quarterly Press.

Cordon, G. (2010, November 28). Royal behavior claim in WikiLeaks documents. Retrieved from http://www.independent.co.uk/news/world/politics/royal-behaviour-claim-in-wikileaks-documents-2146147.html.

Crawford, K. J. (2011). *The strategic project office: A guide to improving organizational performance*. Boca Raton, FL: CRC Press.

Croom, S. (2000). The impact of web-based procurement on the management of operating resources supply. *The Journal of Supply Chain Management*, *36*(1), 4–13.

Cukier, K. N. (2005). Who will control the internet? *Foreign Affairs*, *84*(6). Retrieved from http://www.foreignaffairs.com/articles/61192/kenneth-neil-cukier/who-will-control-the-internet.

Cullen, R. (2006). E-government and the digital divide. In P. Hernon, R. Cullen, & H. Relyea (Eds.), *Comparative perspectives on e-government: Serving today and building for tomorrow* (pp. 291–312). New York: Rowman and Littlefield.

Curtin, G. G. (2007). E-government. In *Encyclopedia of political communications*. Thousand Oaks, CA: Sage. Retrieved from http://www.usc.edu/schools/sppd/bedrosian/private/docs/encyclopedia_of_political_communications.pdf.

Dahl, R. A. (1961). *Who governs?* New Haven, CT: Yale University Press.

Dahl, R. A. (1965). *A preface to democratic theory*. Chicago: Chicago University Press.

Dahl, R. A. (1971). *Polyarchy: Participation and opposition*. New Haven, CT: Yale University Press.

Daniels, M. (2001). *Citizen-centered e-government: Developing the action plan*. Washington, DC: Office of Management and Budget.

Danziger, J., Dutton, W. H., Kling, R., & Kraemer, K. L. (1982). *Computers and politics: High technology in American local governments*. New York: Columbia University Press.

Danziger, J. N., Kraemer, K. L., Dunkle, D. E., & King, J. L. (1993). Enhancing the quality of computing services: Technology, structure, and people. *Public Administration Review, 53*(2), 161–169.

Davis, N. W. (2005). No running around, no run around. Paper presented at Federation of Tax Administrators 21st Annual Technology Conference. Retrieved from http://www.taxadmin.org/fta/meet/tw05_pres/Davis.pdf.

Davis, R. (1999). *The web of politics: The internet's impact on the American political system*. New York: Oxford University Press.

Dawes, S. S., Burke, G. B., & Dadayan, L. (2006). Systems, applications, and products in data processing (SAP). Retrieved from http://www.sap.com/asia/industries/publicsector/pdf/BWP_ROI_Case_Study_Commonwealth_of_PA.pdf.

Dawson, C. (2006, October 16). Measuring the digital divide: Access or competency? *ZDNet Education*. Retrieved from http://www.zdnet.com/blog/education/measuring-the-digital-divide-access-or-competency/585.

de Boer, L., Harink, J., & Heijboer, G. (2002). A conceptual model for assessing the impact of electronic procurement. *European Journal of Purchasing & Supply Management*, *8*(1), 25–33.

Deloitte. (2004). CIO 2.0: The changing role of the Chief Information Officer in government and why it matters in the public sector. Deloitte Development LLC. Retrieved from http://www.deloitte.com/view/en_US/us/Industries/US-federal-government/8e3087895e5fb110VgnVCM100000ba42f00aRCRD.htm.

del Valle, M. (2011). City clerk announces biggest step forward ever in Chicago government transparency with Legislative Information

Center. City of Chicago, Office of City Clerk, Press Release. Retrieved from http://www.chicityclerk.com/news_articles/2011/feb/finaldocmanagereleaseFeb2011.pdf.

Denhardt, R. (1993). *The pursuit of significance strategies for managerial success in public organizations*. Belmont, CA: Wadsworth.

Denhardt, R., Denhardt, J. V., & Aristigueta, M. P. (2002). *Managing human behavior in public and nonprofit organizations*. Thousand Oaks, CA: Sage Publications.

Denhardt, R. B., & Denhardt, J. V. (2006). *Public administration: An action orientation*. Belmont, CA: Wadsworth.

Denning, D. (2000, May 23). Cyberterrorism: Testimony before the Special Oversight Panel on Terrorism, Committee on Armed Services, & U.S. House of Representatives. Retrieved from http://www.cs.georgetown.edu/~denning/infosec/cyberterror.html.

Dovifat, A., Kubisch, D., Brüggemeier, M., Lenk, K., & Reichard, C. (2004). Explaining successes and failures of e-government implementation with micropolitics. *Electronic Government*, 3183, 308–312. Retrieved from http://www.springerlink.com/content/t1qd7djnj84kdda2/.

Downs, A. (1967). *Inside bureaucracy*. Boston: Little Brown.

Drezner, D. W. (2010, *December 5*). Why WikiLeaks is bad for scholars. *Chronicle of higher education*. (The Chronicle Review). Retrieved from http://chronicle.com/article/Why-WikiLeaks-Is-Bad-for/125628/.

Dryzek, J. S., & Niemeyer, S. (2006). Reconciling pluralism and consensus as political ideals. *American Journal of Political Science, 50*(3), 634–649.

Duarte, D., & Snyder, N. (2000). *Mastering virtual teams*. San Francisco: Jossey-Bass.

Dunleavy, P., Margetts, H., Bastow, S., & Tinkler, J. (2006). *Digital era government: IT corporations, the state, and e-government*. New York: Oxford University Press.

Dunlop, T. (2008). On-line voting: Reducing voter impediments. *Policy Study*, *36*, 658–686.

Dutta, S., & Mia, I. (2008). *The global information technology report 2007–2008: Fostering innovation through networked readiness.* New York: Palgrave MacMillan.

Dutta, S., & Mia, I. (2009). *The global information technical report 2008–09: Mobility in a networked world, executive summary.* Geneva: World Economic Forum and INSEAD.

Dutton, W. H., & Eynon, R. (2009). Networked individuals and institutions: A cross-sector comparative perspective on patterns and strategies in government and research. *Information Society*, *25*(3), 198–207.

Dye, T. R. (2010). *Understanding public policy.* New York: Longman.

Edwards, D. (2011, February 14). Assange: WikiLeaks helped spark Tunisia, Egypt revolutions. Retrieved from http://www.rawstory.com/rs/2011/02/14/assange-wikileaks-helped-spark-tunisia-egypt-revolutions.

eEurope. (2005). European Commission Information Society. Retrieved from Eisele, S. (2003, December 2003).Electronic Bracelets Monitor Illegal Immigrants.National Publc Radio. Retrieved from http://www.npr.org/templates/story/story.php?storyId=1550023].

Electronic Frontier Foundation (2011). Digital Millennium Copyright Act. Retrieved from http://www.eff.org/issues/dmca.

Electronic Privacy Information Center. (2011). USA PATRIOT Act (H.R. 3162). Retrieved from http://epic.org/privacy/terrorism/hr3162.html.

Engber, D. (2006, September 8). Why is Chicago so corrupt? And how do you measure corruption, anyway? *Slate*. Retrieved from http://www.slate.com/id/2149240/.

Evans, D., & Yen, D. C. (2005). E-government: An analysis for implementation: Framework for understanding cultural and social impact, *Government Information Quarterly*, *22*(3), 354–373.

Ewusi-Mensah, K., & Przasnyski, Z. H. (1995). Learning from abandoned information development projects. *Journal of Information Technology*, *10*, 3–14.

Federal Communications Commission (FCC). (2006, February 10). FCC Issues 12th Annual Report to Congress on Video Competition. Retrieved from http://hraunfoss.fcc.gov/edocs_public/attachmatch/DOC-263763A1.doc.

Federal Communications Commission (FCC). (2010). *2010 E-Rate program and broadband usage survey: Report*, DA 10-2414. Washington, DC: Harris Interactive, Inc.

Federal Communications Commission (FCC). (2011). Retrieved from http://www.fcc.gov/.

Federal Trade Commission (FTC). (2011). Federal Trade Commission: Protecting America's Consumers. Retrieved from http://www.ftc.gov/.

Fesenmaier, J. (2003). New digital divide report from laboratory for community and economic development (LCED): Measuring outcomes of digital divide investment to Community Technology Centers. LCED: University of Illinois at Urbana–Champaign.

Fildes, J. (2010, September 23). Stuxnet worm 'targeted high-value Iranian assets.' *BBC News*. Retrieved from http://www.bbcnews.com.

Fink, C., & Kenny, C. J. (2003). W(h)ither the digital divide? *The Journal of Policy, Regulation and Strategy for Telecommunications, Information and Media*, *5*(6), 15–24.

Fletcher, P., Bretschneider, S., Marchand, D., Rosenbaum, H., & Bertot, J. C. (1992). *Managing information technology: Transforming county governments in the 1990s*. Syracuse, NY: Syracuse University.

Fletcher, P.D. (Spring 2002a). Policy and portals: A doorway to electronic government. In McIver, William, and Elmagarmid, A.K. (Eds). *Advances in Digital Government*. NY: Kluwer Academic/Plenum Publishers. 231–242.

Fletcher, P. D. (2002b). The Government Paperwork Elimination Act: Operating instructions for an electronic government. *International Journal of Public Administration*, *25*(5), 723–736.

Fletcher, P. D. (2003a). Portals and policies: Implications of electronic access to U.S. federal government information and services. In

G. D. Garson (Ed.), *Digital government: Principles and best practices* (pp. 52–62). Hershey, PA: Idea Group Press.

Fletcher, P. D. (2003b). A government wide strategy for information resources management: The realities of the Paperwork Reduction Act of 1995. In G. David Garson (Ed.), *Public information technology: Policy and management issues* (pp. 74–93). Hershey, PA: Idea Group Press.

Flynn, N. (2001). *The ePolicy handbook: Designing and implementing effective e-mail, internet, and software policies*. New York: American Management Association.

Fonseca, F. (2008, April 4). Navajo Nation to lose internet signal. *USA Today*, on-line. Retrieved from http://www.usatoday.com/tech/wireless/2008-04-04-navajo-Internet-shutdown_N.htm.

Forester, T. (1992). Megatrends or megamistakes? *Computers & society, 22*(1–4), 2–11.

Fortune, J., & Peters, G. (2005). *Information systems: Achieving success by avoiding failure*. Chichester, England: John Wiley and Sons.

Fountain, J. (2001). *Building the virtual state: Information technology and institutional change*. Washington, DC: Brookings Institution Press.

Fountain, J. E. (1992). A customer service literature review. In Kennedy School of Government, *Customer service excellence: Using information technologies to improve service delivery in government* (pp. 13–22). Cambridge, MA: Harvard University.

Frederickson, H. G. (1999). The repositioning of American public administration. *PS: Political Science and Politics, 32*(4), 701–711.

Free Dictionary. (2009). E-government. Retrieved from http://encyclopedia2.thefreedictionary.com/E-Government.

Friedline, D. (n.d.) TiBA solutions' one stop eGovernment framework. Executive summary. Retrieved from http://www.businessonestop.biz/downloads/One.Stop.eGovernment.Framework-Policy.Maker.pdf.

Friedman, T. L. (2005). *The world is flat: A history of the twenty-first century*. New York: Farrar, Straus and Giroux.

Galambos, L., & Pratt, J. (1988). *The rise of the corporate commonwealth: United States business and public policy in the 20th century*. New York: Basic Books.

Garson, D. G. (Ed.). (2000a). *Handbook of public information systems*. New York: Marcel Dekker.

Garson, D. G. (Ed.). (2000b). *Social dimensions of information technology: Issues for the new millennium*. Hershey, PA: Idea Group.

Garson, D. G. (Ed.). (2002). *Public information technology: Policy and management issues*. Hershey PA: Idea Group.

Garson, G. D. (Ed.). (2003). *Public information technology: Policy and management issues*. New York: Marcel-Dekker.

Garson, G. D. (2006). *Public information technology and e-governance: Managing the virtual state*. Sudbury, MA: Jones and Bartlett.

Gartner Research Group. (n.d.) Four phases—the presence, interaction, transaction, and transformation phases. Retrieved from http://www.aoema.org/E-government/Stages-Phases_of_e-government.htm.

Gasco, M. (2006). Evaluating e-government, Academic Conferences International, ACI, ICEG 2006: MINI-TRACKS. Retrieved from http://www.academic-conferences.org/iceg/iceg2006/iceg2006-minitrack.htm.

Gates, H. W. III. (1995). *The road ahead.* New York: Viking.

Gaus, J. M. (1947). *Reflections on public administration.* Tuscaloosa, AL: University of Alabama Press.

Gellhorn, E. (1982). *Regulated industries in a nutshell.* St. Paul, MN: West Publishing Company.

Gellhorn, E., & Levin, R. M. (2006). *Administrative law and process: In a nutshell*. St. Paul, MN: *Thomson/West*.

General Accounting Office (GAO). (2001a). Electronic government: Challenges must be addressed with effective leadership and management, GAO-01-959T. (July 11).Washington, DC: GAO.

General Accounting Office (GAO). (2001b). Testimony by Linda D. Koontz, Director, information management issues, U.S. GAO. Retrieved from http://www.gao.gov/new.items/d021083t.pdf.

General Services Administration (GSA). (2010). GSA website earns largest score increase on customer satisfaction index. Retrieved from http://www.gsa.gov/portal/content/164093.

General Services Administration (GSA). (2011). Retrieved from http://gsa.gov/ACES.

Gerlach, F. (2009). Seven principles of secure e-voting. *Communications of the ACM, 52*(2), 8–9.

Ghafan, A. A. (2003). *A comparative evaluation of e-government approaches in New Brunswick and Dubai.* Doctoral dissertation, University of New Brunswick. Retrieved from http://digitalcommons.hil.unb.ca/dissertations/AAIMQ82530/.

Gibson, R. (2001). Elections on-line: Assessing internet voting in light of the Arizona Democratic Primary. *Political Science Quarterly, 116*, 561–583.

Giuliani, R. (2005). Efficiency, effectiveness, and accountability: Improving the quality of life through e-government. In E. A. Blackstone, M. L. Bognanno, & S. Hakim (Eds.), *Innovations in e-governance, the thoughts of governors and mayors* (pp. 44–56). New York: Rowman and Littlefield.

Gleick, J. (2000). *Faster: The acceleration of just about everything.* New York: Vintage Book.

Gleick, J. (2003). *What just happened: A chronicle from the information frontier*. New York: Vintage Books.

Glenny, M. (2008). *McMafia: A journey through the global criminal underworld*. New York: Knopf.

Goldman S. L., Nagel, R. N., & Press, K. (1995). *Agile competitors and virtual organizations: Strategies for enriching the customer*. New York: Van Nostrand Reinhold, International Thomson Publishing.

Goldschmidt, K.(2001). *Email overload in congress: Managing a communications crisis*, 1–15. Washington, D.C.: Congress On-line Project.

Goldsmith, S., & Eggers, W. D. (2004). *Governing by network: The new shape of the public sector*. Washington, DC: Brookings Institution.

Gordon, T. F. (2009). E-government. Retrieved from www.ercim.org/publication/Ercim_News/enw48/intro.html.

Gorman, S. (2009, April 8). Electricity grid in U.S. penetrated by spies. *Wall Street Journal*. Retrieved from http://on-line.wsj.com/article/SB123914805204099085.html.

Gortner, H., Mahler, J., & Nicholson, J. (1997). *Organization theory: A public perspective*. Boston: Harcourt.

Grant, G., & Chau, D. (2005). Developing a generic framework for e-government. *Journal of Global Information Management*, 131, 1–30.

Gronlund, A. (2002). Electronic government-efficiency, service quality and democracy. In A. Gronlund (Ed.), *Electronic government: Design, applications, and management* (pp. 23–50). Hershey, PA: Idea Group.

Grossman, L. K. (1995). *The electronic republic: Reshaping democracy in the information age*. New York: Viking.

Grunwald, M. (2010, August 26). How the stimulus is changing America. Retrieved from http://www.time.com/time/nation/article/0,8599,2013683,00.html.

Gubbins, M. (2004, April 8). Global IT spending by sector. *Computing*. London U.K.

Guernsey, L. (2001, July 26). Cyberspace isn't so lonely after all. *The New York Times*. Retrieved from http://query.nytimes.com/gst/fullpage.html?res=9C02E4DA163DF935A15754C0A9679C8B63&pagewanted=2.

Habermas, J. (1995). *Between facts and norms: Contributions to a discourse theory of law and democracy* (W. Rehg, Trans.). Cambridge: MIT Press.

Hague, B., & Loader, B. D. (Eds.). (1999). *Digital democracy: Discourse and decision making in the information age*. New York: Routledge.

Hamilton, B. A. (2005). *Beyond e-government*. London: INSEAD, The Business School for the World. Retrieved from http://www.boozallen.com/media/file/151607.pdf.

Hannan, M. T., & Freeman, J. (1977). The political ecology of organizations. *American Journal of Sociology*, *82*, 929–964.

Harris, B. (2002). E-government study reveals trends, progress. *International Government Navigator*. Retrieved from http://www.centerdigitalgov.com/intenreational/story.php.

Hart, T., & Chaparro, B. S. (2004, June 16). Evaluation of websites for older adults: How "senior-friendly" are they? Software usability research laboratory. *Usability News*. Retrieved from http://psychology.wichita.edu/surl/usabilitynews/61/older_adults.htm.

Heady, F. (2001). *Public administration: A comparative perspective*. New York: Marcel Dekker.

Heclo, H. (1977). A *government of strangers: Executive politics in Washington*. Washington, DC: Brookings Institution.

Heclo, H. (1995). Issue networks and the executive establishment. In S. Z. Theodoulou & M. A. Cahn (Eds.), *Public policy: The essential readings* (pp. 46–58). Englewood Cliffs, NJ: Prentice Hall.

Heeks, R. (2001). *Reinventing government in the information age*. London: Routledge.

Heeks, R. (2003a). *Egovernment for development: Success/failure case study* No. 24. IDPM. University of Manchester, UK. Retrieved from http://www.egov4dev.org/success/case/ndb.shtml#title.

Heeks, R. B. (2003b). *Most eGovernment-for-development projects fail: How can risks be reduced?* i-Government Working Paper no. 14, University of Manchester, UK. Retrieved from http://www.sed.manchester.ac.uk/idpm/research/publications/wp/igovernment/index.htm.

Heeks, R. (2004). *The eGovernment for Development Information Exchange project*. Institute for Policy Development and Management, University of Manchester. Retrieved from http://www.egov4-dev.org/success/definitions.shtml.

Heeks, R. B. (2006). *Implementing and managing e-government: An international text*. London: Sage.

Hendricks, J. A., & Denton, R. E. Jr. (Eds.). (2010). *Communicator-in-chief: A look at how Barack Obama used new media technology to win the White House*. Lanham, MD: Lexington Books.

Henry, J., & Hartzler, M. (1998). *Tools for virtual teams*. Milwaukee, WI: ASQ Quality Press.

Henry, N. (2006). Good government: An unstylish idea that warrants a worldwide welcome. In E. E. Otenyo & N. S. Lind (Eds.), *Comparative public administration: The essential readings* (pp. 905–915). London: Elsevier.

Hernon, P. (2006). E-government in the U.K. In P. Hernon, R. Cullen, & Harold Relyea (Eds.), *Comparative perspectives on e-government: Serving today and building for tomorrow* (pp. 55–65). New York: Rowman and Littlefield.

Hernon, P., Cullen, R., & Relyea, H. C. (Eds.). (2006). *Comparative perspectives on e-government: Serving today and building for tomorrow*. Lanham, MD: Scarecrow Press.

Hesseldahl, A. (2005). The U.N. will not bridge the digital divide. Forbes.Com. Retrieved from http://www.forbes.com/2005/02/25/cx_ah_0225tentech_print.html.

Hiltz, R. S., & Turoff, M. (1993). *The network nation*. Cambridge, MA: MIT Press.

Hindman, M. (2008). *The myth of digital democracy*. Princeton, NJ: Princeton University Press.

Hines, A. (1994). Jobs and infotech work in the information society. *The Futurist*, *28*, 9–13.

Hinnant, C. C., Reagor, S., & Sawyer, S. (2003). From keystone to E-Stone: Assessing architectural innovation in state government. National Public Management Research Conference, October 9–11, Georgetown University, Washington, DC. Retrieved from http://teep.tamu.edu/Npmrc/Hinnant.pdf.

Hiskes, A. L., & Hiskes, R. P. (1986). *Science, technology, and policy decisions*. Boulder, CO: Westview Press.

Holden, S. H. (2003). The evolution of information technology management at the federal level: Implications for public administration. In G. D. Garson (Ed.), *Public information technology: Policy and management issues* (pp. 53–73). Hershey, PA: IDEA Group.

Holmes, D. (2001). *eGov: eBusiness Strategies for Government*. London: Nicholas Brealey.

Holzer, M., & Melitski, J. (2003, June 6). A comparative e-government analysis of New Jersey's 10 largest municipalities. Retrieved from http://www.cornwall.rytgers.edu/pdf/Holzer.pdf.

Homburg, V., & Bekkers, V. (2005). E-government and NPM: A perfect marriage? In V. J. J. M. Bekkers & V. Homburg (Eds.), *The information ecology of e-government* (pp. 155–170). Amsterdam: IOS Press.

Horton, S. (2011). Scott Horton interviews Rep. Dennis Kucinich. Transcript of recording from the KPFK 90.7 FM Los Angeles broadcast of March 11th. Retrieved from http://antiwar.com/radio/2011/03/12/rep-dennis-kucinich/.

Huang, A. H. (2002). E-mail communication and supervisor-subordinate exchange quality: An empirical study. *Human Systems Management, 2*, 193–204.

Huckabee, M. (2005). Streamlining in Arkansas. In E. A. Blackstone, M. L. Bognanno, & S. Hakim (Eds.), *Innovations in e-governance, the thoughts of governors and mayors* (pp. 157–168). New York: Rowman and Littlefield.

Humphrey, T. (2009, April 10). Senate OKs bill allowing officials to confer via computer. Retrieved from http://www.knoxnews.com/news/2009/apr/10/tech-sunshine-may-cover-state/.

Huntington, S. (1991). *The third wave*. Norman: University of Oklahoma Press.

Hyde, A. C. (1997). Rethinking the roles of public managers. *The Public Manage, 26*(1), 7.

InfoDev. (n.d.). IT parks: International best practice. Retrieved from http://www.infodev.org.

Information Society Institute (ISI). (2003). Comparative survey of international eGovernment strategies and applications. Retrieved from http://www.uta.fi/laitokset/ISI/english/projects/project61.html.

Internal Revenue Services (IRS). (2009). The American Recovery and Reinvestment Act of 2009. The American Recovery and

Reinvestment Act of 2009: Information Center. Retrieved from http://www.irs.gov/newsroom/.

International Business Machines (IBM). (2009). IBM personal computer: Before the beginning: ancestors of the IBM personal computer. Retrieved from http://www-03.ibm.com/ibm/history/exhibits/pc/pc_1.html.

International Indigenous Portal. (2007). Navajo President Joe Shirley, Jr., addresses international UN conference on information communication, technology. (April 2007). Retrieved from http://iictf.blogspot.com/2007/04/navajo-president-joe-shirley-jr.html.

International Telecommunication Union (ITU). (2007). Bridging the digital divide. *World information society report* (pp. 21–33). Retrieved from http://www.itu.int/osg/spu/publications/worldinformationsociety/2007/WISR07-chapter2.pdf.

Internet World Stats. (2011). Usage and population statistics, China: Internet usage stats and population report. Retrieved from http://www.internetworldstats.com/asia/cn.

Iredell-Statesville County Schools, North Carolina. (2009). Iredell-Statesville Schools. Retrieved from http://www.iss.k12.nc.us/schools.htm.

Jere-Malanda, R. (2009). Tunisia: Looking to the future. *New African, 485*, 52–54.

Johnson, G., & Heilman, J. G. (1987). Metapolicy transition and policy implementation: New federalism and privatization. *Public Administration Review, 47*(6), 468–478.

Jreisat, J. (2002). *Comparative public administration and policy*. Boulder, CO: Westview Press.

Jurkiewicz, C. (2000). Generation X and the public employee. *Public Personnel Management, 29*(1), 55–74.

Kamarck, E. (2004). Government innovation around the world. Faculty Research Working. Paper Series No. RWP04-010, add after 2004 February. Retrieved from http://unpan1.un.org/intradoc/groups/public/documents/apcity/unpan027047.pdf.

Kamensky, J. (2001). Brief history of Vice President Al Gore's National Partnership for reinventing government during the administration of President Bill Clinton, 1993–2001. Retrieved from http://gov-info.library.unt.edu/npr/whoweare/historyofnpr.html.

Kamensky, J. M. (1996). Role of the "reinventing government" movement in federal management reform. *Public Administration Review, 56*(3), 247–255.

Karr, T. (2008, December 9). Obama's Broadband Roadmap. Retrieved from http://www.commondreams.org/view/2008/12/09-8.

Katz, J., & Aspden, P. (1995). Cyberspace and social community development Internet use and its community integration correlates. Retrieved from http://www.nicoladoering.de/Hogrefe/katz2.htm.

Kearney, C., Hisrich, R. D., & Roche, F. (2009). Public and private sector entrepreneurship: Similarities, differences or a combination? *Journal of Small Business and Enterprise Development, 16*(1), 26–46.

Kerwin, C. M. (2003). *Rulemaking: How government agencies write law and make policy*. Washington, DC: Congressional Quarterly Press.

Kestenbaum, D. (2008, August 1). National Public Radio, NPR.org. The digital divide between McCain and Obama. All Things Considered Program. Retrieved from http://www.npr.org/templates/story/story.php?storyId=93185393.

Kettl, D. F. (1993). *Sharing power: Public governance and private markets*. Washington, DC: Brookings Institution.

Kettl, D. F. (1998). *Reinventing government: A fifth year report card.* Washington, DC: Brookings.

Kettl, D. F. (2007). *System under stress: Homeland security and American politics (2nd ed.)*. Washington, DC: CQ Press.

Kettl, D. F., & Fesler, J. W. (2005). *The politics of the administrative process*. Washington, DC: Congressional Quarterly Press.

Khademian, A. M. (2002). *Working with culture the way the job gets done in public programs*. Washington, DC: Congressional Quarterly Press.

Khosrow-Pour, M. (2008). *E-government diffusion, policy, and impact: Advanced issues and practices*. Hershey, PA: Idea Group Inc.

Kimball, L., Noble, S., & Jon, K. (2002). Virtual team tool kit. Washington, DC: Group Jazz Publishing.

Kling, R. (Ed.). (1996). *Computerization and controversy*. San Francisco: Morgan Kaufmann.

Klotz, R. J. (2004). *The politics of internet communication*. New York: Rowman and Littlefield.

Knott, J. H. (1993). Comparing public and private management: Cooperative effort and principal-agent relationships. *Journal of Public Administration Research and Theory*, *3*(1), 93–119.

Koch, E. (2011, January 31). Tunisia, Egypt, WikiLeaks, secrets, politeness and tact. Retrieved from http://erickoch.ca/2011/01/31/secrets-politeness-and-tact/.

Kohno, T. (2004). Analysis of an electronic voting system. *Johns Hopkins University information security institute technical report, TR-2003-19*. Baltimore: Johns Hopkins.

Kotter, J. (1990). *A force for change: How leadership differs from management*. New York: The Free Press.

Kraemer, K. L., & King, J. L. (2006). Information technology and administrative reform: Will e-government be different? *International Journal of Electronic Government Research*, *2*(1), 1–20.

Krigsman, M. (2011, March 21). IT project failures, Minnesota HealthMatch: A perfect storm for IT failure. Retrieved from http://www.zdnet.com/blog/projectfailures.

Kurzweil, R. (2000). *The age of spiritual machines: When computers exceed human intelligence. New York: Penguin.*

Kurzweil, R. (2005). *The singularity is near*. New York: Viking.

Larsen, M., & Myers, M. D. (1999). When success turns to failure: A package-driven process re-engineering project in the financial services industry. *Journal of Strategic Information Systems*, *8*, 395–417.

Laudon, K. C. (1977). *Communications technology and democratic participation*. New York: Praeger. .

Laudon, K. C., & Laudon, J. P. (2003). *Essentials of management information systems*. Upper Saddle River, NJ: Prentice Hall.

Lazer, D. (2002). *How to Maintain Innovation.gov in a Networked World?* Paper presented at the National Workshop on Digital Government, Kennedy School of Government, Harvard University, Cambridge. Retrieved from http://www.hks.harvard.edu/m-rcbg/Director/dgworkshop/lazer.pdf.

Lee, L., & Rosenbloom, D. H. (2005). *A reasonable public servant: Constitutional foundations of administrative conduct in the United States*. Armonk, NY: M. E. Sharpe.

Leigh, D., & Harding, L. (2011). *WikiLeaks: Inside Julian Assange's war on secrecy*. London: Guardian Books and Random House.

LeMay, M. C. (2006). *Public administration clashing values in the administration of public policy*. Belmont, CA: Wadsworth.

Levine, C. H. (1978). Organizational decline and cutback management. In J. M. Shafritz, A. C. Hyde, & J. S. Parkes (Eds.), *Classics of public administration* (pp. 355–368). Belmont, CA: Wadsworth.

Li, B. (2005). On barriers to the development of e-government in China. *Proceedings of the 7th international conference on electronic commerce (ICEC '05)*, August 15–17, 2005. Xi'an, China. (pp. 549–552). Retrieved from http://delivery.acm.org/10.1145/1090000/1089650/p549-li.pdf?key1=1089650&key2=1838576521&coll=GUIDE&dl=GUIDE&CFID=60079787&CFTOKEN=12192707.

Library of Congress (n.d.). Bill summary & status 107th Congress (2001–2002) H.R.2458. E-Government Act. Retrieved from http://thomas.loc.gov.

Lieberman, J. (2002a). U.S. Senator for Connecticut, Official website, Archive. Retrieved from http://lieberman.senate.gov/.

Lieberman, J. (2002b). Text of the E-government Act of 2001 E-government Project. Retrieved from http://lieberman.senate.gov.

Lindblom, C. (1959). The science of muddling through. *Public Administration Review, 19*(1), 79–88.

Lipnack, J., & Stamps, J. (1997). *Virtual teams: Reaching across space, time and organizations with technology*. New York: John Wiley and Sons.

Lipsey, R. J., & Courant, P. N. (1996). *Social and environmental regulation*. New York: HarperCollins Publishers.

Lisowska, G., & Rutkowska, Z. E. (2006). Administration and customer service in Polish social insurance institution (ZUS). Paper presented at the 3rd international pension seminar ONYF, Budapest, January 18–20.

Loader, B. D. (1997). The governance of cyberspace: Politics, technology and global restructuring. In B. D. Loader (Ed.), *The governance of cyberspace* (pp. 1–10). New York: Routledge.

London School of Economics, LSE. Public Policy Group. (n.d.). Government on the web, London, U.K. Retrieved from http://www.governmentontheweb.co.uk.

Long Beach, CA. (2009). Official website. Retrieved from http://www.longbeach.gov/.

Luke, J., & Caiden, G. A. (1999). Coping with global interdependence. In F. S. Lane (Ed.), *Current issues in public administration* (pp. 376–384). New York: St. Martin's Press.

Lyon, D. (1988). *The information society*. Cambridge: Polity Press.

Lyon, D. (1997). Cyberspace sociality: Controversies over computer-mediated relationships. In B. D. Loader (Ed.), *The governance of cyberspace, politics, technology and global restructuring* (pp. 23–37). New York: Routledge.

Makulowich, J. (2000, November 28). A peek at the library of the future. *US Today*. Retrieved from http://www.usatoday.com/life/cyber/ccarch/ccmak009.htm.

Mansell, R., & Silverstone, R. (1996). *Communication by design: The politics of information and communication technologies*. Oxford: Oxford University Press.

Markoff, J. (2008, August 13). Before the gunfire, cyberattacks. *The New York Times*, p. A1.

Markoff, J. (2011, February 16). Computer wins on "Jeopardy!": Trivial, it's not. *The New York Times*. Retrieved from http://www.nytimes.com/2011/02/17/science/17jeopardy-watson.html.

Markus, L. M. (1984). *Systems in organizations: Bugs and features.* Boston: Pitman.

McCracken, D., & Wolfe, R. J. (2004). *User-centered web site development: A human-computer interaction approach.* Upper Saddle River, NJ: Prentice Hall.

McGuire, M., Stillborne, L., McAdams, M., & Hyatt, L. (2001). *The Internet handbook for writers, researchers, and journalists.* New York: Guilford Press.

McLuhan, M. (1962). *The Gutenberg galaxy.* London: Routledge.

McLuhan, M. (1964). *Understanding media: The extensions of man.* New York: McGraw-Hill.

Mendels, P. (1998, May 6). U.S. program wires remote Native American reservations, *The New York Times*, p. B10. Retrieved from http://www.nytimes.com/library/tech/98/05/cyber/education/06education.html#1.

Mercer, J. (1992). *Public management in lean years, operating in a cutback management environment.* Westport, CT: Quorum Books.

Mesa, City of Mesa. (2009). Official website. Retrieved from http://www.ci.mesa.az.us/isd/strategy.asp.

Meskell, D. (2008). The role of the government Chief Information Officer, GSA Office of citizen services and communications, *Intergovernmental Solutions Newsletter 21* (Spring). Retrieved http://www.leighbureau.com/speakers/awilliams/essays/enabling.pdf.

Microsoft, Inc. (2008). Simplifying start-up. *Digital communities.* Wrights media. Retrieved from http://digitalmag.govtech.com/DC/DC_Mag_Dec08.pdf.

Midmarket CIO. (1999, November 5). Definition, digital divide. Retrieved from http://searchcio-midmarket.techtarget.com/definition/digital-divide.

Milakovich, M., & Gordon, G. J. (2004). *Public administration in America.* Belmont, CA: Wadsworth.

Milner, E. (1999). Electronic government: More than just a ''good thing''? A question of''ACCESS.'' In B. Hague & B. Loader (Eds.),

Digital democracy: Discourse and decision making in the information age, (pp. 63–72). New York: Routledge.

Milward, H. B. (1996). Symposium on the hollow state: Capacity, control, and performance in interorganizational settings: Introduction. *Journal of Public Administration Research and Theory, 6,* 193–195.

Milward, H. B., & Provan, K. G. (1998). Measuring network structure. *Public Administration, 76,* 387–407.

Milward, H. B., & Provon, K. G. (2000). Governing the hollow state, *Journal of Public Administration Research and Theory, 10*(2), 359–379.

Mitchell, W J. (1996). *City of bits: Space, place, and the infobahn.* Boston, MA: MIT Press.

Mitev, N. (1996). More than a failure? The computerized reservation systems at French Railways. *Information Technology and People, 9,* 8–19.

Moe, T. M., & Chubb, J. E. (2009). *Liberating learning: Technology, politics, and the future of American education.* San Francisco: Jossey-Bass.

Mollenhoff, C. (1988). *Atanasoff: Forgotten father of the computer.* Ames: Iowa State Press.

Monroe, B. J. (2004). *Crossing the digital divide: Race, writing, and technology in the classroom.* New York: Teachers College Press.

Moon, J. M. (2002). The evaluation of e-government among municipalities: Rhetoric or reality? *Public Administration Review, 62*(4), 424–433.

Moon, J. M. (2005). From e-government to m-government? Emerging practices in the use of mobile technology by state governments. IBM Center for the Business of Government. Retrieved from http://www.uquebec.ca/observgo/fichiers/28540_mgovernment.pdf.

Morris, D. (2000). *Vote.com.* New York: Renaissance Books.

Moscaritolo, A. (2009, January 1). Optimism for Obama's cybersecurity platform. *SC Magazine: For IT security professionals.* Retrieved from http://www.scmagazineus.com/optimism-for-obamas-cybersecurity-platform/article/123422/.

Mossberger, K., Tolbert, C. J., & Stansbury, M. (2003). *Virtual inequality: Beyond the digital divide*. Washington, DC: Georgetown University Press.

Myerson, M. (1996, April 30). Everything I thought I knew about leadership is wrong. *Fast Company Magazine, 2*. Retrieved from http://www.fastcompany.com/online/02/meyerson.html.

Nalbandian, J. (2000). The manager as political leader: A challenge to professionalism. *Public Management, 82*(3), 7–12.

National Association of Schools of Public Affairs and Administration (NASPAA). (n.d.). Enter the MPA/MPP public policy challenge. Retrieved from http://www.naspaa.org/youtubechallenge/.

National Institute of Aging (NAI). (2002). *Older adults and information technology: A compendium of scientific research and web site accessibility guidelines*. Washington, DC: U.S. Government Printing Office.

National Institute of Standards and Technology (NIST). (2002, December). ITL Bulletin, advising users on information technologies: Security of public web servers. Retrieved from http://csrc.nist.gov/publications/nistbul/b-12-02.pdf.

National Partnership for Reinventing Government (NPRG). (2001). History of the national reinventing government, accomplishments 1995–2000, NPR was the longest-running reform effort in the history of the federal government. Retrieved from http://govinfo.library.unt.edu/npr/whoweare/appendixf.html.

National Telecommunications and Information Administration (NTIA). (1995). Report, Falling through the Net: A Survey of the "Have Nots" in rural and urban America (July), Washington, DC: Department of Commerce.

National Telecommunications and Information Administration (NTIA). (1998). Report, Falling Through the net II: New data on the digital divide. (July). Washington, DC: Department of Commerce.

National Telecommunications and Information Administration (NTIA). (2000). (October). *Falling through the net: Toward digital inclusion*. (4th Report). Washington, DC: U.S. Department of Commerce. Retrieved from http://www.ntia.doc.gov/ntiahome/fttn00/contents00.html.

Navajo Nation Community Development (NNCD). (n.d.). Retrieved from http://www.nndcd.org.

Neagu, S. (2009, July 30). How does Skype work? Technology explained. Retrieved from http://www.makeuseof.com/tag/technology-explained-how-does-skype-work/.

Nebraska, State of. (1994, February 16). Energy and cost savings through telecommunications and teleconferencing. *Usage Report*. http://www.nlc.state.ne.us/epubs/E5700/B044-1994.pdf.

Neef, D. (2001). *e-Procurement: From strategy to implementation*. Upper Saddle River, NJ: Prentice Hall.

New Zealand. (n.d.). Networking government in New Zealand. Retrieved from http://www.e.govt.nz/plone/archive/about-egovt/programme/networking-government.html?q=archive/about-egovt/programme/networking-government.html.

Nguyen, T. (2011). Tunisia's Twitter revolution: Is the revolt in Tunisia the next Twitter revolution? (January 14). Retrieved from http://www.tednguyenusa.com/tunisias-twitter-revolution/.

NIC. (2011, March 22). Utah.gov's groundbreaking solution. Retrieved from http://www.egov.com/Insights/BestPractices/Pages/InnovativeeGov.aspx.

NICUSA (2011, March 21). Egovernment Insights. Retrieved from http://www.nicusa.com/Insights/BestPractices/Pages/Innovativee-Gov.aspx.

Nigro, L., Nigro, F., & Kellough, E. J. (2007). *The new public personnel administration*. Belmont, CA: Wadsworth.

Nilsen, K. (2006). E-government in Canada. In P. Hernon, R. Cullen, & H. Relyea (Eds.), *Comparative perspectives one-government: Serving today and building for tomorrow* (pp. 66–83). New York: Rowman and Littlefield.

Norris, D. F., & Moon, J. E. (2005). Advancing e-government at the grassroots: Tortoise or hare? *Public Administration Review*, *65*(1), 64–75.

Norris, P. (2001). *Digital divide: Civic engagement, information poverty and the Internet in democratic societies*. New York: Cambridge University Press.

North Carolina, State of. (2009). North Carolina e-procurement home page. Retrieved from http://eprocurement.nc.gov/.

Northrop, A. (1999). The challenge of teaching information technology in public administration graduate programs. In G. D. Garson (Ed.), *Information technology applications in public administration: Issues and trends* (pp. 7–22). Hershey, PA: IDEA Group.

Northrop, A. (2002). Lessons for managing information technology in the public sector. *Social Science Computer Review*, *20*(2), 194–205.

Norton, P. (2008, February 1). Directgov: The right direction for e-government or a missed opportunity? *Journal of Information, Law and Technology*. Retrieved from http://www.allbusiness.com/media-telecommunications/telecommunications/11925399-1.html.

Nowell, G. (2009). Public vs. private managers: A new perspective. *Journal of Business and Economics Research*, *7*, 3. Retrieved from http://www.cluteinstitute-onlinejournals.com/archives/abstract.cfm?ArticleID=2676.

Obama, B. (2007, February 10). Presidential announcement speech in Springfield, Illinois. Retrieved from http://www.whitehouse.gov/issues/technology.

Odden, L. (2006, March 7). Wal-Mart blog PR backfires. *On-line marketing blog, business blog consulting*. Retrieved from http://kevin.lexblog.com/2006/03/articles/public-relations/walmarts-blog-strategy-backfires-large-law-firms-take-note/.

Odgerel, U. (2009). Adaptability of e-government policy in Mongolia: Comparative study with Japan. Retrieved from http://wwb.worldbank.org.

O'Donnell, O., Boyle, R., & Timonen, V. (2003). Transformational aspects of e-government in Ireland: Issues to be addressed. *Electronic Journal of E-Government*, *1*(1), 22–30.

Office of the Federal Register. (n.d.). *Federal Register*. National Archives and Records Administration. Retrieved from http://www.gpoaccess.gov/fr/index.html.

Office of Management and Budget (OMB). (2000). Memorandum for heads of executive departments and agencies, circular number A-130. Retrieved from http://www.whitehouse.gov/omb/circulars/a130/a130trans4.html.

Office of Management and Budget (OMB). (2002). E-government strategy: Implementing the President's management agenda for e-government: Simplified delivery of services to citizens. Retrieved from http://www.whitehouse.gov/omb/inforeg/egovstrategy.pdf.

Office of Management and Budget (OMB). (2003a). *Implementing the president's management agenda for e-government: The E-government strategy*. The White House Archives. Retrieved from http://www.cio.gov/documents/2003egov_strat.pdf.

Office of Management and Budget (OMB). (2003a). Federal enterprise architecture program management office. *The technical reference model (TRM) Version 1.1*. Retrieved from http://links.enterprisearchitecture.dk/links/files/FEA-RM_TRMv1.pdf.

Office of Management and Budget (OMB). (2004). Recommended policies and guidelines for federal public websites: Final report of the interagency committee on government information (ICGI). Retrieved from http://cio.gov/documents/ICGI/web-guide lines.html.

Office of Management and Budget (OMB). (2005). *Enabling citizen-centered electronic government 2005–2006 FEA PMO Action Plan*. Washington, DC: Office of Management and Budget, White House.

Office of Management and Budget (OMB). (2006a). *Analytical perspectives, budget of the United States government, fiscal year 2007*. Washington DC: Office of Management and Budget, White House.

Office of Management and Budget (OMB). (2006b). *Circular A-11: Preparation and submission of budget estimates*. Washington, DC: Office of Management and Budget, White House.

Office of Management and Budget (OMB). (2007). Sourced from FEA Consolidated Reference Model Document Version 2.3 October 2007. Retrieved http://whitehouse.gov/omb.

Office of Management and Budget (OMB). (2011). *Circular no. A-130 Revised*. Management of Federal Information Resources. The White House. Retrieved from http://www.whitehouse.gov/omb/circulars_a130_a130trans4.

Office of Management and Budget, OMB. (2004).Recommended policies and guidelines for federal public websites: Final report of the interagency committee on government information (ICGI). (June). Retrieved from http://cio.gov/documents/ICGI/web-guide lines.html.

Office of Personnel Management. (1996, August). The National performance review. OMB. Retrieved from http://www.opm.gov/perform/articles/056.asp.

Oksuz, O. (2007, June). The impact of new communication technologies on public administration: A comparative analysis on the e-government policies in Britain and Turkey. *Civil Academy Journal of Social Sciences*,5.2 *85*(15). Retrieved from http://findarticles.com/p/articles/mi_7071/is_2_5/ai_n31636788/.

O'Leary, R. (2006). *The ethics of dissent managing guerrilla government*. Washington, DC: Congressional Quarterly Press.

Oliver, E. L. (2004). *E-government reconsidered: Renewal or governance for the knowledge age*. Regina, SK: Canadian Plains Research Center.

O'Looney, J. A. (2002). *Wiring governments: Challenges and possibilities for public managers*. Westport, CT: Quorum Books.

One Laptop Per Child Foundation. (2011). Cambridge, Massachusetts. Retrieved from http://laptopfoundation.org/.

Organization for Economic Co-operation and Development (OECD). (2001). Public management committee. E-government: Analysis framework and methodology. Retrieved from http://www.olis.oecd.org/olis/2001doc.nsf/c5ce8ffa41835d64c125685d005300b0/0b677ed527d35bc0c1256b21004f4b6a/$FILE/JT00118445.PDF.

Organization for Economic Co-operation and Development (OECD). (2006). Management in government comparative country data, e-government. Retrieved from http://www.oecd.org/document/0/0, 2340,en_2649_34129_35611008_1_1_1_1,00.html.

Osborne, D., & Gaebler, T. (1992). *Reinventing government*. New York: Addison Wesley.

Osborne, D., & Plastrik, P. (1998). *Banishing bureaucracy: The five strategies for reinventing government*. New York: Plume Book.

Ostrom, E. (1994). Constituting social capital and collective action. *Journal of Theoretical Politics*, *6*(4), 527–562.

Otenyo, E. E. (2010). Game On: Video games and Obama's race to the White House. In J. A. Hendricks & R. E. Denton Jr. (Eds.), *Communicator-in-chief: A look at how Barack Obama used new media technology to win the White House* (pp. 123–138). Lanham, MD: Lexington Books.

Otenyo, E. E., & Lind, N. S. (2004). Faces and phases of transparency reform in local governments. *International Journal of Public Administration*, *27*(5), 287–307.

O'Toole, L. (1997). Implementing public innovations in network settings. *Administration and Society*, *29*(2), 115–138.

Parliamentary Affairs. (2006, April). E-government in Britain—A decade on. *Parliamentary Affairs*, *59*(2), 250–265.

Pavlichev, A., & Garson. D. G. (2003). *Digital government: Principles and best practices*. Hershey, PA: IDEA Publishing Group.

Peters, B. G. (2009). *American public policy: Promise and performance*. Washington, DC: CQ Press.

Peterson, S. (2003, January 30). *ERP of a different color*. Government technology. Retrieved from http://www.govtech.com/gt/39204.

Pfeffer, J. (1998). Understanding organizations: Concepts and controversies. In D. Gilbert, S. Fiske, & G. Lindzey (Eds.), *Handbook of social psychology* (pp. 773–777). New York: McGraw-Hill.

Pfeffer, J., & Salancik, G. R. (2005). External control of organizations: A resource dependence perspective. In J. M. Shafritz, S. Ott, &

Y. S. Jang (Eds.), *Classics of organization theory* (pp. 521–532). Belmont, CA: Thomson Wadsworth.

Pima County. (2009). Pima County Public Library Website. Retrieved from http://www.library.pima.gov/.

Pins, J. E. J. (Ed.). (2002). *E-government and its implications for administrative law-regulatory initiatives in France, Germany, Norway and the United States*. New York: T.M.C. Asser Press.

Plenert, G. (2001). *The eManager value chain management in an eCommerce world*. Los Angeles: Blackhall Publishing.

Postman, N. (1993). *Technopoly: The surrender of culture to technology*. New York: Vintage Books.

Pressman, J., & Wildavsky, A. (1973). *Implementation*. Berkeley: University of California Press.

Prins, J. E. J. (2007). *Designing e-government*. New York: Kluwer Law International.

Prins, J. E. J., Eifert, M. M., Girot, C., Groothuis, M., & Voermans, W. J. (Eds.). (2002). *E-government and its implications for administrative law regulatory initiatives in France, Germany, Norway and the United States*. New York: Cambridge University Press.

Putnam, R. (1996). The strange disappearance of civic America. *The American Prospect, 24*, 34–46.

Putman, R. (2000). *Bowling alone: The collapse and revival of American community*. New York: Simon and Schuster.

Pyrillis, R. (2007, May). IT across the Navajo Nation. *FedTech*. Washington, DC. Retrieved from http://fedtechmagazine.com/article.asp?item_id=277&sv=popular.

Raab, C. D. (1997). Privacy, democracy, information. In B. D. Loader (Ed.), *The governance of cyberspace: Politics, technology and global restructuring* (pp. 155–174). New York: Routledge.

Rawls, J. (1971). *A theory of justice*. Cambridge, MA: Harvard University Press.

Reddick, C. G. (2009). *Handbook of research on strategies for local e-government adoption and implementation: Comparative studies*. Hershey, PA: Idea Group Inc.

Reddick, R., & King, E. (1997). *The online journalist: Using the Internet and other electronic resources*. Fort Worth, TX: Harcourt Brace.

Reno v. American Civil Liberties Union, 521 U.S. 844 (1997).

Richter, W. L., & Burke, F. (2007). *Combating corruption, encouraging ethics: A practical guide to management ethics*. Lanham, MD: Rowman & Littlefield.

Riggs, F. (1961). *The ecology of public administration*. New Delhi: East Asia Publishing.

Robbins, S., & Judge, T. (2009). *Organizational behavior*. Upper Saddle River, NJ: Prentice Hall.

Rohr, J. A. (1986). *To run a constitution: The legitimacy of the administrative state*. Lawrence: University Press of Kansas.

Rosenbloom, D. H., & Carroll, J. D. (2000). *Constitutional competence for public managers: A casebook*. Itasca, IL: F. E. Peacock.

Rosenbloom, D. H., Caroll, J. D., & Carroll, J. D. (2000). *Constitutional competence for public managers: A casebook*. Itasca, IL: F. E. Peacock.

Rosenbloom, D., & Kravchuk, R. S. (2005). *Public administration understanding management, politics, and law in the public sector*. New York: McGraw Hill.

Rosenbloom, David H., & Lee, Yong. (2005). *A reasonable public servant: Constitutional foundations of administrative conduct in the United States*. Armonk, NY: M. E. Sharpe.

Royal Pingdom. (2011). Internet 2010 in numbers. Retrieved January 12, 2011, from http://royal.pingdom.com.

Rutgers University. (n.d.). Best practices. Retrieved from http://andromeda.rutgers.edu/~egovinst/website/bestpracpg.htm.

Rutgers University. (n.d). E-government institute, Newark, NJ. *Best Practices in E-government Resource List*. E-governance. Retrieved from http://spaa.newark.rutgers.edu/home/ncpp/institutes/e-governance-institute/best-practices.html.

Sanger, D., & Markoff, J. (2009, May 29). Obama outlines coordinated cyber-security plan. *The New York Times*. Retrieved from http://www.nytimes.com/2009/05/30/us/politics/30cyber.html.

Sappington, D. (1991). Incentives in principal agent relationships. *Journal of Economic Perspectives*, *5*(2), 45–66.

Savas, E. S. (2005). *Privatization in the city successes, failures, lessons*. Washington, DC: Congressional Quarterly Press.

Scharpf, F. W. (1993). Coordination in hierarchies and networks. In F. W. Scharpf (Ed.), *Games in hierarchies and networks: Analytical and empirical approaches to the study of governance institutions* (pp. 125–165). Boulder, CO: Westview Press.

Schelin, S., & Garson, G. D. (2004). *Humanizing information technology: Advice from experts*. Hershey, PA: Cyber Tech.

Schlosberg, D., & Dryzek, J. S. (2002). Digital democracy: Authentic or virtual? *Organization and Environment*, *15*(3), 332–335.

Schlosberg, D., Zavestoski, S., & Shulman, S. (2007). Democracy and e-rulemaking: Web-based technologies, participation, and the potential for deliberation. *Journal of Information Technology & Politics*, *4*(1), 37–55.

Schmitt, E. (2010, July 26). In disclosing secret documents, WikiLeaks seeks "transparency." *The New York Times*, p. A11.

Scholl, H. J. (2001). Applying stakeholder theory to e-Government: Benefits and limits. October 3–5 proceedings of the 1st IFIP Conference on E-Commerce and E-Government. Zurich, Switzerland.

Schoofs, R. (2007). Abolish the periodicals department! *Scholarly Publications*. Paper 1. Retrieved from http://scholarworks.gvsu.edu/library_sp/1.

Schumpeter, J. (1947). *Capitalism, socialism and democracy*. New York: Harper and Brothers.

Scott, W. R. (2003). *Organizations: Rational, natural, and open systems* (5th ed.). Upper Saddle River, NJ: Pearson Education.

Scottsdale, City of. (2009). *The general plan*. (April 2). Retrieved from http://www.scottsdaleaz.gov/generalplan.asp.

Seifert, J. W., & McLoughlin, G. J. (2007, July 23). *State e-government strategies: Identifying best practices and applications*. CRS Report for Congress, Order code RL34104. Washington, DC: Congressional

Research Service. Retrieved from http://www.fas.org/sgp/crs/secrecy/RL34104.pdf.

Sennett, R. (1974). *The fall of public man*. New York: Knopf.

Servon, L. J. (2002). *Bridging the digital divide: Technology, community, and public policy*. Malden, MA: Blackwell.

Shafritz, J. M., Hyde, A. C., & Parkes, S. J. (2004). *Classics of public administration*. Belmont, CA: Wadsworth.

Shafritz, J. M., Ott, S. J., & Jang, Y. S. (2005). *Classics of organization theory*. Belmont, CA: Wadsworth.

Shafritz, J. M., & Russell, E. W. (2003). *Introducing public administration*. New York: Longman.

Sharma, S. (2004). Assessing e-government implementations. *Electronic Government: An International Journal, 1*(2), 198–212.

Shiels, M. (2009, April 9). Spies 'infiltrate US power grid'. BBC News. Retrieved from http://news.bbc.co.uk/2/hi/technology/7990997.stm.

Shulman, S. W. (2005). E-rulemaking: Issues in current research and practice. *International Journal of Public Administration, 28*, 621–641.

Shulman, S. W., Schlosberg, D., Zavestoski, S., & Courard-Hauri, D. (2003). Electronic rulemaking: New frontiers in public participation. *Social Science Computer Review, 21*(2), 162–178.

Silva, M. (2009). Call it the YouTube factor. *The Swamp*, Tribune's Washington Bureau. Retrieved from http://www.swamppolitics.com/news/politics/blog/2009/09/ youtube_factor_tide_has_turned.html.

Simon, C. A. (2007). *Public policy preferences and outcomes*. New York: Pearson Longman.

Simon, H. (1957). *Models of man: Social and rational*. New York: Wiley and Sons.

Sittenfeld, C. (1999, September 30). Leader on the Edge. *Fast Company, 28*. Retrieved from http://www.fastcompany.com/online/28/rswan.html.

Slevin, J. (2000). *The Internet and society*. Cambridge: Polity Press.

Smiley, J. (2010). *The man who invented the computer: The biography of John Atanasoff, digital pioneer*. New York: Doubleday.

Snellen, I. T. M., & Van De Donk, W. B. H. J. (Eds.). (1998). *Public administration in an information age: A handbook.* Amsterdam: IOS Press.

Solop, F. I. (2001). Digital democracy comes of age: Internet voting and the Arizona democratic primary election. *Political Science and Politics, 36*, 289–293.

Sriramesh, K., & Rivera-Sanchez, M. (2006). E-government in a corporatist, communitarian society: The case of Singapore. *New Media & Society, 8*(5), 707–730.

Stanforth, C. (2010). Analysing e-government project failure: Comparing factorial, systems and interpretive approaches. *iGovernment Working Paper No. 20*. Institute for development policy and management. University of Manchester, U.K. Retrieved from http://www.aspanet.org/scriptcontent/custom/staticontent/2006PDworkshops/egov.cfm.

Stapenhurst, R., & Kpundeh, S. J. (Eds.). (1999). *Curbing corruption: Towards a model for building national integrity*. EDI Development Studies. Washington, DC: World Bank.

Starling, G. (2005). *Managing the public sector*. Belmont, CA: Wadsworth.

State businesses collect "SCBOS Bucks" at first anniversary of web-based tool. (2006). *South Carolina Business Journal, 25*(7), 1. Retrieved from http://findarticles.com/p/articles/mi_qa5513/is_200607/ai_n21394954/.

Steele, L., & Holzer, M. (2003, June 27). Rutgers University. Retrieved from http://andromeda.rutgers.edu/~ncpp/roundtable/cases.htm.

Stiglitz, J. M., Orszag, P. R., & Orszag, J. M. (2000). *The role of government in a digital age*. The Computer and Communications Industry Association. U.S. Global Change Research Program. Retrieved from http://globalchange.gov/index.php.

Stillman, R. J. II. (2005). *Public administration concepts and cases*. New York: Houghton Mifflin.

Stone, A. (1997). *How America got on-line: Politics, markets, and the revolution in telecommunications*. Armonk, NY: M.E. Sharpe.

Stone, D. (2002). *Policy paradox: The art of political decision making*. New York: W. W. Norton.

Street, J. (1992). *Politics and technology*. New York: Guilford Press.

Strutton, A. (2010, July 29). Rogue website author local lad. *The Townsville Bulletin*. Retrieved from http://www.townsvillebulletin.com.au/article/2010/07/29/158481_news.html.

Sussman, G. (1997). *Communication, technology, and politics in the information age*. Thousand Oaks, CA: Sage.

Sweeney, T. W. (1998, October 2). Out of isolation and onto the Internet by the year 2000. *Access America: e-gov e-zine*. Retrieved from http://govinfo.library.unt.edu/accessamerica/text/services_rockyridge.html.

Tan, C. W., Pan, S. L., & Lim, E. T. K. (2005). Managing stakeholder interests in e-government implementation: Lessons learned from a Singapore e-government project. *Journal of Global Information Management, 13*(1), 31–53.

Tang, P. (1997). Multimedia information products and services: A Need for "cybercops"? In B. D. Loader (Ed.), *The Governance of Cyberspace* (pp. 190–208). New York: Routledge.

Templeton, B. (2004). *10 big myths about copyright explained: An attempt to answer common myths about copyright seen on the net and cover issues related to copyright and USENET/Internet publication*. Retrieved from http://www.templetons.com/brad/copymyths.html.

Theoharakis, V., & Serpanos, D. (2001). *Enterprise networking: Multilayer switching and applications*. Hershey, PA: Idea Group.

TiBA Solutions. (2005). iSolution methodology: SCBOS South Carolina Business One Stop. Retrieved from http://www.tibasolutions.com/casestudies/scbos/QSPT0005-402TiBASolutionsSouthCarolinaBusinessOneStop.pdf.

Toffler, A. (1981). *The third wave*. New York: Bantam Books.

Tremlett, G. (2010, January 5). Mr Bean ousts Zapatero from Spain's EU website. *The Guardian*. Retrieved from http://www.guardian.co.uk/technology/2010/jan/05/mr-bean-hacker-zapatero.

Truman, D. B. (1951). *The governmental process*: *Political interests and public opinion*. New York: Alfred A. Knopf.

Turban, E., King, D., Lee, J. K., & Viehland, D. (2004). *Electronic commerce 2004: A managerial perspective*. Upper Saddle River, NJ: Prentice Hall.

Ulziikhutag, M. O. (2006). Adaptability of e-government policy in Mongolia: Comparative study with Japan. Retrieved from http://wwb.worldbank.org/.

Underprivileged Children's Education Programs-Bangladesh (UCEP). (2011). Special Program: Cyber Schools Foundation. Retrieved from http://www.ucepbd.org/special/02.htm.

Unisys. (2009, January 15). Unisys awarded RFID III contract by U.S. Department of Defense for radio frequency identification technology. Retrieved from http://www.reuters.com/article/2009/01/15/idUS138446+15-Jan-2009+BW20090115.

United Nations. (2003a). UN global e-government survey. Department of Economic and Social Affairs and the Civic Resource Group. Retrieved from http://unpan1.un.org/intradoc/groups/public/documents/un/unpan016066.pdf.

United Nations. (2003b). *World public sector report 2003: E-government at the crossroads*. New York: United Nations Press.

United Nations. (2004). Global e-government readiness report 2004. Towards access for opportunity. Retrieved from http://www.unpan.org/egovernment4.asp and http://www2.unpan.org/egovkb/global_reports/04report.htm.

United Nations. (2005a). UN global e-government readiness report 2005: From e-government to e-inclusion. Retrieved from http://www.unpan1.un.org/intradoc/groups/public/documents/un/unpan021888.pdf.

United Nations. (2005b). Economic and Social Commission for Asia and the Pacific. *Designing e- government for the poor*. Geneva: United Nations Publication.

United Nations, Division of Public Administration and Development. (2005). *Global e-government readiness report, 2004*. New York: United Nations.

United Nations Economic Commission for Africa. (2004). Resources on e-government. Retrieved from http://www.uneca.org/aisi/nici/egov.htm.

United States Agency for International Development. (2006). Best practices in ICT policy, enabling e-government for developing countries, dot-GOV project, Dot Com Alliance, Washington DC. Retrieved from http://www.usaid.gov.

United States Department of Justice. (2006). Office of Justice Programs. Retrieved from http://www.amberalert.gov/.

United States Postal Services (USPS). (2001, January 16). Postal service joins forces with AT & T, IBM to deliver Netpost. Certified to federal government. Press Release # 01-005. Retrieved from http://www.usps.com/news/2001/press/pr01_005.htm.

United States Government. (2011). Recovery.gov: Track the money. Retrieved from http://www.recovery.gov/Pages/default.aspx.

United States Postal Service (USPS). (2011). Privacy impact assessments (PIA). Retrieved from http://www.usps.com/privacyoffice/pia.htm.

van Dijk, J. (2005). *The deepening divide: Inequality in the information society*. Thousand Oaks, CA: Sage.

Vaughn, J., & Otenyo, E. (2007). *Managerial discretion in government decision making: Beyond the street level*. Sudbury, MA: Jones and Bartlett.

Vogt, S. (2003). Government: Online but not in line. *Information world review*. Retrieved from http://www.computing.co.uk/information-world-review/features/2084029/government-online-line]http://

www.iwr.co.uk/professional-and-library/3007071/Government-on-line-but-not-in-line the correct source?].

Wagner, W. P. (n.d.). *Business transformation was the goal.* Retrieved from http://en.sap.info/business-transformation-was-the-goal-part-1/180.

Wagner, W. P., & Antonucci, Y. L. (2004). An analysis of the imagine PA public sector ERP project. *37th Hawaii International Conference on System Sciences*, (January 5-8) 1–8.

Walton, A. (1999, January). Technology vs. African-Americans. *Atlantic Monthly*, *283*(1), 14–18. Retrieved from http://www.theatlantic.com/issues/99jan/aftech.htm.

Warren, K. F. (1997). *Administrative law and the political system* (3rd ed.). Upper Saddle River, NJ: Prentice Hall.

Warschauer, M. (2003a). Dissecting the "digital divide": A case study in Egypt. *The Information Society: An International Journal*, *19*(4), 297–304.

Warschauer, M. (2003b). *Technology and social inclusion: Rethinking the digital divide*. Cambridge, MA: MIT Press.

Webopedia. (2009). E-government. Retrieved from http://isp.webopedia.com/TERM/E/e_government.html%20%2810.

WebReference.com. (2009, March 23). Introduction to RSS. Retrieved from http://www.webreference.com/authoring/languages/xml/rss/intro/.

Weerakkody, V., Jones, S., & Olsen, E. (2007). E-government: A comparison of strategies in local authorities in the UK and Norway. *International Journal of Electronic Business*, *5*(2), 141–159.

Weik, M. H. (1961). The ENIAC story. Ordnance Ballistic Research Laboratories, Aberdeen Proving Ground, MD. ENIAC patent (No. 3,120,606), filed June 26, 1947, and issued 1961. Retrieved from http://ftp.arl.army.mil/~mike/comphist/eniac-story.html.

Weinschenk, C. (2010). A pretty picture for teleconferencing. IT business edge. Retrieved from http://www.itbusinessedge.com/cm/blogs/weinschenk/a-pretty-picture-for-teleconferencing/?cs=44223.

West, D. M. (2003a). *Achieving e-government for all: Highlights from a national survey*. Working Document, Commissioned by the Benton Foundation and the New York State Forum of the Rockefeller Institute of Government. Retrieved from http://www.benton.org/publibrary/egov/access2003.html.

West, D. M. (2003b). Global e-government full report. Taubman Center for Public Policy at Brown University.

West, D. M. (2004). E-government and the transformation of service delivery and citizen attitudes. *Public Administration Review, 64*(1), 15–27.

West, D. M. (2005). *Digital government: Technology and public sector performance*. Princeton, NJ: Princeton University Press.

West, D. M. (2006). E-government report, Brookings Policy Reports, Inside Politics.Org. Retrieved from http://www.insidepolitics.org/egoc05intpressRelease.pdf.

West, W. (2005). Administrative rulemaking: An old and emerging literature. *Public Administration Review, 65*(6), 655–668.

White House. (2001, February 11). Press Release. Executive Order, 2001, President Bush. Retrieved from http://www.whitehouse.gov.

WikiLeaks: Royal family member "made inappropriate remarks." (2010, November 28). *The Telegraph*. Retrieved from http://www.telegraph.co.uk/news/.

Wikipedia. (2009). E-government. Retrieved from http://en.wikipedia.org/wiki/EGovernment.

Wilhelm, A. (2000). *From democracy in the digital age*. New York: Routledge.

Williams, A. (2005). The District's Business Resource Center: The best in e-customer service. In E. A. Blackstone, M. L. Bognanno, & S. Hakim (Eds.), *Innovations in E-governance: The thoughts of governors and mayors* (pp. 114–131). New York: Rowman and Littlefield.

Winseck, D. (1998). *Reconvergence: A political economy of telecommunications in Canada*. Cresskill, NJ: Hampton Press.

Withrow, J., Brinck, T., & Speredelozzi, A. (2002). Comparative usability evaluation for an e-government. Ann Arbor, MI. Retrieved from http://www.diamondbullet.com/egovportal.pdf.

Wong, W., & Welch, E. (2004). Does e-government promote accountability? A comparative analysis of website openness and government accountability. *Governance*, *17*(2), 275–297.

World Bank. (2006). Designing and implementing e-government: Key issues, best practices and lessons learned. Retrieved from http://web.worldbank.org/WBSITE/EXTERNAL/TOPICS/EXTINFORMATIONANDCOMMUNICATIONANDTECHNOLOGIES/EXTEDEVELOPMENT/0,,contentMDK:20415171~menuPK:828158~pagePK:64020865~piPK:51164185~theSitePK:559460,00.html.

World Bank. (2009). E-government. Retrieved from http://web.worldbank.org/.

World Bank. (2011). eGovernment: Case studies, Washington, DC: World Bank Group. Retrieved from http://go.worldbank.org/0QQ3Z9HT61.

World Broadband Statistics Report (2010.). World broadband statistics: Short report Q4. Retrieved from http://point-topic.com/dslanalysis.php .

Woyke, E. (2009, April 3). Korea bridges digital divide: Korea's IT agency has advice for the Obama administration. Forbes.com. Retrieved from http://www.forbes.com/2009/04/02/internet-broadband-korea-technology-korea-09-broadband.html.

Yuki, G. (1994). *Leadership in organizations*. Englewood Cliffs, NJ: Prentice-Hall.

Zavestoski, S., Shulman, S., & Schlosberg, D. (2006). Democracy and the environment on the Internet: Electronic citizen participation in regulatory rulemaking. *Science, Technology, & Human Values*, *31*, 384–408.

ZDNet UK. (2005, July 1). Computerization and e-government in social security: A comparative international study. Retrieved from http://whitepapers.zdnet.co.uk/0,39025945,60144710p-39000361q,00.htm.

Zeller, T. Jr. (2006, February 27). Cyberthieves silently copy your passwords as you type. *The New York Times*. Retrieved from http://www.nytimes.cm/2006/02/27/technology/27hack.

Zhang, J. (2002). Will the government serve the people? The development of Chinese e-government. *New Media and Society*, *4*(2), 163–184.

Zittrain, J. (2008). *The future of the Internet and how to stop it*. New Haven, CT: Yale University Press.

Zizek, S. (2011, January 20). Good manners in the age of WikiLeaks. *London Review of Books*, *33*(2), 9–10. Retrieved from http://www.lrb.co.uk/v33/n02/slavoj-zizek/good-manners-in-the-age-of-wikileaks.

Zwerdling, D. (2005). *Morning Edition*. (March 2, 7:30. Transcript). Electronic anklets track asylum seekers in US. Washington, DC: National Public Radio.

Index

www.ingramcontent.com/pod-product-compliance
Lightning Source LLC
LaVergne TN
LVHW022300060326
832902LV00020B/3196

* 9 7 8 1 9 3 4 8 4 4 1 7 5 *